THE
PHILOS
OF CRIME AND
PUNISHMENT

C000127269

Ilham Ragimov

THE PHILOSOPHY OF CRIME AND PUNISHMENT

Goodge & Wyse
INTERNATIONAL

Originally published in Russian as
Философиа преступления и наказания

First published in English
in 2015 by
Goodge & Wyse
PO Box 2131
London W1A 5SU
England

© Ilham Ragimov 2015

ISBN 978-1-908755-88-9 (hardback)
978-1-908755-89-6 (paperback)

The right of Ilham Ragimov to be identified as the
author of this work has been asserted by him in accordance
with the Copyright, Designs and Patents Act 1988.

All right reserved. No part of this publication may be
reproduced, stored in or introduced into a retrieval system, or
transmitted, in any form, or by any means (electronic, mechanical,
photocopying, recording or otherwise) without the prior written
permission of the publisher. Any person who does any unauthorised
act in relation to this publication may be liable to criminal
prosecution and civil claims for damages.

A catalogue record for this book is available from
the British Library.

A catalog record for this book is available from
the Library of Congress.

Typeset & designed by Goodge & Wyse

Printed & bound in Great Britain

Contents

Ilham Ragimov

Ilham Ragimov was born in 1951 in Tovuz, in the Republic of Azerbaijan.

In 1975, he graduated in law with honours at Leningrad State University, and in 1978 completed his postgraduate Candidate of Legal Sciences at the same university. He then worked at the Institute of Philosophy and Law of the Academy of Sciences of the Republic of Azerbaijan before becoming departmental head at the Ministry of Justice of Azerbaijan in 1980. From 1982 until 1992 he was head of the Office of Legislation of the Ministry of Justice and was a member of its board. In 1988 at Leningrad University, he became the youngest doctor of sciences in the field of post-Soviet criminal law, and qualified as professor in 1996.

Between 1992 to 1996 he was director of the Scientific Research Institute for Judicial Expertise, Criminalistics and Criminology. He was the first author of the concept of reforming the system of judicial law in Azerbaijan prepared in 1992-1993, and the following year he set up a state programme to combat crime. In 1994 he took up the chair of the Union of Lawyers of Azerbaijan, and since 2006 he has been vice-president of the International Union of Lawyers. He has worked at the oil company Lukoil, and was also president of the Sindo-Ryu Karate Do Federation of Azerbaijan.

In 2004 he became an academician of the Russian Academy of Security, Defence and Law Enforcement, the second Azerbaijani ever to be elected. In 2009, he was elected honorary board member of the International Fund for Cooperation and Partnership of the Black Sea and the Caspian Sea.

From 1996 to 2000 he taught law at various universities, and was also vice-rector of the Higher Diplomatic College. He has written more than a hundred articles on criminal and correctional labour law, as well eight studies on fundamental issues of law and procedure, the latest of which are *Crime and Punishment* and *The Philosophy of Crime and Punishment*, which have been translated into several languages.

Ilham Ragimov is the recipient of awards that include the Defence and Law Enforcement Order of Peter the Great of the second degree from the Russian Academy of Security (the first Azerbaijani to be so honoured), Honoured Lawyer of the Republic of Azerbaijan, the International Order of the Crescent and Star of the first degree (highest) and the title of Chevalier of the International Order of Crescent and Star from France's International Committee for Human Rights, the Albert Einstein Award from the International Foundation for Albert Einstein founded by the Global Business Leadership Council, and the honorary title of Doctor Honoris Causa from the Bulgarian Academy of Sciences.

*

Introduction

O people! Discuss the nature of things
And you shall know the truth!
—*Quran, Surah 2: Al-Baqarah (The Cow)*

Having been occupied with the study of punishment long enough, I finally came to understand that knowledge of any subject can never be truly complete and definitive. No natural, social or spiritual concept can be thoroughly and absolutely understood by mankind. Yet man strives for the truth, or at least hopes to discover it through deep and continuous research in a given subject.

Delving ever deeper into the subject of punishment, I became all too well aware that a juridical approach in itself would prove too limited and narrow to gain knowledge of this complicated area, and that I needed to step outside of the boundaries of legal and criminal studies. I became aware too that without a philosophical understanding of the concept of crime and its causes, it is not possible to understand the philosophical meaning of the concept and essence of punishment, for it is only through knowing what crime is that one may regard a given person's deed as such and thus call the reaction to it punishment.

Working from these fundamental conclusions, I decided to look at punishment within the context of the concept of crime and its causes—not only from the juridical perspective but also from the philosophical. As a result, I needed to retreat from a number of my previously expressed propositions on the subject. And yet I found comfort in the words of the American philosopher, poet and publicist James Russell Lowell that "the foolish and the dead alone never change their opinions".

I am not entirely sure that I shall find the truth, since the areas of interest to me here touch upon the fields of scientific knowledge where debate still rages on. I endeavour only to test my own convictions against these emerging arguments. Will I find success? Well, I can look to Georg Hegel's words of encouragement: "Daring in the pursuit of truth, trust in the power of reason are the preconditions to philosophical study. Man must respect himself and declare himself worthy of the best. No matter the high regard we have for the greatness and power of spirit, it will always fall short. The hidden essence of the Universe does not carry a force capable of withstanding the daring of knowledge; it must reveal itself to man, spread the riches and depths of its nature before his eyes and give him the chance to enjoy them."[1]

At first sight, the philosophy of crime and punishment as a subject seemed to me to be hopelessly muddled and it seemed to require a preliminary introduction in the shape of a voluminous number of philosophical definitions and concepts that I almost lost heart and turned back. However, I reminded myself always that learning is the process of the mind's striving from ignorance to knowledge, from lack of understanding to understanding, from mystery to the truth. As D. A. Kerimov so rightly says, "knowledge is as infinite as the world; life, existence, including the existence of law, are infinite".[2]

At the same time, I understood clearly that such a path to knowledge presumes overcoming a variety of obstacles and difficulties. There certainly could be no progress without referring to the distinguished work of our predecessors; this is the universal law of evolution, according to which the present is the son of the past and the father of the future (Gottfried Leibniz). There is nothing in our world, in our life, which has not been discussed before, or, as they say in such cases, everything new is well-forgotten everything old. No commentary, no retelling, even the most conscientious and qualified, can bring about the kinds of impressions that may be gained through direct acquaintance with the works of the great thinkers of the past—they can never express the real essence of ideas presented in days gone by. Of this I became deeply convinced in my study of the history of philosophy, religion, law and the other sciences dealing with crime and punishment.

One issue that has always been raised in the science of criminal law is this: can we confine ourselves to merely the juridical boundaries of studying crime and punishment? Will this allow us to reach our intended targets? Countering M. V. Dukhovskiy, who was one of the first to demand an expansion of the scientific boundaries of criminal law, A. F. Kistyakovskiy had the following to say: "If the author rejects the idea of criminal law as a science studying only crime . . . as a separate phenomenon, without studying its reasons . . . then one might ask him what would the author suggest our

1   Hegel, G. W. F. *Encyclopedia of the Philosophical Sciences*, Moscow, 1974, vol. 1, p83.
2   Kerimov, D. A. *Methods of Law: Subject, Functions, Problems of the Philosophy of Law*, Moscow, 2011, p7.

science to do, when the standards of public life, over which it has no mastery, are such that one must first study only crime and the punishment imposed for it?"[3]

Undoubtedly, juridical studies of crime and punishment are not only important but also necessary. As M. P. Chubinskiy stresses, "this must be recognised and remembered once and for all, no matter what the reformative suggestions".[4] But we require the facts of psychological and physical life serving as the basis of the concept of crime and punishment, as well as knowledge of the nature, habits, and inclinations of the criminal, the methods and means of criminal acts. The philosophical foundation of a man's behaviour is also required, including that of a criminal, as well as the right to impose punishment for the crime and so on.

Yet the science of criminal law does not provide this essential, vital knowledge and information. For this reason, if we seek to explain the cause of man's criminal behaviour and, consequently, understand the essence of crime and punishment, we are compelled to look to the achievements of other sciences. Here we mean adapting the methods and means of sciences that do not deal with law in order to examine and explain the issues of criminal law, crime and punishment. This would seem to undermine Enrico Ferri's assertions to the effect that "the justice system of the future will focus on the criminal as a biochemical individual, who acts in this or that particular social environment", hence no attempts at reconciliation "can take root"; there is no middle way; the new methods required for the advancement of science "are not compatible with studying of crime as an abstract juridical entity".[5] Meanwhile, the modern criminal justice system focuses precisely on crime as a juridical and philosophical entity, employing the results of psychology, psychiatry, genetics and medicine when studying the criminal personality.

In other words, at the moment the issues of crime and punishment are firmly established among those issues studied and discussed not only by criminology and criminal legal science, but also by philosophy, sociology, psychology, theology and so on. Sometimes it is extremely difficult, and in some cases even impossible, to define this or that concept, even if it is widely used in everyday life and seemingly self-explanatory. As a result, ordinary people, when meeting and discussing crime, criminals and punishment, do not waste their time in penetrating the essence and substance of these concepts. Such terms are simple

3 Quoted from: Sergievskiy, N. D. 'Philosophical Methods and Science of Criminal Law', in Sergievskiy, N. D. *Selected Works*, Moscow, 2008, p208.
4 Chubinskiy, M. P. *Essays on Criminal Policy*, Moscow, 2010, p24.
5 Ferri, E. *Criminal Sociology*, 1893, pp 14, 580, 584.

and commonplace to them, and, most importantly, clear to them. And this gives them the opportunity to understand each other very well. As Augustine of Hippo wrote: "If they do not ask me about the meanings of particular concepts, I know what is being discussed. If they ask me to explain their essence to others, I am incapable of doing that." The complexity and difficulty of explaining the concepts of crime and punishment stem from their philosophical essence. Because of this, first and foremost, an integrated and thorough philosophical approach to these phenomena is required with the aim of revealing their philosophical essence, although this is clearly a rather difficult task.

Y. V. Golik has the following caution: "He who decides to plunge into the abyss of philosophical issues of the law will take an interesting and exciting but very 'dangerous' path. The problem is that philosophy is one of those sciences in which there is no consensus of research opinion on any of the issues. Very often these opinions differ so much that there is no commonality at all. Arguments are infinite, and they have been going on not for decades or even centuries, but for millennia."[6] The statement has complete justification, but I recommend that researchers proceed from the Russian V. I. Vernadskiy's statement: "I understand perfectly that I may be enticed by the wrong, the deceiving, that I may follow the path that leads me into the thickets; but I cannot fail to follow it, I despise all chains on my thoughts, I cannot and shall not make them follow the path that, while practically important, does not allow me to understand the issues tormenting me at least somewhat better . . . And this search, this striving is the basis of any scientific pursuit."

There are many questions that thinking people ask themselves at some point on a particular question and for which this or that specific science or practice cannot offer a simple and unambiguous answer. The task of philosophy is precisely to study these matters and, where possible, to explain them. How is the world organised? Is it developing? Who or what determines the laws of development? Is man mortal or immortal? How can man understand his destiny? What are the cognitive possibilities of man?

In short, we can state justifiably that philosophy has contributed greatly, if indirectly, to all of the advancements ever achieved by mankind. Philosophy is unified and diverse—man cannot manage without it in any sphere of his life. As Bertrand Russell said: "All . . . fields of knowledge border the unknown in the world surrounding us. When a man enters the borderline areas or goes beyond them, he gets from science to the field of speculation. His speculations are also a kind of study, and that, besides everything else, is philosophy."

6   Golik, Y. V. *Philosophy of Criminal Law*, Saint Petersburg, 2004, p7.

Philosophy includes a wide range of fields, among them the philosophy of law among them which studies in a broad sense the consequences of these or those legislative principles. We should not forget that the matters of good and evil and the concept of justice are referred to as a philosophical discipline which we call ethics, i.e. these are ethical and not legal categories. Therefore the concepts of 'crime' and 'punishment' should be referred to as philosophical categories, since the law, legal sciences, criminal law and criminology in particular are not able to answer the questions that are of interest here.

Philosophy serves as the scientific basis, the foundation for research on certain issues of other sciences, including legal. Thus, for example, the concepts of retribution, punishment, suffering and so on may be examined only through philosophy. The following magnificent words were written by the jurist and social philosopher Y. V. Spektorskiy: "All three fields of philosophy—ethics, metaphysics and gnosiology—are most closely connected with jurisprudence. As Dante's Devil said, *'Tu non pensavi ch'io löico fossi!'*— 'You did not suppose that I was a logician!'—just as jurisprudence might proclaim: 'You did not suppose that I was a philosopher!' The understanding of this should elevate and ennoble it, it should put it higher than the reproaches it has to listen to too often; to wit, as if it were only engaged in slavish pedantry or empty and harmful pettifoggery. But *noblesse oblige*. The understanding of it binds as well. It makes jurisprudence treat philosophy and its issues with great attention. If in general, as Plato once said, "the lack of interest in philosophy is sooner a feature of self-satisfied ignorance than superiority of real knowledge, the lack of such interest on the part of a lawyer is disregard for his own profession—a disregard which is even more unforgivable as the death of jurisprudence from an attack of alien sciences may be the result of it."[7]

It would appear that this is the most thorough and convincing answer to the proponents of positivism, who consider legal science to be self-sufficient and that philosophy, ethics and other sciences should not be called upon to reveal and understand the essence of legal phenomena. This cannot be put better than by Hegel, who stated that "jurisprudence is a part of philosophy".[8] Indeed, can jurisprudence truly manage without philosophy in revealing the essence of concepts and understanding of legal issues? If we proceed from the fact that philosophy seeks to answer the theoretical questions that sciences cannot hope to solve, then the answer can only be negative. In principle, all sciences have a common basis and the same goal,

7 'Philosophy and Jurisprudence', *Juridical Bulletin*, vol.. 2, Moscow, 1913.
8 Hegel, G. W. F. *The Philosophy of Right*, Moscow, 1990, pp 17–18.

namely to study nature and reveal its laws for the benefit of mankind. However, we should not forget the words of the ancient treatise, the *Arthashastra* (Old India, fourth century BCE): "Philosophy has always been considered the lamp for all sciences, the means for doing any deed, the foundation for all regulations." History attests that it is philosophers who in all times have posed questions and tried to answer them before lawyers, which is natural since the essence of philosophy is to speculate on the general issues of 'The World–Man'. Consequently, if man is the object of punishment and at the same time serves as the subject of crime as well, we should accept that it is impossible to explain the essence of the system 'Crime–Man–Punishment' without philosophy. In this regard, the legal sciences, criminal law and criminology in particular are powerless, for, as Kant said, "philosophy is really nothing else than the 'practical science of man'."[9]

Philosophy treats crime and punishment from the standpoint of their place and role in the common social mechanism, justifying or blaming their juridical nature in terms of ethics and spiritual and moral standards.[10] For this reason, in order for the science of crime and punishment to be convincingly constructed from a methodological point of view and to be maximally efficient for society, it should be oriented not only towards juridical disciplines but also, first and foremost, towards philosophy and thence only via its study towards all the humanitarian sciences, joined with the help of philosophy to the broader system of scientific knowledge.

Sometimes philosophers and lawyers compete in accusing each other, without understanding each other. Philosophers consider lawyers incapable of expressing independent opinion freely, as they obey the requirements of formal laws. Lawyers suppose that philosophers say a lot of wonderful things that are far removed from practical use. To be fair, we should underscore that philosophy sometimes tries to explain many phenomena by overly complex concepts and categories not easily comprehensible for the purposes of jurisprudence. And this creates certain problems for their practical use. In fact, philosophy itself is not as difficult as the language it speaks. The paradox is that the more difficult to comprehend, the more complex, confusing the philosophical idea is, the greater the genius the philosopher is considered to be.

I am convinced that anyone with the courage to take upon themself the research of such a difficult and ungrateful issue as crime and punishment must carefully and attentively study not only the thoughts of outstanding

---

9 Kant, I. *From Manuscript Inheritance*, Moscow, Progress, 2000, p78.
10 See: Sych, K. A. *Criminal Penalty and Its Classifications: Experience of Theoretical Modelling*, Saint Petersburg, 2002, p75.

lawyers but also those of philosophers, psychologists, sociologists and writers whose research is related to these institutions of criminal law. However, we should never forget that the philosophy of law is a fundamental science within the system of legal sciences, and that the sectoral sciences have mostly applied value in comparison with it. The advancement of both the former and the latter depends on their unity and mutual penetration.

Weber stressed that "philosophy was born on the very day when thought refused to explain nature by way of fantastic creatures, who were instead relegated to the field of fables, and proceeded to unite all substances by either eternal power and eternal mind, or, speaking its language, by basic laws and causes."[11] It follows that any philosophy relating to any phenomenon entails the study of the reasons for the origin of this phenomenon, the conditions of its existence and related changes. Hence it seems that the philosophy of crime and punishment was born when man started thinking about behaviour that causes harm to other people and the community at large, as well as about how to prevent such phenomena.

As the philosophers of ancient times emphasized, we are only capable of knowing the truth about the concept and essence of crime and punishment through the means of philosophical categories, and it is these categories that are methodologically universal means, instruments and methods for understanding the nature of society.

Based on these provisions, I shall endeavour to answer the following questions that have a philosophical essence: What is crime beyond criminal law? Where are the reasons and origins of man's behaviour, criminal in particular? What is the essence of punishment? Where did it come from? What to punish for and why? Whom to punish and how? Who has the right to punish and who gave this right? Is it required by society at all and what is its future?

*

---

11 Weber. *History of Philosophy*, Kiev, 1882, p10.

I
Crime

I

The Concept and Essence of Crime

As a logical step towards a scientific understanding of the concept of 'crime', the thing defined by the word 'crime' needs to be clearly established. In other words, we should start by accepting that using 'crime' as applied to merely the study and description of crime as a legal category is not enough; we need seek an explanation of crime both as a phenomenon and as a philosophical concept. The traditional legal, formal and customary meaning of crime does not offer any opportunity to learn its true nature and essence, and hence the meaning of punishment and its social purpose. The main disadvantage of any number of definitions across the world, in my view, lies in the fact that rather than analysing any actual causational relationship, the dogma of criminal law was and is vigorously preoccupied with the analysis of offences as listed in the Criminal Code, and ignoring similar phenomena beyond that code.

E. B. Kurguzkina rightly says that "comprehension of the genuine concept of crime cannot fully lie within legal science and it should go beyond",[1] an observation that draws on Hegel's own statement that legal science as a science of positive law does not deal with the meaning of law—and, accordingly, with the meaning of crime—but with that which in this place and at this time is correspondingly power-authoritatively established (i.e. made positive) as law. Consequently, criminal law as a legal means in its approach to the understanding of criminal deeds proceeds not from reason but from authority, i.e. from a powerful establishment.[2]

From a practical point of view, then, we may ask the question: what should

1   Kurguzkina, E. B. 'Understanding of Criminal Deeds', *Philosophical Sciences*, 2008, no. 5, p84.
2   See: Hegel, G. W. F. *The Philosophy of Right*, Moscow, 2007, p283.

be considered a crime? The answer is a simple one: crime is a punishable offence. This is how criminal law understands crime. More specifically, criminal law dogma traditionally provides the following definition of crime: "A criminal act is an act that violates the rules of law and order."

In his Epistle to the Romans, Paul the Apostle declared: "Where there is no law there is also no transgression" (Rom. 4:15). In the twentieth century, Louk Hulsman expressed the same idea in different wording: "Law says where there is a crime; law creates 'crime'."[3] However the formal legal definition of crime fails to answer the following questions: What are the general features of those acts which across the times and nations are considered 'criminal' and thus punished? Which acts are criminal by their nature? Is it possible to identify one act at least that is considered criminal in all the codes? Is it possible to identify those features that are common to all types of crime in different social types?

We can agree with E. A. Pozdnyakov when he says that the legal approach to crime and its definition are formal and that they do not in the least satisfy the needs of those who seek a deeper insight into the phenomenon of crime and to reveal its underlying grounds and reasons.[4] The purely formal nature of the concept of crime enables any authority that is dominant for reasons such as political, to create systems that require this concept. Despite efforts for greater objectivity in criminal law, the criminalisation and decriminalisation of acts still cannot be free from the voluntarist approach of those directly involved in lawmaking. Furthermore, there may be cases of the intentional criminalisation of acts which, while not a danger to society, are considered as such only for a narrow circle of authorities in defence of their violation of the public interest.[5] This is especially typical for countries with an authoritarian and undemocratic regime of control.

Y. V. Golik makes the point that long and incalculable attempts by lawyers to provide a complete and comprehensive concept of crime have not yet led anywhere.[6] Being dissatisfied with the legal definition of crime, some experts have decided to develop this concept regardless of criminal laws. Thus, Emile Durkheim, following his predecessor Raffaele Garofalo, formulated a sociological definition of crime that would differ from the legal one, though even though the ancient philosophers were aware of the social significance of crime. Gabriel Tarde, working within the French sociological school,

3   Hulsman, L. Picnes. Perdue. Paris, 1982, p68.
4. See: Pozdnyakov, E. A. *The Philosophy of Crime*, Moscow, 2001, p58.
5. Kurguzkina, E. B. Op. cit, p84.
6. See: Golik, Y. V. 'Philosophy of Criminal Law: Modern Formulation of the Problem', *Philosophy of Criminal Law*, Saint Petersburg, 2004, p24.

believes that crime must be explained primarily as a social phenomenon and its origins as historical.[7]

According to Hegel the essence of crime is its insignificance in terms of the inviolability of right as an absolute value: "Something changes through crime and the object exists in this change, but this existence is the opposite of itself, and thus it is insignificant; as a right right is removed and it means insignificance. It is right being absolute that cannot be removed, therefore manifestation of crime is insignificant in and of itself, and this insignificance is the essence of the criminal act."[8]

Crime is a purely mental rather than external phenomenon, according to P. A. Sorokin: "A particular act may or will be criminal not in and of itself, but only in the case where in a psychic experience of someone else it is qualified as criminal."[9] It follows that Sorokin understands crime as a conflict of heterogeneous behaviour patterns existing in a given society.[10]

Another opinion is to consider crime solely from a biological point of view, where "crime is an expression of the inability of an individual to refuse homeophagy (cannibalism, direct or indirect attacks on life); it involves satisfying our instincts and stresses regarding our neighbours instead of looking for 'meeting our needs in the external world'."[11] Meanwhile, advocates of utilitarianism start from the fact that "crime is an act committed by a member of a social group, and considered by the other members of this group as an act so detrimental to the group or perceived as having such a degree of antisocial attitude of the executor, that the latter, in their effort to protect their welfare, react to it publicly, openly and collectively."

Following this argument, their conclusion that crime is not only a governmental but also a social phenomenon. Enrico Ferri, in disagreeing with Leonce-Pierre Manouvrier[12] declaring the social nature of crime as exclusively a phenomenon, called crime a "natural and social phenomenon", since crime, being a social phenomenon, at the same time is a manifestation of the biological side of an individual.[13]

The imperfection of the above, added to the many other related definitions we shall encounter, is connected with the fact that the legal definition

7 Tarde, G. D. *Criminal and Crime. Comparative Crime. Crowd Criminality*, comp. and foreword by V. S. Ovchinskiy, Moscow, 2004, p7.
8 Hegel, G. W. F. *The Philosophy of Right*, Moscow, 1990, p145.
9 Sorokin, P. A. *Crime and Punishment, Feat and Reward*, Saint Petersburg, 1914, p85.
10 Ibid., pp 128–130.
11 Bahar. 'Une nouvelle définition du crime basée sur la science biologique', *Revue pénitentiare*, 1895, p739.
12 Manouvrier, L. P. 'Les aptitudes et les acts', *Bull. de la soc. d'anthr.*, Paris, 1890; new edn, 1893.
13 Ferri, E. *Criminal Sociology*, Moscow, 2005, p102.

of crime does not lie in the answer to the question: is a single act prohibited by law enough to establish the concept of crime? Recently, along with the legal definition of crime, formal usage has adopted the term 'crime' in a criminological sense, understood as a culpable act constituting a significant risk to society, regardless of its recognition as a crime by law.[14] Simultaneously, D. A. Shestakov suggested singling out imaginary crime as an act unreasonably forbidden by law under penalty of law.

What act should be regarded as criminal and what should not is a question to which there is no decisive answer. According to Athenian law, Socrates was a criminal and yet we now understand that his criminal act not only helped his country but all of mankind, while in Sparta babies born weak or deformed were exterminated as being unable to grow up to serve and thus judged unfit for the state.

Before the Revelation of the Quran, the Arabs did not regard the burying of newborn girls alive as a crime and it was not even condemned, because for a family, women were considered a burden or deadweight if unable to work. It was also associated with a lack of men needed for war fighting. Defiant and honest, the statesman Aristides was expelled from Athens just for the fact that his rivalry with Themistocles was harmful in the defence against the Persian invaders, breaking the unity and agreement of all parties. As for Zoroaster, who followed later, the most serious crime was to bury the dead in the ground. Instead, corpses were left to dogs or birds of prey, while the Greeks considered not wrapping the dead in a shroud the greatest crime.

There are many such examples to be found in the history of any nation. G. V. Maltsev is right in stating that "one has been and remains unchanged: every community, ancient or modern, classifies to the category of criminal acts those acts of its members that are experienced as appearing dangerous to the common cause, causing harm to the society and its individual members, threatening the collapse of the social organisation. All this is now summarised in the concept of the social danger of the criminal act."[15]

From all this it follows that 'crime' is essentially a term applied to certain social situations. The same act, in terms of substance in different historical times, in different societies and in different social contexts, can be regarded as anti-social, socially neutral or socially approved. Thus, during the Arab Caliphate, the Caliph Umar, guided by a commandment that doubt softens punishment, vacated the sentence for theft in a year of famine. As T. Tarde points out, "the system of virtues, as well as the system of crime and vice,

14   See: Shestakov, D. A. *Criminology: Crime as a Feature of Society*, Short Course, Saint Petersburg, 2001.
15   Maltsev, G. V. *Vengeance and Retaliation in Ancient Law*, Moscow, 2012, p420.

changes with the course of history".[16] Indeed, there have been nations where theft and plundering were not only not considered crimes but, on the contrary, deemed virtues. As a consequence of its structure and general conditions, every society will create a certain amount of certain crimes. The concept of crime is associated with the ideas prevalent in a particular community, ideas that promote what constitutes criminal and what entails criminal penalties. And, of course, what does not.

The actual grounds for classifying certain acts as criminal and others as administrative or civil may be identified only on the basis of knowledge about the course of the historical development of a particular nation. The same behaviour that is frowned upon by society at this time and in this place may be approved at another time and in another place. And it is extremely difficult to determine which behaviour is approved and which is disapproved. It is impossible to study crime beyond time and space by taking it out of the social environment in which it exists. Hence who should be considered a criminal and when, is also a matter of time and historical period.

On this, Sorokin points out that "when comparing specific acts called criminal by various codes, it turns out that you cannot specify any act which would be considered as such by all codes. Even such crimes as murder are not always or everywhere considered crimes."[17]

There are indeed situations where, for any number of reasons, the state of a society along with its common norms and values lose their binding nature, and their rationale and fairness begin to be questioned by the overwhelming majority of the population. In the Soviet period, for example, profiteering and cheating customers were considered crimes even though the population of the country understood the pointlessness and injustice of the criminalisation of these acts.

The consumption of alcohol has a long tradition in many parts of the world, and for some nations it may even be regarded as a characteristic feature. It was also found that some violent crimes are committed in a state of alcoholic intoxication. Every year tens and possibly hundreds of thousands die as a result of alcohol abuse, which raises the question of whether this is a phenomenon that is harmful to both the individual and the whole of society? Why should the consumption of drugs be considered a danger to society and a crime, while alcohol abuse is not?

Back in the days of the USSR, Soviet criminal legislation regarded

16   Tarde, G. D. *Comparative Crime*, Moscow, 1907, p33.
17   Sorokin, P. A. 'Crime and Punishment', *Feat and Reward: Sociological Studies on the Basic Forms of Social Behaviour and Morality*, foreword by V. V. Sapova, Moscow, 2006, pp 128–130.

committing a crime under the influence of alcohol as a mitigating circumstance in sentencing. This stance has since been dropped and henceforth it is possible that drinking, i.e. drinking alcohol, may come to be considered a crime.

In fact the number of acts that may be defined as crimes is increasing. For example, the law may impose liability for female prostitution, based on the fact that the number of women working in the sex industry is steadily increasing, although this phenomenon (i.e. the act) existed in ancient times, when such women were stoned to death, and when public opinion pursued them with indignation.

Once the nations of the Caucasus (as with many other nations) had the custom of kidnapping girls. This was not a crime, because the kidnappers did not pursue the goals of bringing harm to the girl or her family. Instead, she was offered the opportunity to marry and create her own family. From the moral viewpoint, we may assume that this custom was vicious, because the girl would in all likelihood object to being married without love. However, the common life of Caucasians in those days was that the vast majority of girls were married off without even being acquainted with their husbands. In other words, custom and tradition did not consider such acts as criminal, they were completely normal. Later, during the Soviet period, this act was regarded as kidnapping and a crime—a relic of times past. So there is no such act that could be considered a crime at all times and by all nations.

Laws, including criminal, prescribe good customs and proscribe bad ones. However, there have been many cases where the legislature and the public recognised as socially dangerous and harmful customs that, in fact, were useful, and vice versa. For example, in Persia, the law did not consider as criminal a sexual relationship between mother and son, while socialising with a gentile woman was classified as an incomparably more dangerous felony. Customs are therefore like sources and principles from which laws derive; indeed, the etymology of the word 'custom' reveals it to be a form of the ordinary, i.e. habitual, repetitive conduct.[18] D. A. Dril believed that "a custom is not a common rule for future actions established in advance as mandatory, but only a solution, though due to frequent recurrence, a generalised solution, yet nevertheless allowing changes considering new features and occasions."[19]

---

18   See: Dal, V. *Explanatory Dictionary of the Living Great Russian Language*, Saint Petersburg/Moscow, 1881, vol. 2, pp 637–638.
19   Dril, D. A. *Crime and Criminals: The Doctrine of Crime and Measures to Combat It*, Moscow, 2010, p224.

It would be wrong to consider that a legal custom is something archaic, a remnant from the times of pre-industrial society. Rather, any custom, including a legal one, is a living, evolving element of the social regulation of contemporary social life.[20]

Blood vengeance is one such custom that has long been prohibited and yet it endures in places. And there should be nothing surprising in this. A non-Caucasian views blood vengeance as a relic of times past, an animal law of merciless retaliation. Perhaps it is so. However, the law of blood vengeance is much harder and more flexible than most European laws. Blood vengeance does not simply arise or disappear spontaneously: from birth, every Caucasian knows all the rules of blood vengeance and carries them in their heads. In practice, blood vengeance constitutes the sole obstacle to mass murder. It was only because of blood vengeance that an order satisfactory to all was able to survive in the Caucasus. Fear and rules (conditions) of vengeance contributed to this, yet served also as the basis for relationships among the tribes and other peoples. Of course we should note too that pursuing one's enemy until the end of one's life was considered a sacred duty for Caucasians.

What then is blood vengeance exactly? We can say that it is a sacred duty that theoretically leads to an endless cycle because each act of vengeance generates a new round, and so on without end. "Not only blood vengeance, but all forms of punishment—from the most primitive to the most advanced—are an expression of revenge."[21]

In fact, killing out of revenge is the response of an individual to unfair improper behaviour that causes death or any injury to him or a member of his family, clan, tribe or group. It cannot be defence against an attack, because the act arises after harm is inflicted, and because it is too late to speak of protection from imminent danger. Blood vengeance may be directed not only against the person who caused the harm but also against other group members. According to Erich Fromm, the person starts to administer justice when losing faith. "In his thirst for revenge he no longer needs the authorities, he is the 'supreme judge' and, in the act of revenge, he feels both as an angel and God . . . and this is his finest hour."[22]

A noteworthy incident, in the Lankaran district of Azerbaijan in the early 1990s, involved R., a minor who shot dead his father's murderer in front of the whole courtroom. This transpired in our time, not in the past, not in ancient times of yesteryore. Why then is revenge such a deep-rooted and

20   See: Lapaeva, V. V. *Law Sociology*, Moscow, 2011, p177.
21   Menninger, K. A. *The Crime of Punishment*, New York, 1968.
21   Oppenheimer, H. *Historical Research on the Origin of Punishment*, Moscow, 2012, p77.
22   Fromm, E. *The Anatomy of Human Destructiveness*, Moscow, 2004, p380.

intense passion? Might it be that the person is inherent in the elementary sense of justice? In the real-life example just given, the minor killer R. was convinced that the court would hand down an unjust sentence and so he decided to administer justice himself.

According to psychologists, the desire for revenge as a deep personal feeling is inherent in everyone, regardless of nationality and religion. That makes it hard to agree with Fromm's claim that an individual who attains the level that corresponds to the Christian or Buddhist ideal of a man is devoid of vengeful feelings. For a start, the Bible admits revenge, and secondly, we can also speak here of a Muslim complying with all of the principles of Islam. If we follow Fromm's reasoning, it turns out that killing out of revenge disappears thanks to the spiritual and religious development of a human being. Currently, it is near impossible to find a person who has reached such a level, while, on the contrary and given present conditions, sectarian killings would appear to have reached a peak. In fact, in its time, blood vengeance has played a social role in ensuring the stability of society, and proved a powerful deterrent against violent crime.

In Mecca, before the advent of Islam, there were no trials, no jail and no punishment. The tribe held its members accountable to customary law. In particular, when many girls were born, an Arab found a simple way to kill them. Ruthless desert customs allowed for the burying alive of unwanted daughters in the ground so that they would not be a burden for the tribe and would not reduce the proportion of boys suckling breast milk. Once at the sanctuary of the Ka'aba, a little girl was passing by the Prophet Muhammad. He called the child, gently stroked her head and began to sing children's songs to her. Members of the Quraysh tribe who were sitting around shook their heads in disapproval as they looked at the girl and the Prophet, since girls were considered worthless creatures. One elderly Quraysh, who could no longer tolerate such impudence, went up to Muhammad and demanded: "Why are you caressing this child? Do you not know that it is even allowed to kill girls with impunity?" At this the Prophet stood up and revealed a new ayah of the Quran: "Treat your parents with great kindness; if either or both of them attain old age; do not kill your children out of poverty; we will provide for you and them" (Surah 6, ayah 152). And this is how a significant law of Islam arose, one that put an end to the custom that had existed in the desert for centuries.

Sometimes customs and traditions are so deeply rooted in the minds and in the living conditions of people that their cancellation or prohibition occurs in stages, rather than immediately. For example, a ban on alcohol, according to the Quran, was imposed at a time when a few believers came to prayers intoxicated and their actions provoked unhealthy attention. There was then revealed in the Quran the following ayah: "They ask you about wine and gambling. Say, 'In them is great sin and [yet, some] benefit for people. But their sin is greater than their benefit' " (Surah 2, ayah 219).

Here we should note that Heinrich Oppenheimer, most likely due to ignorance of the Quran, offers the wrong reasons for the prohibition against alcohol in Islam when he writes: "We can be sure that the motive of retribution for drunkenness in Muslim, Chinese and Mexican law lies in the sphere of belief in magic, and alcohol, like other poisons, was considered as possessing supernatural properties due to its specific action."[23] As is clear from the ayah above, the Quran does not strictly forbid alcohol or gambling, there is no liability here. Conversely, it even refers to the benefits of these activities.

The fact is that the Arabs, in the centuries of pre-Islamic times, had long held their own customs and moral values. In particular, they boasted of drinking wine, not because it was in itself a source of pride but because it seemed a manifestation of generosity (*karam*), more precisely a means of encouraging the soul to extravagance. Even a cursory glance at the collections of pre-Islamic poetry will reveal the large number of poems in praise of wine.

The same may be said of gambling (*maysir*), considering that this activity is one of the manifestations of generosity, since everything they had won, or everything that had remained for the winners net their rates, was spent on food for the poor. This ayah of the Quran affects people through persuasion rather than coercion. Later there appears ayah 43 of Surah 4 (An-Nisa' [The Women]), where Allah sends people the following message: "O you who have believed, do not approach prayer while you are intoxicated until you know what you are saying." Here the attitude towards alcohol is more strict, but still it is not considered a sin, or in legal language, a crime.

There are other ayahs of the Quran dealing with alcohol and gambling that specifically prohibit and penalise them: "O you who have believed, indeed, intoxicants, gambling are but defilement from the work of Satan, so avoid them that you may be successful" (Surah 5: Al-Ma'idah [The Table], ayah 90); "Satan only wants to cause between you animosity and hatred through intoxicants and gambling and to avert you from the remembrance of Allah and from prayer. So will you not desist?" (Surah 5, ayah 91). On the basis of these statutes, there are Muslim countries who consider such acts criminal, and for which severe penalties are stipulated.

---

23 Oppenheimer, H. *Historical Research on the Origin of Punishment*, Moscow, 2012, p77.

It is useful to note here that in the Quran and other sources of Islamic law, matters related to the various institutions of criminal law, including the institution of crime, are covered in detail. According to Muslim law, the rules of conduct are governed by religious, legal, moral norms, customs, rules of courtesy and etiquette. According to the Quran, human life is under the constant control of Allah, who evaluates each action in terms of its compliance with religious requirements (standards). The scripture repeatedly emphasizes that Allah sees everything done by people and that "nothing on earth and in the sky is hidden" from Him. Hence any criminal behaviour is not only a deviation, a violation of law followed by punishment in this life, but at the same time it also acts as a religious sin entailing punishment in the afterlife. This means that according to the Quran, crime can be regarded as a deviation from the requirements of legal norms, as well as a religious sin.

The issues of crime and punishment are set out in the legal norms of Surah 4 (Al-Nisa' [The Women], ayahs 33–34, 94–95) of the Quran. However, despite the religious and legal nature of these ayahs, the Quran cannot be considered a legal code in the modern sense. When studying the concept of crime, Muslim legal scholars considered two fundamental philosophical and theological origins. First of all, they believed that all the actions and even the thoughts of people are somehow predetermined by the will of Allah. Conversely, the framework established by the Quran is flexible enough to allow an individual to choose the option of their behaviour in many real-life situations. Therefore, the Quran gives the general direction, basic principles and rules for the protection of the five core values: religion, life, intellect, progeny and property.

From the point of view of the main representatives of the Muslim and legal theory of crime, criminal behaviour (crime) in the formal legal sense means committing an act prohibited and punishable by Allah. At present, the Quran is rarely used as a legal tool in Muslim countries but continues to operate in a spiritual sense as a means of preventing crime, which introduces contradictions between criminal law and religious dogmas. This is perfectly natural because, no matter how deep and fine, certain, universal and multidimensional the Quran has been, many of its provisions and rules cannot be literally and directly reflected, or implemented, in the modern criminal legislation of contemporary Muslim states.

The essence of crime, therefore, cannot be detected by mere theoretical and applied criminological legal research without the involvement of sociological, psychological, statistical, philosophical means of cognition. Criminology does not offer any comprehensive legal, economic, sociological, psychological recommendations about crime; it simply informs society about the state of crime and suggests the appropriate means to combat this phenomenon. There is always something mysterious and mystical in the criminal act, it is located at deep levels impervious to criminological analysis. And this is why the problem arises of the lack of analytical tools available to criminology and other related disciplines.

Judging by objective properties, crime is the affront of a specific person against the order of human, group and individual relationships established in the society. This makes the crime *social*, for the interaction of several units is the essence of social phenomena. By committing a crime, the perpetrator engages in an interaction with other members of society, i.e. the local social group and society in general. However, not all kinds of interactions should be understood as social interaction, only those not present anywhere except the human community, i.e. between people or organisations. It should also be emphasized that crime is a social phenomenon since acts of behaviour are invariably accompanied by mental experiences.

Consequently those interactions between people not having any relationship to mental forms are not included in social phenomena—and we know that criminal behaviour is always accompanied by mental experiences. As Sorokin puts it: "Every interaction between anyone, once having a mental nature, is a social phenomenon."[24] The community of individuals being in mental interaction with each other is a social group or a social unit, therefore crime is a result of the lack of the conditions required for the possibility of correct mental interaction between people, resulting in no identical manifestations of the same mental experiences by different members of society. In other words, social conditions in society create unequal opportunities for its members, this leads to improper mental interaction between them and, thus, to conflict.

But the issue does not lie only in the external social conditions. Due to the individuality of human nature, members of a society or group differently understand and accept certain conditions of the society in which they live. Eventually this leads to a contradiction of interests of the individual and society, which sometimes ends in crime. As a result, we have a particular social group separated from society, which is characterised by repetition, mass character, typicality, public danger, and so becomes the starting point of sociological analysis.

Thus the subject of the sociology of crime eventually centres around

24 Sorokin, P. *Crime and Punishment: Feat and Reward*, Saint Petersburg, 1914, p19.

human behaviour in general and criminal behaviour in particular, meaning that crime can be regarded as a sociopsychological phenomenon. Nevertheless this is still not enough to understand the essence of crime since it also requires philosophical understanding and knowledge. In recent years, philosophical studies have focused on the problems of crime and criminality: E. A. Pozdnyakov published his monograph *The Philosophy of Crime*; D. S. Babichev's thesis for his Candidate of Legal Sciences degree was entitled 'Political and Legal Studies of the Philosophy of Criminality'; A. P. Dubnov and V. A. Dubovtsev published their study *The Philosophy of Criminality: The Criminalisation of Russian Society* in 1999; and a more recent publication is *The Philosophy of Evil and the Philosophy of Criminality* (2013), a solid monograph written by A. I. Alexandrov.

None of these authors distinguish between the concepts of the 'philosophy of crime' and the 'philosophy of criminality'. As Babichev in particular writes: "The study of the philosophy of criminality involves consideration of the phenomenon of criminality as an inescapable reality of life that is capable of continuous existence and development."[25] He even suggests that when studying the philosophy of criminality one should draw on the knowledge gained in the fields of philosophy, philosophy of law, sociology and other liberal sciences.[26]

Along with the concept of the philosophy of criminality, Babichev also repeatedly refers to the 'philosophy of crime'. In his view, the study of the philosophy of criminality supposes a philosophical understanding of the nature of the phenomenon of the offence and consideration of its essence from a position of the absolute manifestation of 'evil' coming from a man. According to the author, this 'evil', as a phenomenon contained in man constituting his essence and guiding his actions, generates criminal origins in him. It cannot be denied, since Babichev correctly believes that the causes of criminal behaviour are to be found in man himself. Thus he provides an answer to the philosophical question of why a person commits a crime, and so, whether he likes it or not, confirms the validity of the use of the concept of 'philosophy of crime' and not 'philosophy of criminality'.

Alexandrov's arguments on the use of the philosophy of criminality are not so convincing. Working along this concept, he in fact ends up discussing the philosophy of crime: "The philosophy of criminality should adequately comprehend the philosophical and theoretical meaning and essence of the phenomenon of the offence, the boundaries and degree of its relation to

25   Babichev, D. S. 'Political and Legal Studies of the Philosophy of Criminality',
     Candidate of Legal Sciences thesis, Ufa, 2004, p40.
26   Ibid, p22.

lawful behaviour, identify the main causes and conditions of the occurrence and preservation of the viability of criminal behaviour, and develop - methodological prerequisites for, if not its eradication, then at least, its minimisation. These are its research tasks as a fully independent and promising area of research."[27]

Firstly, when examining the phenomenon of offence (including crime naturally), the causes and origins of criminal behaviour are the main subjects in the philosophy of crime since the question of what constitutes a crime and wherein lie the roots of this phenomenon is answered not by the philosophy of criminality but of crime. Alexandrov returns to this, reiterating: "When carrying out the philosophical study of crime, one needs to answer a number of questions: why does one commit a crime; which properties inherent in him are pushing him to actions qualified as crime?"[28] If these issues are attributed to the philosophy of criminality, then we can ask what questions exactly should be answered by the philosophy of crime? If we proceed from the fact that it does not matter, it then turns out that there is no difference between criminality and crime, although Alexandrov goes on to consider these phenomena as communication between the public and the individual, quantity and quality.[29]

Secondly, Alexandrov, in my opinion, is mistaken his argument that the philosophy of criminality should develop methodological prerequisites for, if not its eradication, then at least its minimisation. In fact, we are talking about criminal policy to combat crime and this is not the goal of philosophical investigation but of criminology and criminal law. However, in order to ensure the correct application of the concepts of the philosophy of crime and the philosophy of criminality, the relation, autonomy and correlation of the concepts of crime and criminality should be considered. The need to distinguish between these concepts is that the methodological approach to the study of the causes of criminality and crime in general depends on the way of understanding their relationship. In other words, if criminality is qualitatively different from crime, if these phenomena are not uniordinal, then the hopelessness of studying criminality via the knowledge of specific criminal acts is quite obvious and natural.

Criminality and crime can be seen concept-wise as the ratio of a part towards the whole, so understanding this particularly requires using the philosophical categories of the whole and the discrete. Even thinkers from

27 Alexandrov, A. I. *The Philosophy of Evil and Philosophy of Criminality*, Saint Petersburg, 2013, p65.
28 Ibid., p69
29 Ibid., p85.

the past, starting with Aristotle, faced insurmountable difficulties in defining such concepts. A study deep enough in this direction was carried out by Hegel, who sought to overcome these difficulties. We, as lawyers, can only use what is widely accepted in our research, as Hegel says, "a thing as *this* thing is their purely quantitative ratio, it is a simple aggregation of their 'also'. It consists of one or the other specific quantity of one substance and also of a certain amount of some other substance, and also of something different: the thing is a connection involving the absence of any connections."[30]

A. Leps adds the conclusion that "criminality as a thing consists of various crimes that have only a quantitative ratio for different crimes, or their groups, or 'their mere accumulation', or their 'also'. Likewise, we can say that criminality as a sum of different crimes has no connection between different crimes."[31] Leps proceeds from theory to practice and argues "nowadays, modern criminology sums up the crimes committed within a specific territory over a certain period of time, and it turns into a completely new phenomenon called criminality as the phenomenon of essence considered dynamically, its structure is studied, it is compared with the number of the population, etc. Of course, these 'notes' are of certain operational importance in the daily work of agencies related to law enforcement. But one often tries to give such 'notes' scientific value, although the case is far from scientific."[32]

So Leps believes that criminality as a new phenomenon is the result of the sum of separate crimes within a particular territory. He emphasizes the quantitative and statistical nature of the criminality concept, there is no objection to it. At the same time, Leps notes that the new criminality concept has a structure, dynamics, tendency, nature and so on. The question then arises: can criminality as a phenomenon of essence characterised by these features possess only quantitative characteristics without any qualitative properties? There are many other linked fundamental questions of not only theoretical but also practical importance. Can certain crimes exist independently within criminality as a whole, or are they inseparable from it? How are separate crimes combined in criminality, i.e. in a natural or in an artificial way? Are there qualitative or quantitative features? Does the interaction of separate crimes in criminality lead to the emergence of new qualities of the whole not peculiar to the crimes as a part? Which occurs first: a separate crime as part of a whole, or criminality as a whole?

30   Hegel, G. W. F. *Science of Logic*, Saint Petersburg, 2002, p448.
31   Leps, A. 'Hegel's Philosophy and Criminality as a Phenomenon of Essence', *Legal Sciences and Education*, 2012, no. 35, p167.
32   Ibid, pp 468–470.

Nowadays, criminality is characterised as a negative social and legal phenomenon and also as a social phenomenon, or as both a social and philosophical and legal phenomenon, as one of society's parameters, characterising the state of the social mechanism and mismatch between its constituent parts.[33]

Alexandrov provides an interesting definition of criminality where, in answering the question of what criminality is, he observes that "criminality is the mass solution of human problems violating a criminal ban".[34] What conclusion follows from this definition? The mass solution of human problems emphasizes the conscious, organised, focused yet not spontaneous nature of crime. In other words, in order to solve their problems, a certain group of people, i.e. a certain mass gathered together, agrees in advance and comes to a single mass decision with respect to the violation of the criminal ban against committing crimes in a certain period of time within a particular territory. The nature of these crimes does not matter. But is such mass solution possible?

There is another position which was no less prevalent in the former Soviet Union and in foreign criminology, namely that criminality is the totality of all the specific crimes committed in a certain period of time in a given society or region.[35] Some believe that this definition is formal and defines the normative aspect of criminality while not actually revealing the nature of this social phenomenon.[36] We know that any social phenomenon appears as an element of the social system that is society. Within the framework of this system, all social phenomena and processes in their interaction are analysed, and criminality is among these phenomena. Taking a statistical approach, sociology provides public material on qualitative and quantitative changes in criminality. Based on such data, criminology examines the state, dynamics and structure of criminality, i.e. everything that is associated with criminality statistics comprising the acts committed by people in the society and against the interests of the society.

The unique feature of criminality consists of the fact that every single

33   See: *Criminology: A Textbook*, ed. by V. N. Kudryavtsev & V. E. Eminov, Moscow, 1997; *Criminology for Law Schools*, ed. by A. I. Dolgova, Moscow, 1997; Spiridonov, L. I. *Sociology of Criminality*, Moscow, 1978, etc.

34   Alexandrov, A. I. Op. cit, p71.

35   See: *Criminology*, ed. by I. I. Karpets, V. N. Kudryavtsev, N. F. Kuznetsova, A. B. Sakharov, Moscow, 1976; *Criminology*, ed. by V. G. Zvirbul, N. F. Kuznetsova & G. M. Minkovskiy, Moscow, 1979; Vermet, M. *Major Criminology Issues*, translated from Hungarian, Moscow: Progress, 1978; Holyst, B. *Criminology: Major Issues*, translated from Polish, Moscow, 1980, etc.

36   See: Shapiev, S. 'Criminality and Society', (criminological theoretical and applied research), thesis Doctor of Law, Saint Petersburg, 2000, pp 31–32.

crime results from conscious human activity, and the figures on criminality are formed spontaneously, i.e. criminality statistics may not reflect reality. Of course, we cannot be limited only by statistical analysis of criminality without talking about the issues of its social and historical origins. Criminality is at the same time a relatively massive, historically volatile, social phenomenon of a criminal and legal nature. However, the social nature of criminality is caused by the social essence of a particular crime and not by the fact that criminality has social roots and causes. What does this mean?

The fact is that human behaviour is a phenomenon belonging to a social category and crime is known for being a behaviour type. Therefore, before studying criminal behaviour as a phenomenon of the social category, we need to define what we mean by social behaviour. L. Gumplowicz said: "Under social phenomena we understand relations arising from the interaction between human groups and communications."[37] According to G. Simmel, social phenomenon or society 'exists where several individuals are interacting."[38] As we can see, the difference in views between Gumplowicz and Simmel is that the former considers the group to be an element of interaction rather than the individual, although there is no essential differ-ence since "a few individuals" can also be considered a group.

From a sociological point of view, social phenomenon is, first of all, the interaction of various centres or the interaction with specific characteristics. However, every human interaction is inevitably accompanied by internal processes that take place between the persons involved. In other words, by analysing social phenomena, in particular the behaviour of people within a group, and attempting to break down their infinitely diverse actions into cat-egories, one should always begin with an analysis of the mental experiences accompanying any act of human behaviour. It follows that the analysis of mental experiences will provide a key to explaining all human actions, including those that are criminal. This is possible, of course, when psycho-logical categories and concepts are applied to social phenomena. Consequently, a social phenomenon will be an interaction that possesses a mental nature quite independent of who makes it or what it results in.

What then is mental interaction? From the psychological point of view (the inner one), this sort of interaction reduces to exchange, wishes and generally everything that can be described as a mental experience. It is not necessary for the interaction to be longlasting. If an interaction is short or

37   Gumplowicz, L. *The Outlines of Sociology*, Saint Petersburg, 1899, pp 113, 105, 106, 116, 265, ff.
38   Simmel, G. *Sociologie*. Leipzig, 1908, pp 5–7, 31–39.

accidental, it is enough for a mental experience, such as when committing a crime without any certain or planned preparation, that is, spontaneously.

Criminal sociality lies precisely within the interactions of individuals through the concept of 'crime', i.e. resulting from the commission of specific criminal offences. If crime ceased, then of course the application of the concept of 'criminality as a social phenomenon' would no longer be needed. Thus if we consider criminality to have a statistical numerical value (e.g. 24,000 crimes were recorded as being committed in Azerbaijan for 2011), it is not really possible to speak about the social nature of criminality, because statistical recording does not derive *per se* from human interaction, just as social phenomena include no characteristics of gender, age, height, weight, hair colour and so on. The situation changes when criminality is considered as a collection of individual and specific crimes, where its repeatability, mass nature, typically and the importance of public danger are established, i.e. if its characteristics and properties are fixed. In this case, criminality as a social phenomenon becomes the starting point for sociological and criminological research. Here again we may turn to Hegel: "The whole consists of the parts, without them it is nothing . . . So the whole and the parts are dependent on each other . . . each of them is independent in and of itself, they are two independent existences indifferent to each other . . . the whole is equal to the parts and the parts are equal to the whole."[39]

Based on the logic of the relationship between a part and the whole, we turn directly to the analysis of this in respect to the phenomena of crime and criminality. By 'part' we understand it as a singular phenomenon, i.e. a specific crime, a set of properties, qualities, traits that determine its specificity and particularity, which thus differentiate it from all other parts, i.e. crimes. For example, murder is distinct from rape, although both are included as parts of the same whole. Even with the whole set of individual criminal manifestations, the absolute identity of at least two of these is excluded, for there are no two crimes exactly the same or similar subjects committing them. However, clearly there is no specific crime that exists in isolation, by itself, without any relationship to other criminal phenomena. Theft as a crime cannot be understood without understanding the substance of robbery, otherwise we cannot give either the appropriate qualifications. In fact, no crime can appear, exist or disappear without communication or interaction with other phenomena from social, political, legal, spiritual and moral life. But if individual crimes (parts) are interconnected and they are interacting, then they have an element in common that refers them all to the same whole (criminality).

39   Leps, A. Op. cit, p173.

This commonality, being inherent in all crimes without exception, is the essence of a criminal act. It seems then that *evil* as a philosophical category is the essence of crime, and through the category of evil we can construct a comparative description of certain crimes. For example, murder differs from rape in many aspects, but they are united by evil as common to both of these phenomena. Consequently, since there are no absolutely similar, identical crimes, there is no absolute distinction between them—differences only arise in the degree and nature of evil. Therefore, in viewing the whole when referring to crime, there should be understood the unity of properties and qualities that are inherent in all of the parts without exception.

Kerimov writes: "The emergence of the whole can only take place if its parts really exist, the union of a certain set of which creates a kind of integral organisation."[40] All this gives us the grounds to state that criminality (as the whole) cannot exist without the individual crimes (as the parts), and vice versa; they are organically linked, dependent and conditioned. It should be stressed that criminality as a formation of the whole does not include only certain essential properties of a crime but the totality of the characteristics and features, i.e. criminality includes crime in its entirety. As a result, a new formation, i.e. criminality, acquires the properties that constitute the essence of crime: *evil*. Thus, both crime and criminality have a common essence, evil; criminality as an integral formation is not just a simple set of crimes.

Criminality as a whole with respect to individual crimes, i.e. to the parts, is objective in nature, regular, its formation is a necessity. L. O. Volt notes that "any whole differs from any mechanical unit in that it has some patterns of order and its parts are organised".[41] Accordingly, criminality should be considered a system, because, as V. G. Afanasyev notes, "there are no words, every whole is a system",[42] because the totality of crimes, the interaction of which determines the availability of new integrative qualities not peculiar to the generating ones, is a system. Criminality also evidences a certain structure.

One feature of criminality as a whole is the obligatory presence of a common structure integrating individual crimes as parts and marking them. In this structure V. I. Sviderskiy sees "the principle, the way, the law of connection of the elements of the whole, the system of relations of elements within this whole".[43] The structure of criminality characterises the inner

40 Kerimov, D. A. *The Methods of Law*, p212.
41 Volt, L. O. 'The Ratio of the Structure and Elements', *Philosophy Issues*, 1963, no. 5, p45.
42 Afanasyev, V. G. *The Problem of Integrity in Philosophy and Biology*, Moscow, 1964, pp 8–10.
43 Sviderskiy, V. I. *Some Features of Development in the Objective World*, Leningrad, 1964, p135.

form of its organisation, within which individual crimes are included in another whole by their various features. So for example, groups of juvenile crime, core crimes, crimes related to the economic block and so on are formed.

Criminality is changeable and unstable. The level of criminal stability depends on the nature, properties and dynamics of individual crimes. Hence it can be said that certain crimes, i.e. the parts, stand primary in relation to criminality (the whole) but secondary to old crimes. This applies to those acts which later receive the status of criminal. Kerimov explains that "the whole is the foundation for the existence, operation and development of the parts. Therefore, whatever value the parts might have in the whole, they are ultimately subordinate in relation to the whole."[44]

Yet as a result of the parts, i.e. the individual crimes, criminality as the whole exists and changes. After all, only through the examination and detailed analysis of specific crimes is one able to deepen one's knowledge of the essence of crime, to discover new laws and to particularise known laws of its development. This does not detract from the value of the whole, which is the object of study of the general causes of criminality. We can therefore see that individual crimes (as the parts) and criminality in general (as the whole) constitute an independent area of study. As K. Fisher puts it: "The whole is independent, and the parts are just a moment of this unity; however, they have their independence to the same extent, and reflective unity is only a moment."[45]

Recognition of criminality as a social phenomenon inevitably leads to recognition of its conditionality by specific social causes. In other words, if criminality, as opposed to an individual crime, is not an act of free will then its existence is also brought about by some kind of stable acting forces or causes independent of human will. Criminality consists of acts committed by people in the community and against the interests of society. Any social change, no matter how insignificant it may seem, directly or indirectly affects the level and dynamics of criminality. However, such changes cannot be associated with the causes of criminality since, as well as existing social conditions, they have an impact on criminality via individuals acting negatively on their behaviour.

Sociology and criminology have repeatedly returned to seek out what affects the state, level, structure and dynamics of the manifestations of criminality and negative definitions in general. A myriad of factors was revealed

44 Kerimov, D. A. Op. cit, p219.
45 Fisher, K. *Hegel: His Life, Doubts and Teachings*, Moscow; Leningrad, 1933, p390.

in the areas of economy, politics, demography and even space. This spurs the question of whom do they affect? Do they affect the personality, the individual or criminality as a statistical aggregate of individual crimes? What should we investigate in this case: the influence of these factors on people or on criminality, which is impossible without individual crimes? When we try to answer the question of the causes of crime, we start looking for the answer by referring to the individual who committed the crime as the subject of the act, and the question concerning the causes of criminality recedes into the background. This fits in with G. Manhein's view where he asserts that "it is time to reject searching for the causes of criminality"[46] and to study the mechanism of the origins of human behaviour, in particular criminal behaviour.

It is impossible to study the phenomenon of criminality only on a philosophical level, apart from the legal reality, since criminality is a complex multifaceted and, above all, social and legal phenomenon with its own inherent characteristics and patterns of development. Since criminality and crime are different concepts there cannot be any equal mark between them. Using a statistical approach, sociology throws up objective material on qualitative and quantitative changes in criminality. Based on this, criminology needs to study the state, dynamics and structure of criminality, i.e. everything connected with criminal statistics. As for the causes of human criminal behaviour, this does not belong to the field of criminology but to other fields such as philosophy, psychology, biology and genetics—in a word, all those sciences that study human nature in its broadest sense. It is a logical assumption that we need to analyse the causes of human criminal behaviour and the conditions and circumstances that lead to the commission of a criminal act rather than the causes of criminality.

Criminality results from the synthesis of material, i.e. the processing of statistical material not with a view to determining the causes of human criminal behaviour but for practical and theoretical use in the fight against this phenomenon. This is why we cannot speak of the 'philosophy of criminality'. We should use the term 'sociology of criminality' as criminality is at the same time a social and legal phenomenon. The subject matter of both the sociology and philosophy of criminality eventually focuses on human behaviour in general and on criminal behaviour in particular.

Looking at the philosophy of crime, there exist both the sociology and psychology of crime. Since crime is both a sociopsychological and a philosophical and legal concept, it is not possible to agree with Pozdnyakov's

46   Manhein, G. *Comparative Criminology*, London, 1965, p208.

statement that crime "as a definition should be of a legal nature and it simply cannot be something else".[47] But before we are able to understand the essence of the philosophy of crime we need to first understand the freedom of the human will, which is the task of philosophy as a science.

The philosophy of crime is more specific in terms of the research subject and naturally depends on the approach to the solution of questions in philosophy in general. It seeks to answer the question why a person in a given situation commits a criminal act. N. A. Neklyudov believes that the philosophy of crime involves the study of crime on the basis of criminal statistical data: "The philosophy of crime as an act is but a distraction of statistics of quality and quantity."[48] He argues that the philosophy of crime as an act is not intended to examine the ratio between a criminal act and our spirit—be it a product of unconditional arbitrariness or the relative liberty of a person, a product of their ill will or simply a consequence of inevitable fate, the judge—rather this is the task of philosophy in general and the philosophy of criminal law in particular; in short subjective philosophy.

So for Neklyudov there is an objective philosophy of crime, the starting point of which is external conditions, and a subjective philosophy, i.e. ill will as the cause of crime. In other words, the subject matter of objective philosophy is solely those external circumstances from which ill will as the subject matter of subjective philosophy might benefit most. Thus, he reasons, from the standpoint of the objective philosophy of crime, committing a criminal act is caused not only by ill will, as it is incorporeal, but also by external conditions.

For a start, one can hardly agree with the assertion that a science that studies crime based on criminal statistical data should be termed as the philosophy of crime. It is rather the science of criminology engaged in the analysis of statistical data with a view to making recommendations to combat crime. Secondly, studying a criminal and a crime beyond time and space by artificially taking them out of their social environment and the conditions of the social community life in which they exist and with which they are bound by organic inseparable connections is impossible and makes no sense. And finally, when we talk about the philosophy of crime, we talk about a *deed*, one that is directly linked to a person with no connection to the outside world, in other words we are talking about a 'pure act'. In this case then, we are looking for an answer to the question of whether a person was free to choose

47 Pozdnyakov, E. A. *Philosophy of Crime*, p82.
48 Neklyudov, N. A. *Criminal Statistical Studies*, Moscow, 2010, p5.

their behaviour when committing a crime or not. We are not interested in the conditions and circumstances in which this person was placed and which, in fact, could contribute to this, which is why it makes no sense to divide the philosophy of crime into subjective and objective. The philosophy of crime is an eternal quest for answers to the questions of whether a person is free to choose their behaviour and where the origins of a criminal act lie.

*

2

Causes and Origins of Criminal Behaviour

Historical Background

Studying the causes of crime has a long history of development saturated in all manner of established theories, original concepts and intriguing ideas by philosophers, lawyers, psychologists, sociologists, religious thinkers, doctors and even authors. Some of them, upon closer inspection, appear primitive to say the least and even, at times, ridiculous and incomprehensible. Nevertheless, they are of great interest to us in studying the causes of crime. As a result, nowadays the following generally accepted approaches to determining the causes of crime exist: regulatory and legal, philosophical, ethical, religious, anthropological (the result of the biological and natural qualities of a person), sociological and so on. It is also possible to divide the history of this issue by following its successive periods.

In prehistoric times, this was a subject for philosophers who briefly commented on the concept and causes of crime, so to speak, superficially, when considering general scientific questions of philosophy. The social significance of crime and its causes was already grasped by the ancient philosophers since the time of Solon, Pythagoras, Protagoras, i.e. before the great Greek thinkers Plato and Aristotle. In his Socratic dialogue *Gorgias* Plato examines the causes of crime not as the disease of a criminal's soul but as the disease of a state, whose cure falls within the duties of the government. In other words, the philosopher sees the causes of crime in the social roots of society and not in the individual.

Unlike Plato, however, Aristotle's views were of a more solid character because he almost always spoke about the causes of crime not from the abstract and philosophical, as Plato did, but from the criminal and political point of view. Aristotle also considered the causes of crime as a social evil that must be fought and, if possible, prevented. Stoics, the philosophy of which had a cosmopolitan character, on the contrary believed that crime was a perversity of human nature. Still, the ancient philosophers were not able to create any established theory of crime and its causes, although their views on this have played an invaluable role in the development of the science of criminal law.

The second period begins with the appearance of the classical school of criminal law and is associated with two great events: humanism and the Reformation. Chubinskiy rightly observes that without either of these the natural and legal doctrine that led to the flourishing of new criminal and legal studies could not have arisen.[1] Politicians, philosophers and lawyers now started thinking about new approaches to the causes of crime. Among these were the likes of Hugo Grotius, Hobbes, Spinoza, Locke, Fichte, Gomel, Feuerbach. Without any doubt, they have made a huge contribution to the struggle with outdated and outmoded views on the concept of crime and its causes, and, accordingly, the methods of combating these phenomena. But, unfortunately, none of them was able to do what Cesare Beccaria did. As Ferri writes: "Neither the Romans, who greatly developed civil law, nor the medieval lawyers, could elevate criminal law to the height of a philosophical system. Guided rather by feelings than by strictly scientific aspiration, Beccaria was the first to give impetus to the teaching of crime and punishment."[2]

Indeed, the formation of the classical school of criminal law was closely connected with Beccaria, upon whose principles was subsequently built a system of criminal law in the civilised world. The scientific method of this school was the *a priori* study of crime as an abstract legal entity. One of the most brilliant representatives of this school, Francesco Carrara, said: "Crime is a legal phenomenon, the violation, not the action."[3] The best representatives of the Russian classical school defined crime as a phenomenon embracing a sphere of 'legal relations'[4] and the object of pure legal research, as expressed by N. S. Tagantsev, as "studying the legal construction of criminal acts".[5]

Thus, the classical school stated that a criminal act as the actual relationship outside the legal concept should not become a subject for study by a

1   Chubinskiy, M. P. *Essays on Criminal Policy*, Moscow, 2010, p136.
2   Ferri, E. Op. cit, p22.
3   Carrara. *Programma, parte generale*, 6th edn, 1886, pp 1, 21–23.
4   Nabokov, V. D. *Collection of Articles on Criminal Law*, Saint Petersburg, 1904, p8.
5   Tagantsev, N. S. *Russian Criminal Law*, Saint Petersburg, 1902, vol. 1, p16.

criminologist, since for criminal law, according to V. D. Nabokov, "crime and punishment are concepts".[6] This structure of the concept of crime inevitably led to neglecting the identity of the criminal as the subject of a criminal act. This opened the opportunity to attack the classical idea via the question of whether it is possible to examine a crime without the identity of the person who committed it. Ferri wrote on this subject, saying: "For the classical criminalist, the identity of a criminal has quite a secondary importance, like a patient once had to a doctor. The criminal appears to him as a creature to which are applied the theoretical formula being the product of theoretical speculations, an animated mannequin, on the back of which the judge sticks the number of the Criminal Code article and who becomes the number himself at the execution of the sentence."[7]

Furthermore, the classical school was accused of exhausting the substance of the science of criminal law by defining crime as a legal phenomenon, thereby restricting the limits of its study of crime as an exclusively legal phenomenon.[8] But the most powerful and consistent accusation against the classical school targeted the fact that it took the free will of people resulting in the commission of a crime as an implicit postulate, meaning that it is precisely free will that determines whether to commit or not to commit a crime, whether that be to commit it one way or another and whether in a greater or lesser extent.[9]

In reality, the classical school did not deny the possibility of studying criminals. It merely left them unattended. It approached criminals essentially from one direction only, considering the crime committed, although it did acknowledge the impossibility of studying crime without considering the subject who committed it. Hence the assertion that the classical school regarded crime simply as a legal entity, as an act without a figure, ignoring the impact of human and sociological factors on crime, is not true. This is confirmed in particular in Beccaria's *Crime and Punishment*, as Chubinskiy rightly points out, "after Beccaria, a powerful reformist stream began widely developing and, in the end, swept away the old order of criminal justice and caused the creation of a new order, in sharp contrast to the previous one considering its principles and institutions."[10]

It should also be stressed that Montesquieu, whose works had such a strong influence on Beccaria, was more a positivist than all of his

6   Nabokov, V. D. Op. cit, p5.
7   Ferri, E. Op. cit, p32.
8   See: Charykhov, H. M. *Doctrine on the Factors of Crime*, Sociological School for the Science of Criminal Law, Moscow, 1910, p1.
9   Ferri, E. Op. cit, p33.
10 Chubinskiy, M. P. Op. cit, p218.

predecessors, except perhaps for Bacon, in the sense that he not only expressed ideas that were fruitful to criminal policy but also sought to justify them. It is clear that the rich sociological, anthropological and statistical material used by the later positivists was available neither to Beccaria nor to Montesquieu, who largely used only historical material.

In my opinion, the position of the classics was that the study of the psychophysical organisation of the subject of crime should not and cannot be the subject matter of legal, especially criminological research because the study of the physical, biological, psychological essence of a person is an independent field of anthropological and sociological research. Otherwise, along with the concept of crime set forth in criminal law and called the 'legal definition', a term employed in criminology should also be used, i.e. the 'material' or criminological definition.

At the beginning of the nineteenth century, statistics began to be mainly engaged in the study of crime. It seems that it would be right to consider this as the beginning of a new, third period of studying the concept and nature of crime in relation to the identity of a criminal. In contrast to physical and biological phenomena, social phenomena, which include crime, are impossible to study experimentally. And so the observation method needs to be sufficient when researching the field of sociology.

One of the most useful and effective tools for such observations is statistics. As Tarde writes: "Statistics is something like an evolving public feeling: for society, it is like animal vision and by determination, gradualness, increasing abundance of its charts, curves and coloured maps it makes this analogy more and more striking with every passing day. In fact, an eye is nothing but a wonderful machine for the fast, instant and original calculation of optical vibrations, which it transmits to us in the form of a continuous series of visual pictures like a constantly updated atlas."[11]

Crime statistics evolved in Belgium and France under the guise of a chapters of moral statistics. A group of scientists who, having no intention of studying crime or focusing on moral statistics as the subject matter of their research, observed crime as an immoral act. They dealt with the issues of crime based not upon *a priori* evidence but upon conclusions drawn from the real life of society. Scientific criminal statistics came to be born between 1825 and 1830, and the forefather of the field is considered to be Adolphe Quetelet, a professor at Brussels University.

As Krone once said, criminal statistics is "the first condition of success in the fight against criminality and it plays in this fight the same role as the

---

11   Tarde, G. D. Op. cit, p81.

intelligence service plays during war".[12] Using digital data, Quetelet studied the question of whether the actions of a person with moral sense and thought occur with certain regularity. And he came to the following bold conclusions: "Society in and of itself bears the germ of the committed crimes. Society itself one way or another inevitably creates crimes and a criminal is a criminal weapon in its hands; every social form generates a certain number and a certain kind of crimes necessarily committed in its environment."[13]

Quetelet believed that crimes would remain constant and unchanged until their causes were explored and addressed so as to effect change, although this was known before him to many of those who were seriously pursuing this line of thought. What was new and important was the fact that on the basis of an analysis of statistical data on the status of criminality, Quetelet struck a powerful blow against the belief in the possibility of the fight against crime by criminal penalties. In particular, he argued that criminal penalties cannot prevent growth in criminality without affecting its social factors. This should be unconditionally accepted, although we know that punishment cannot cause any effective direct action on social factors. At the same time, by estimating the value of criminality factors such as sex, age, climate, economic conditions and social status, he set out to investigate the biological factors of criminality.

Quetelet was so fascinated by his statistics that he began to set up parameters for those who had a known propensity towards crime. The statistician's merit lies in the fact that before him, the causes of crime had been estimated only theoretically, but now it was possible with the help of numbers to point the causes of crime more or less precisely, which promised success if following the path specified by a scientific process. Another no less important merit of statistics is the study on the basis of statistical data and the reasons for the wrongful act, as well as crime motives, although criminalists have almost never used these data, while this is where many useful things can be learned for the proper application of criminal penalty not only as prevention, but also as repression.

As is evident, the main challenge facing statisticians was to help determine the causes of crime and sources of specific criminal behaviour through numerical indicators. At the same time, it should be appreciated that statistics is not yet talking about the totality of the conditions and individual factors that determine crime. Hence B. M. Bekhterev notes: "Statistics in general

---

12 Krochue. *Der gegenwärtige Stand der Geff ngnisswissen Schaft, G Zeitschz f.d. ges. Strafzechtw*, 1881, vol. i, p75.

13 Quetelet, A. *Physique sociale. Essai sur le développement des tacultés de l homme*, 2nd edn, 1869, vol. i, p312; vol. ii, p358.

operates by large numbers; therefore it does not give us precise instructions on the particular conditions that more closely define the nature of crime. Only the totality of the factors affecting a person and including not only common factors, but also those more private and intimate, defines crime and its nature."[14]

Quetelet conducted several studies of influences on the occurrence of crimes. He drew up a wonderful chart demonstrating how the seasons have a measurable effect on the propensity towards crime. He argued that statistics allowed for predicting crime within a particular territory. In particular, he concluded that the number of crimes committed each year remains more or less unchanged and that the movement of crime is so uniform that it is possible to compile a criminality chart with almost the same accuracy as a death chart: "How sad is the situation of the human race. Almost with the same precision with which we determine the number of births and deaths, can we predict how many persons would stain their hands with the blood of their neighbours, how many would be forgers and poisoners."[15] Of course it is hard to concur because in reality it is impossible to predict with accuracy the state, dynamics and rate of criminality since such a phenomenon is spontaneous, although today a degree of predictions as to the development of criminality are being developed. Quetelet's inaccuracy in this respect is easily forgiveable since he had statistical data that was available to him only for a brief period of time. It should also be borne in mind that, as a mathematician, he drew his conclusions based on numerical data, meaning that he studied the number of crimes and misdemeanours outside of their relationship to the social conditions of society.

While exploring the physical laws governing moral order, Quetelet admitted that the 'average person' has a certain propensity towards crime, specifically that an individual is exposed to some extent to the possibility of committing a crime. The conclusions he drew on the impact of climate, sex and age on criminal human behaviour were of a primitive nature and have subsequently proved questionable. Nevertheless the merits of statistics cannot be underestimated, indeed, as was noted at the International Statistical Congress in London in 1860, "criminal statistics for a legislator is the same as a map, a compass and a lot to a mariner".

So, long before the emergence of the positive school of criminal law studying crime and its causes, statistics had already dealt with issues of

14   Bekhterev, B. M. *Objective and Psychological Method Applied to the Study of Criminality*; Dril, D. A. *Criminality and Criminals: The Doctrine on Criminality and Measures to Combat It*, Moscow, 2010, p708.

15   Quetelet, A. *Physique sociale. Essai sur le développement des facultés de l'homme*, 2 ed. 1869, vol. I, p312; vol. II, p358.

criminality. Admittedly it involved the nature of figures, hieroglyphics, which still had to be translated and examined using data provided by other sciences. This is the path followed by anthropologists and sociologists, as well as all those who took up the study of the causes of crime, resulting in the question of whether the changing composition of numbers is compatible with the concept of free will, which is the basis of the classical school of criminal law.

Rejecting the basic provisions of the classical school on the causes of crime, i.e. free will, the positivist school began to look for the cause elsewhere. Anthropologists began to assert and prove that crime is not a product of free will but a necessary result of the physical and spiritual individuality of crime. Heaping criticism on the classical school and its view of free will, H. M. Charykhov wrote: "Both a theorist and a practitioner had before them only the concept of murder, violence, theft, fraud. And thanks to the unfortunate theory of 'free will', the subject brought to crime became the true culprit of the murder, theft, fraud. But these delusions, like any errors, were to be inevitably eliminated. The fall of the doctrine of free will was the beginning of the conquest of the positivist teaching on crime."[16]

Anthropologists initially searched for the causes of crime in the physical nature of the environment: the impact of weather, climate, thermometric, geological and other factors. Soon they focused on man: they started searching for the causes of crime in his anthropological, physiological and mental organisation. It was argued that by committing a crime, a person is engaged in it not only by his animal (physiological, biological) nature, but also by his mentality, the content of which is not exhausted by experiences generated by the state of his body. The formation of criminal behaviour, according to anthropologists, involves "everything that we have seen, heard, and so on. In short, all our relationships to the outside world".[17] Indeed Cesare Lombroso believed that the study of crime committed by animals would further a better understanding of crime committed by people, just as the anatomy and physiology of animals helped to better understand human nature. But is it even possible to examine animal crime in order to better define human crime? Lombroso, for his part, believed in its possibility not only for animals but even plants.

The subject of anthropology, or the doctrine of man, is the knowledge of his nature. Anthropology allowed him to establish a direct relationship between heredity and the criminal behaviour of a person. Can anyone

16 Charykhov, H. M. Op. cit, p133.
17 Manouvrier, L-P. 'La genèse normale du crime', *Bul. de la Société d'Anthropologie*, Paris, 1893, p456.

nowadays believe that criminal behaviour 'as such' is inherited? I suspect that even Lombroso himself did not believe this. He argued that every crime is a return to the habits of primitive man, and that every criminal is distinguished by the physical and mental characteristics of a savage.

Although the anthropological school failed to construct a concept of crime—and therefore its teaching as a theoretical system, in contrast to the classical school, remained logically incomplete—the anthropologists made the transition from the dogmatic, logical study of the classics to the positive knowledge of crime and the criminal. In other words, instead of abstract structures and abstractions of the concept of crime, the real phenomenon in its particular manifestation was considered. Ultimately Lombroso concluded that "crime is a phenomenon as natural and necessary as birth, death, conception and mental illness, the initial version of which it often is".[18]

His disciple Garofalo attempted to fill the gap in the theoretical system where he set out to establish a natural scientific concept of crime and thereby elevate the anthropological doctrine to the level of a natural scientific theory of crime. The attempt was unsuccessful. Then one more representative of this theory, J. Bahar, decided to formulate a "new definition of crime on the basis of biological science",[19] according to which the desire to take the life of a similar species is a manifestation of that hereditary instinct towards cannibalism common to all humans and animals. This instinct pushes a person to sacrifice the weaker for the sake of nutrition.

Once the anthropological theory of born criminals was rejected by society, particularly among those administering justice, Ferri announced in 1882 the creation of a new school, which he called 'criminal sociology' and in which he introduced experimental data from anthropology, physiopsychology, psychopathology and criminal statistics, as well as the measures to combat crime indicated by science (through prevention and repression). The purpose of the new school, he explained, is "to explore the natural genesis of crime, both in the criminal and in the environment in which he lives, in order to treat different causes by different means".[20]

In the end, Ferri comes to the following conclusion: "When we talk about the criminal type and of a born criminal, we mean the physiopsychological predisposition towards crime, which in some individuals may or may not lead to criminal acts (similar to how a predisposition towards mental illness may or may not lead to insanity) if it is constrained by favourable

18   Lombroso, C. *L'homme criminel*, Paris, 1895, vol. ii, p150.
19   Bahar, J. 'Une nouvelle définition du crime basse sur la science biologique', *Revue pénitentiaire*, 1895, pp 739–740.
20   Ferri, E. *Criminal Sociology*, Moscow, 2005, p22.

environmental conditions, but as soon as these conditions become unfavourable, they are the only positive explanation of inhuman and antisocial criminal activity."[21] Thus he indicates that crime, whatever form it may take and whatever category it may fall into, has complex origins and nature that are biological, physical and social. Therefore, certain actions can be imputed to a person, and therefore he is responsible for them because he lives in a society.

Eventually we found ourselves with the sociological school that made the issue of crime and punishment the object of study of three independent and at the same time closely related disciplines, forming a system of the science of criminal law: criminal sociology (criminology), criminal policy and criminal dogmatics. Essentially, this school is apologetic, in that while paying serious attention to the social factor of criminality, it does not deny on behalf of the majority of its representatives either much of the anthropological data or legal studies that form the core of the classical school. Tarde, being a representative of the sociological school, observes that "crime is a social phenomenon, like any other, but at the same time it is as antisocial as cancer, participating in the life of the organism but promoting its mortification".[22]

In principle, all the representatives of this school believed that crime was nothing but a response to social injustice, a result of the imperfect and unsatisfactory organisation of society, the radical reform of which would minimise the incidence of criminality and perhaps altogether destroy it. The sociological school supposes that crime is a necessary result of the social environment in which the criminal grew up and lives. Charykhov, one of the representatives of this school, wrote: "So, social environment determines and motivates the forms of social development. Crime as a form of social and individual human action, as a form of social development, cannot be regarded and studied outside the influence of the factors that determine and drive the forms of social development in general. And so crime as a special case of the general process of development is determined by the factors of social environment, rather than spatial environment."[23]

Considering crime as a sociological entity rather than a physiological entity, Manouvrier believed that "a person always acts in accordance with his physiological organisation, but the nature of his actions is entirely determined by the external environment. Only the human ability to act

21   Ibid, p114.
22   Tarde, G. D. Op. cit, p198.
23   Charykhov, H. M. Op. cit, p19.

depends on anatomy and physiology. And the way of acting depends on the environment."[24]

We can draw a number of conclusions from this. Firstly, if social environment is everything, if it becomes so damaged that it favours the development of perverse and criminal natures, then reforming efforts should be directed precisely towards this environment and the conditions of its functioning. "Societies have such criminals as they deserve"[25] and it turns out that growth and decline in criminality depend mainly on social factors, i.e. on factors that can be modified and corrected by society more easily than others. Secondly, we can conclude that the lower a man stands on the social ladder, the greater the chance of him committing a crime. Thirdly, having divided factors for crime into two groups, namely social and individual, the sociological school assigns precedence in determining the causes of crime to social factors as the primary category. Hence the absence of primary, i.e. social factors, *ceteris paribus*, would not lead to the origin and emergence of personal (derivative) causes, i.e. psychophysical properties. It follows that one should look for personal causes as the causes of crime; causes which, first of all, should be sought in the surrounding social environment, since the causes of crime lie in man himself while his causes lie in the environment. A criminal, i.e. a 'microbe', is an element that gains significance only when it finds fertile ground. Fourthly, the social factors of crime refer to the totality of the effects of the social environment, and the individual—to the impact of the individual human environment (List, Charykhov).

So what is the downside of this school? It is stated that crime is a social phenomenon determined by social factors. This is it. Is the nature of this phenomenon conservative or evolving? There is no answer to this question. Seeing a direct causal link between social factors and a criminal phenomenon, representatives of the sociological school using the positive method do not go beyond this, in other words they do not seek to discover the logic upon which the social environment creates such a social phenomenon as crime.

And finally, the sociological school makes no clear distinction between social and individual factors, nor between economic reasons and conditions for that matter. So the sociological school does not form a particularly complete and coherent system since, disagreeing as it does on a number of

24 Manouvrier. 'Les aptitudes et les actes', *Revue scientifique*, 1891, p592 (Second Congress in Paris, 1889).
25 Lacassagne. 'Marche de la criminalité en France', *Revue scientifique*, 1881, no. 22, p167.

significant issues with the anthropological school, it nevertheless is close to it in many aspects. This explains why these directions cannot be represented as two hostile and strictly separate camps.

The proponents of the economic direction of studying crime and its causes, having a rich theoretical and practical base, are quite popular. The fact that criminality serves as an unusually sensitive barometer of the economic situation of society is undeniable. This is clearly evidenced by the comparative analysis of the state of criminality in different countries with different economic developments. In *Utopia*, for example, More points to an economic reason that causes the poverty and misery of many thousands of people and forces them to lead a criminal life, while Gian Domenico Romagnosi clearly states that economic poverty leads to crime: "We can find examples of the poor who turned to robbery being compelled by poverty and slavery. Subsequently, when detainees were asked why had they chosen such a desperate job, the danger of which was known to them, they said that they were aware of the danger but that they preferred to take this risk than to lead the miserable life they were leading."[26]

Engels conducted his own criminal study using statistics. As a result, he concluded that the extraordinary growth of criminality in England was linked to the difficult economic situation to be found there. Earlier, Voltaire had spoken out for the widest prevention of crimes requiring primarily the legislator to research what crimes are most relevant to the weaknesses of human nature. Indicating, for example, the fact that property crimes are committed mainly by the poor and that laws are made by the rich, he opposed any neglect of the causes of these crimes. Additionally, in the fight against beggary and vagrancy, demonstrational execution is not needed as much as concern for the eradication by reasonable measures of the phenomenon called beggary.

Bentham rightly notes that if a person is deprived of the means of subsistence, the fear of punishment cannot stop him because an irresistible motive draws him to crime if the satisfaction of his needs is impossible according to the law. The surest means therefore is not to expect poverty but to prevent it. Bentham's system is distinguished by its remarkable thoroughness and originality, and none of his predecessors had penetrated so deeply into crime-generating recesses or found any similarly effective means of crime prevention.[27]

We can see that even Homer in the *Odyssey* (xvii, 286) had an opinion on

---

26 Romagnosi, G. D. *Genesi del diritto penale*, Milan, 1841, p294.
27 See Bentham, J. *Introduction aux principes de morale et de jurisprudence*, 1789.

this when he said: "But a ravening belly may no man hide, an accursed plague that brings many evils upon men." Certainly the philosophers of the Golden Age did not ignore the impact of material conditions on criminality. Thus, Xenophon saw in poverty a powerful incentive for criminal behaviour. In *Symposium* he says by means of Kallias that "men who have money for necessities are less inclined to crime".

So no one can seriously doubt that poverty and beggary have a significant impact on the status of criminality. However, we must not forget that wealth and luxury also play an important role in committing crimes. It all depends on the type and nature of the crime. Plato in *Republic* notes that the material extremes, luxury and poverty, are equally dangerous. Therefore the philosopher advises governors to ensure that luxury and poverty do not appear in the state: the former develops moral turpitude, idleness and commitment to innovation, the latter base feelings and the desire to do evil regardless of the love for innovation.

Aristotle offers a particularly pertinent thought in Book 1 of *Rhetoric* where he notes that wealth and poverty in and of themselves do not impel a person to commit a crime. However, the poor will seek money as they need it, while the rich will seek the pleasure without which they decisively could do while bathing in luxury. Yet both groups are prompted to act thus not for reasons of wealth or poverty but simply passion. And so, according to Aristotle, the sources of crime are passion, a desire generated by poverty and wealth. It follows that the absence of these two elements eliminates passion and hence crime. In the same work, Aristotle also highlights a key fact, that a crime is easier to commit in poverty where there is nothing to lose.

Indeed, external factors, including socioeconomic, have a certain impact on the individual and lead him to such a psychophysical state that, for a certain part of the population, results in crime. However it is clear that not all individuals who find themselves in this situation choose the criminal path. In the world, there are only six percent who are criminals of the total global population, which is why one of the most contentious and difficult issues is to establish the link between crime and economic conditions. It should be borne in mind that these conditions are both individual in nature, i.e. they are applied only to a particular individual, and general in nature, ie. they are applied to the economic situation, the state of society, people in general. Hence it seems appropriate to refer the concept of 'economic conditions' both to the life of society and to the life of each individual. When we talk about the economic causes of crime, we should not focus on the active cause, but on the causes that influenced human will, that is, on the

Something forcing the individual to make this decision and not the other. And this *Something* is in the hands of the individual. This *Something* may be influenced not only by the economic situation, but also by other factors of a different nature, including psychophysical, because the individual is at the same time a biological being.

The answer to the question of whether the main cause, or one of the main causes, of crime is the economic inequality due to which citizens are divided into poor and wealthy is that the economic condition of the society, as well as its social environment, are conditions for the emergence of the causes of crime. In other words, beggary and poverty can influence criminal behaviour without being the main causes of crime. The cause lies within the man himself. Even under the conditions of collectivism, egalitarianism crimes, especially economic ones, continued to exist, although such acts were most severely punished, including by the death penalty. Therefore, improving the economic situation of the masses at any rate does not lead to the extinction of criminal manifestations—we can only talk about their decrease. If the vast majority is experiencing the influence of economic conditions on criminal behaviour, there is no reason to assume that these conditions apply to them more than to the minority that is economically better off. But how then can we explain that, after all, the poor make up the main contingent of the army of criminals? Does this mean that they are the vast majority?

Analysis of criminal statistics in Azerbaijan related to a fixed period has demonstrated an undeniable connection between criminality and economic conditions in the country. And yet at the same time, this analysis reveals the fact that crime bears equally clear traces of very different phenomena such as political, ethnic relations, changes in the social and political structure of the state and forms of governance. For example, the Karabakh conflict, lasting for more than twenty-five years to date, has had a severe impact on the status, nature and rate of criminality in Azerbaijan—not only because of the grievous economic and social situation of the refugees from Armenia and Karabakh, but to a greater extent because of the mental state of the entire population of the republic.

A special approach to the subject was formed after the October Revolution. The Bolsheviks, in the words of M. V. Kozlovskiy, considered axiomatic the position that a criminal was a product of the social environment, and that all of his actions, all of his motivations, depended neither on him nor on our 'will'. Nevertheless, forensic scientists of the young Land of the Soviets in the 1920s were unanimous in the view that "no crime can be explained solely by external causes, ignoring the features of the person committing it".[28] Of course, this approach of scientists and the science of criminal law in explaining the concept of crime and its causes was not consistent with the philosophy of Marxism, which declared: "The theory that considers punishment a *result of the criminal's own will* is only a speculative expression of the ancient *jus talionis* (the right of identical retaliation)—an eye for an eye, a tooth for a tooth, blood for blood."[29]

The Bolsheviks were convinced that the sources of crime lay in the resistance of the overthrown exploiting classes, supported by the entire international bourgeoisie and the petit-bourgeois element of anarchy, bourgeois habits and skills to which a sufficiently broad strata of the working people were still committed. So armed, they believed that with the elimination of these causes, crime would be automatically eliminated. The scientific explanation of the concept of crime and its causes therefore found itself at odds with the policy and doctrine of the socialist state in the fight against crime. As a result, from the beginning of the 1930s, Soviet criminology was forced to change its attitude towards the understanding of the concept of crime, and therefore towards the explanation of the roots of criminal behaviour.

A. N. Traynin noted in those years that "bad heredity, physical or mental abnormalities are not critical in the movement of criminality as social phenomena are determined by social levers and these factors themselves are only derived from the social foundations of human life".[30] This approach lasted until the beginning of the 1960s, up to the point when Soviet scientists started paying attention to the criminal personality, when there then arose a discussion about the relationship between the social and the biological in human criminal behaviour, which continues today.

In fact, the history of the teachings on criminal nature can be represented as the history of the struggle between two directions: the sociological and the biological. Everything is reduced to solving the following issues: whether there is any relationship between the hereditary properties of an organism and human behaviour, including criminal, and, if there is, what is the level of quantified 'contribution' of the biological to the various functions of the human body, the psychological processes and human behaviour. If, prior to the nineteenth century, this issue was not so acute, then advances in medicine and genetics eventually began to generate hope in mankind that these sciences would help to answer the questions that concern us here. Why does a person commit a crime? What are the origins of this behaviour? How can they be eradicated?

28   See: *The Proletarian Revolution and Law*, 1918, no. 1, p27.
29   Marx, K. & Engels, F. *Works*, 2 edn, vol. 8, p531.
30   Traynin, A. N. *Criminal Law: The General Part*, Moscow, 1929. pp 141–142.

The position of Marxism-Leninism was crucially that social phenomena, which include crime, cannot be explained from a biological point of view. Yet at the same time another problem arose since a man is also a biological being, so man and his behaviour should be examined from sociobiological points of view. Otherwise, i.e. if everything is reduced to the social environment and it is assumed that the natural, biological element in a man plays no role in his criminal behaviour, we must then wait until society solves all of the social problems of the people and the need for their punishment disappears, as people should not be to blame for the shortcomings of the social conditions of society. Victor Hugo, in *Les Misérables*, asks through his character Jean Valjean "whether human society could have the right to force its members to suffer equally in one case for its own unreasonable lack of foresight, and in the other case for its pitiless foresight; and to seize a poor man forever between a defect and an excess, a default of work and an excess of punishment."

In our view, one should not seek an overall comparison of the social and the biological as acquired and inherited by a man, rather we should try to uncover the specific interaction, analysis of the mechanism of action of factors in explaining the causes of behaviour. It is understandable that a man changes but does not eliminate or destroy the natural and the biological in him. Genetic diversity creates the unique, unrepeatable biological individuality of each person, however science has proven that biological differences among people, even ethnic groups and races, are negligible in comparison with their unity—indeed, many psychological properties are inherited. This is not, however, an indication that there is a relationship between the human physical structure, mental make-up and criminal behaviour (as asserted by psychiatrists E. Kregmer and R. Funes), and G. Kaiser rightly stresses: "The study of crime as a product of heredity has been very poor . . . We should definitely recognise the failed attempt to explain criminal behaviour by hereditary factors."[31]

One could argue the existence of hereditary causes of crime, if it were possible to establish that the genetic development patterns of people living in a certain time within a certain territory were the same as in criminality movement patterns. Thus the basis of the discussion on the role of the biological can be eliminated, provided that the genetic factor is not the decisive cause of the behaviour, including criminal, and plays a minor role compared to social causes. After all, the methods and forms of preventing criminal

---

31   Kaiser, G. 'Genetics and Crime', *Proceedings of the II International Symposium on Criminology*, San Paulo, Brasil, 1975, pp 7–8.

manifestations depend on the solution to this problem. If it is found that the causes of criminal behaviour are associated with biological factors, then we must invent ways of bringing a medical impact on the criminals such as forms of genetic control. In fact, the vast majority of Soviet and modern legal scientists believed and continue to believe that criminality is not a biological category, an opinion shared by philosophers. For example, according to P. N. Fedoseev, "it would be absurd to seek the roots of criminality in the biological qualities of a person, but at the same time we must take into account some of the individual differences between people."[32]

In fact, could an unreasonable man truly fulfil the role of a thinking, active creature capable of unlimited progress if his thoughts and actions were of an innate, genetically-programmed nature? Science has demonstrated that "the brain's enormous plasticity, and people's ability to be taught and trained, exclude the fatal genetic programme value."[33] This means that people with a normal genetic programme may control themselves, and that in case of programme disturbance, the brain is affected to some extent—in other words, affecting the genetic programme causes a sharp contradiction between social needs and biological possibilities.

It was during the 1920s when heated debate began over the relationship between the social and biological determinants of criminal behaviour in the USSR, when close attention was paid to the study of the criminal personality. Without going into the history of the clash of these opposing views, it is notable that this debate still continues. In 1969, I. I. Karpets categorically declared that "there cannot be any peaceful coexistence of the social and the biological in the issue of the nature of criminality".[34] It became clear that legal science and, above all, criminology was not able to solve this problem, since it concerned the nature of man, his essence, the causes of his behaviour in general and criminal behaviour in particular. Most likely, the answer to the question of the causes of criminal behaviour should be provided by geneticists, biologists, psychiatrists and psychologists, i.e. those representatives of the sciences that directly study the nature of man as a biological being.

Fromm, the founder of the theory of destructiveness, believed that deviation of human behaviour cannot be explained only by the influence of psychological reasons putting mental disorders in dependence on the social

32   Fedoseev, P. N. 'Issues of the Social and the Biological in Philosophy and Sociology. Part of the Biological and the Social in Human Development', *Philosophy Issues*, 1976, no. 3, p29.

33   See: Belyaev, D. K. *Modern Science and Issues of Human Studies*, Ibid. 1981. No. 3, p15.

34   Karpets, I. I. *Criminality Issues*, Moscow, 1969, p32.

environment phenomenon.[35] In Soviet criminology, no one ever claimed that there were natural-born criminals, 'criminal types' or that crime was a biological concept. There were not and had never been any open or covert supporters of Lombroso's theories. Currently, however, it is generally accepted that man is subject not only to the laws of social development, but also to the laws of nature, biological laws, and that he is the unity of the two determinations—the biological and the social. Therefore, biological research must go hand in hand with the sociological study of crime, i.e. the scientific study of crime as a kind of social phenomenon and the presentation of the social conditions of the crime based thereon. As Karpets says, "a man cannot be separated from the conditions of his existence, as it is impossible to explain the reasons for his behaviour, including criminal, and the causes of crime by general biological factors",[36] for man is a social being yet he is a biological being as a part of nature.

P. N. Fedoseev adds that there are many unclear aspects regarding the mechanism of interaction between the biological and the social, particularly in the field of psychology.[37] In this he is absolutely correct but the question is faced head-on: whether the biological or the social has the advantage in human behaviour, namely the criminal. B. S. Volkov believes that "biological characteristics have a great influence on the formation of human social attitude."[38] According to I. S. Noy, "it is undeniable for today's modern science that a newborn enters this life being 'programmed' to a certain extent".[39] We believe that when studying the causes of crime, we cannot have unwarranted bias towards psychological and psychiatric factors without sufficient clarification of the influence of the objective social conditions on these factors.

Crime then is a complex phenomenon, so the question of whether the biological or the social in criminal human behaviour is primary or secondary has no perspective. The key is that the criminal act is possible in the presence of these factors. We should talk not about the priority of one factor or the other, but about the interaction of the biological and the social, i.e. the person and the environment.

35 See: Fromm, E. *Anatomy of Human Destructiveness*, Moscow, 1994, pp 244–310.
36 Karpets, I. I. *Modern Issues of Criminal Law and Criminology*, Moscow, 1976, p33.
37 Fedoseev, P. N. 'Issues of the Social and the Biological in Philosophy and Sociology', *Part of the Biological and the Social in Human Development*, Moscow, 1977, p29.
38 Volkov, B. S. *Deterministic Nature of Criminal Behaviour*, Kazan, 1975, pp 80, 85–86.
39 Noy, I. S. *Methodological Issues of Soviet Criminology*, Saratov, 1976, p79.

A Religious Explanation for the Causes of Crime

On one of the ancient temples there is the inscription: "I am what is, was, will be, and no one has learned my being." We believe that it is impossible to know the philosophical essence of crime without specifying its causes. At the same time, it is obvious that the answer to the eternal question of why a person commits a crime lies in direct proportion to our knowledge of the meaning of human behaviour in general. But it is clear that this is necessary to understand human essence and nature to the extent we are interested in, and then to proceed to study human behaviour, including criminal. This is the sequence which will allow us to consider the issue at hand.

The dictum "Know thyself", inscribed at the front of the temple of Apollo at Delphi, has been a kind of benchmark for philosophers since ancient times. Undergoing perfection for centuries has been the human ability to deeply and subtly reflect the most important things: themselves, their place in the world, the sense of their own existence, justice, the origins of good and evil. Slowly, gradually, man approached the knowledge of truth—as Montaigne writes: "The worst state of a man is when he ceases to be conscious of himself and control himself."[40] It follows that the best state of a man is when he is able to know and understand himself, as well as control himself. But is this possible? Plato says: "Do your own thing and know thyself." Did the philosopher mean to tell us that if a man wants and tries, he always gets his own, i.e. that he will be able to unravel the mysteries of human nature? Yet up to this day, man remains a mystery not fully amenable to knowledge, as many philosophers warned at the time. Thus, Montaigne wrote: "A man is an amazing, earthly, truly fickle and ever staggering creature. It is not easy to get a steady and uniform idea about him."[41] More specifically this was expressed by Pascal: "There is no issue more unsolvable for a man than himself."[42]

A man is the most incomprehensible creature of nature to himself, because it is difficult for him to comprehend what a physical body is, harder still to comprehend what the spirit is, and entirely unclear how the physical body might be connected to the spirit. Moreover, where did man descend from in the first place? The history of the creation of Adam, the first man, is to be found in the Holy Scriptures of the Jews, Christians and Muslims, and the description of the Creation is more or less the same in the Jewish and

---

40 Montaigne, M. *On Human Nature: Montaigne, La Rochefoucauld, Pascal*, Moscow, 2009, p110.
41 Ibid, p19.
42 Ibid, p368.

Christian sources. According to Genesis, Adam was created from the "dust of the earth", while the Talmud describes the Lord God as kneading Adam's body from the mud.

Meanwhile, the Islamic version of Adam's creation is different and in it we can find a great deal of amazing details from the Quran, for example: "That is the Knower of the unseen and the witnessed, the Exalted in Might, the Merciful, Who perfected everything which He created and began the creation of man from clay" (Surah 32: As-Sajdah [The Prostration], ayahs 6-7). A passage that most fully reveals Adam's mission may be found in Surah 2: Al-Baqarah (The Cow): "And when your Lord said to the angels, 'Indeed, I will make upon the Earth a successive authority.' They said, 'Will You place upon it one who causes corruption therein and sheds blood, while we declare Your praise and sanctify You?' Allah said, 'Indeed, I know that which you do not know: (ayah 30).

And so begins the story of Adam, the first man on Earth. At the behest of the Lord, the angels descended to Earth to collect all kinds of soils contained thereon: red, white, brown, black; soft and pliable, solid and sandy . . . And then the Lord created Adam with handfuls of that soil. His descendants were destined to become as diverse as any handful of soil taken from any part of the world from which their ancestor was created, with accordingly different appearances and qualities.

In the Quran, the soil from which Adam was created has many names, which to a certain extent helps us to imagine the process of his creation. A separate name of soil was used for each stage. That which the angels gathered from around the Earth was called soil. Sometimes the Lord calls it clay. After being mixed with water, clay or soil turns into mud. Then, the matter left to dry is called 'viscous' clay. After some time, it turns dark and exudes an odour, it becomes black, smooth clay. From this substance the Lord created Adam's body. His soulless body dried up for a while and turned into what is referred to in the Quran as 'sounding clay'. Adam was thus created from a material close to potter's clay, which rings when tapped lightly. The amazing thing is that this idea gained acceptance and confirmation. It was discovered that the simplest clay contains the basic elements of biological life and so, apparently, it is for good reason that from ancient times up to the present time people have been using clay for treating a variety of diseases.

Since ancient times in many nations there have been myths and legends that man was created from clay. For example, in Macedonian legends, the Lord sculpted people from clay using his own hands, taking care "so that the parts of the body were not attached wrongly so that man would not be offended". But then he decided to speed up the process of making people and made a man-mould, which he filled with clay. The adoption of this form of mass production mean that quality suffered. Some people turned out with a crooked hand or foot, others were blind or bald, and others proud or stubborn. This is how the good (made by the Lord's own hands) and the bad (moulded) people were created. Interestingly, in Sumerian myths, the gods Enki and Ninmah also moulded humans from clay, and at first they made good people. They then became drunk and created abnormal beings.

The creation of people from clay is therefore described in the myths of the ancient Greeks and Egyptians, a number of Indian tribes of North America and the peoples of Africa. It is the biblical story of the creation of man from clay that, no doubt, is known to most. According to scientists, even the Hebrew word for 'man' has a connection to the word 'earth, red soil'.

At the beginning of the twentieth century, the Russian scientist V. I. Vernadskiy, when studying clay, found a number of interesting properties attesting to the ancient myths of the creation of man. Found in the composition of clay were *all of the macro and micro-elements present in our body*. The most interesting thing was that they were contained in clay *almost in the same proportions*. Recently, American scientists made a sensational discovery, confirming at a higher level Vernadskiy's conclusions. They found that ordinary clay contains the basic elements of biological life, constituting the membranes of human cells and other biological organisms. It should be noted that cell membranes are not only involved in the formation of cells, but also contain the genetic code of an organism—ribonucleic acid (RNA), which is the basis of all life.

Geologists and soil scientists distinguish between up to forty kinds of clay. They differ in composition, texture and colour—there is blue, white, red, yellow, green, gray and even black clay. The colour and shade of clay, as well as its properties, are determined by its chemical composition, which also determines its therapeutic properties. The healing properties of clay are determined by its unique ion-exchange properties. It can supply cells with missing elements and absorb what is in excess. Thus, clay is able to normalise the mineral composition of the body and regulate metabolic processes.

So, one of the versions is that man was created by God. But can we ever truly know that which we have not created? After all, without knowing ourselves, we cannot explain our behaviour and, therefore, understand the causes of criminal acts. In fact, why do people, knowing good and evil, sometimes choose the latter? As Pozdnyakov correctly points out, this is "evidence of the phenomenal absurdity of human nature, because of which mankind suffers, is penalised and punished throughout its history—though rightly".[43]

---

43   Pozdnyakov, E. A. *Philosophy of Crime*, pp 155–156.

Perhaps God himself gave us a kind of instinct for inhumanity? Hobbes wrote on this subject: "A man by nature is an evil and destructive creature; he resembles a killer that may be kept away from his hobby only by the fear of a stronger killer."[44] The angels certainly warned God that man would sin and shed blood. However, the culprit of criminal and sinful human nature turned out to be the Serpent, who "was more subtle than any beast of the field which the Lord God had made", and who persuaded Eve with tricks and cunning to try the fruit of the forbidden Tree of Knowledge of Good and Evil. The woman at first refused, saying that God had forbidden them to eat from this tree, as anyone eating the fruit would die. The Serpent told her that she would not die, "you will be like God, knowing both good and evil". Finally, the woman, persuaded by the Serpent, violated the will of God, and then gave the fruit to Adam. The couple learned of good and evil, realised their nakedness and hid from God.

The Tree of Knowledge of Good and Evil symbolised God's priority to decide instead of humans, and for humans what is good and what is evil. Before the Fall from grace, evil had already existed in the world in the face of the fallen angels, and Adam, who gave the names to the animals, knew what was good and evil. According to John Chrysostom, God originally created an autocratic man, otherwise he would not punish him for violating the commandments or reward him for their observance. The Fall then represented the desire of man to usurp God's right to decide what was good and what was evil. Misconduct was followed by punishment: the Serpent was cursed and doomed to crawl on his belly and eat dust; the woman was doomed to "bear children in weakness" and to be ruled by her husband; the man was doomed to toil the ground in sorrow and by the sweat of his face all the days of his life as "cursed is the ground for thy sake". People were no longer immortal, and after death they had to return to the ground in the form of the dust from which Adam was created.

After that, God clothed people and banished them from the Garden of Eden "to work the ground from which [they] had been taken". So that people would not be able to enjoy the fruits of the Tree of Knowledge of Good and Evil, a cherubim with a "flaming sword which turned in every direction" was placed at the entrance. This means that evil is inherent in the depths of human nature, that in its irrational freedom, in its apostasy from divine nature, it has an internal source.[45]

Why, unlike the animal lacking a sense of cruelty, is the human inclined

---

44   For details see: Hobbes, T. *Leviathan. 4.2. About the State, Works*, 2 volumes, Moscow, 1991, vol. 2, p324.
45   See: Berdyaev, N. A. *Mindset of Dostoevsky*, Moscow, 2001, p237.

to its manifestation? Fromm writes: "A man is the only living being that can destroy his own kind without any benefit for himself."[46] It cannot be that God created us with bloodthirsty tendencies. Where then lie the origins of evil? Jeffrey Burton Russell offers the following words from Rousseau: "Man, do not look far for the creator of evil, it is you."[47] According to Freud, human actions are led by animal instincts. He claims that man is possessed by these instincts, as they are predicated on his nature.[48]

According to religious beliefs, evil human behaviour, violence, crime are the result of the impact of 'evil' forces on humans. Thus Augustine argues: "A man is free to choose his actions, and he commits crimes only under the influence of an evil will, the result of the introduction into him of evil forces."[49] Why does God allow a person to become a criminal, i.e. to commit evil? Y. V. Romanets writes that "God denies evil as the ultimate aspect, but admits it as a means to gain the love of good".[50] We find such reasoning in the observations of Archimandrite Platon (Igumnov) when he says: "The propensity towards virtue has true spiritual value in the case where it is a consequence of the defeated propensity towards sin."[51]

According to Augustine, the pleasantness of health is clearer when the burden of disease is experienced: "Since everyone is born of a corrupted process, first, by necessity, they become like Adam, evil and carnal, and then, when reborn, they grow into Christ, become kind and spiritual . . . although not every evil man will become good, no one however will become good who was not evil."[52] Does this mean that God allowed us to do evil, i.e. to commit crime, on condition that we must repent? "For the good that I want, I do not do, but I practise the very evil that I do not want" (Rom. 7:19).

Having created us, God laid out at the same time the rules of behaviour and determined in detail what a godly man should do, what would happen to him if he does not do the proper deeds, and how he might atone for his past and become a pious man again. Having endowed man with the qualities of good and evil, God at the same time requires us not to commit evil, but, on the contrary, to constantly strive to be good. Therefore, first of all, in determining people's behaviour, religion is based on the concepts of

---

46   Fromm, E. *Anatomy of Human Destructiveness*, Moscow, 1994, pp 189–190.
47   Russell, J. B. *Prince of Darkness*, translated from English by I. Y. Larionova, Saint Petersburg: Evrazia, 2002, p347.
48   See: Freud, S. *The Ego and the Id*, Tbilisi, 1991, pp 374–380.
49   *Works of St Augustine*, Kiev, 1901, p41.
50   Romanets, Y. V. *Ethnical Grounds of Law and Law Enforcement*, Moscow, 2012, p302.
51   See: Archimandrite Platon (Igumnov). *Orthodox Moral Theology: The Holy Trinity Lavra of St. Sergius*, 1994, pp 224–228.
52   St Augustine. *The City of God*, vol. 3, Moscow, 1994, p43.

good and evil, which translated into legal language means 'right, human, legal or illegal, harmful and criminal behaviour'. The Quran says: "So whoever does an atom's weight of good will see it. And whoever does an atom's weight of evil will see it" (Surah 99: Al-Zalzalah [The Earthquake], ayahs 7–8). And also: "Whoever comes [on the Day of Judgment] with a good deed will have ten times the like thereof [to his credit], and whoever comes with an evil deed will not be recompensed except with the like thereof; and they will not be wronged' (Surah 7: Al-A'raf [The Heights], ayah 8). A similar reminder from God may be found in the New Testament: "And will come forth, those who did good deeds to a resurrection of life, those who committed evil deeds to a resurrection of judgment" (John. 5:29).

Particular attention should be paid to the fact that in the divine passages, the commission of good and evil depends entirely on man and is done for his own good. In other words, the behaviour of any man depends on the freedom of his will. And this means that man is fully responsible to God for his acts. "If you do good, you do good for yourselves; and if you do evil, [you do it] to yourselves" (Surah 17: Al-Isra' [The Night Journey], ayah 7). Or: "Whoever does righteousness, it is for his [own] soul; and whoever does evil [does so] against it. And your Lord is not ever unjust to [His] servants" (Surah 41: Fussilat [Explained in Detail], ayah 46). Clearly this last expression "your Lord is not ever unjust to [His] servants" emphasizes that human action is voluntary, depending upon man himself, and that no one is forcing him. We can only conclude that God gave man the freedom of choice in his behaviour.

Now according to the Quran, Allah declared the supremacy of reason, he praised reasonable people. Reason keeps man from what can hurt him. So, the main element of the divine passages is the commandment, which can act as a specific requirement—prohibition, obligation or permission—or as a general principle. It should be noted that the Quran in many of its ayahs (verses) emphasizes the reward for good deeds, it arouses people's firm belief, without which they cannot follow the 'straight path', and therefore the Almighty called the book the guide for the theopathic. That is why the Quran is called the Great Scriptures, and why the other divine passages, which are rightly called Sacred, contain obvious truth and vast knowledge: "Indeed, this Quran guides to that which is most suitable and gives good tidings to the believers who do righteous deeds that they may have a great reward: (Surah 17, ayah 9).

From all this we come to understand that God, having created us, would see man as virtuous only. And in fact, he naturally is so from birth. The actions of the forces of 'evil' begin where man, namely his soul and spiritual world, begins. This means that while we exist, living within us are two souls or two forces, which are one and the same, each leading us to its own side: one to good, the other to evil. And from this standpoint, we can conclude that if the forces of evil are stronger, the person will commit a crime. Montaigne remarked that "the greatest difficulty for those who are engaged in the study of human actions is to reconcile them with each other and give them a single explanation, for our actions are usually so sharply contradicting each other, it seems unlikely that they proceeded from the same source."[53]

So the fundamental position of religion is that man is not perfect, because his nature is stamped indelibly with the original sin of his ancestors Adam and Eve, furthermore he is inclined to succumb to the temptations of the Devil. Thus ensnared in the grip of this temptation, man steps upon the path that leads to crime, i.e. to denial. In this regard, the natural question arises of whether a man can choose his behaviour in terms of religion. If we acknowledge that man is the creation of a Supreme Being, then only He was destined to fully appreciate the essence of the being created by Him, and hence the origins of his behaviour, including criminal. But did God give man the ability to freely dispose of his behaviour?

It is a question that was posed by Augustine in his letter for the Apostle Paul: "Might it be that from ignorance man does not have the free will to choose what he actually has to do, or might this be because of carnal instincts, which by their nature are even more amplified by the destructive force of original sin? He, seeing how to do the right thing and wanting it, cannot, however, do it." Augustine himself was trying to prove that there is no free will, and that man's life is predetermined by God, who gives him bliss or lays a curse upon him. Hence, a person commits a crime within the will of God. Therefore, the root cause of crime is the will of God. If this is so, it turns out that people cannot or are not able to answer for their actions, including crime. This leads to the issue of responsibility for acts committed. Why does God bestow bliss to some, and why are others cursed? Why do some become criminals by His will, and others noble? And finally, why does God wish the people he created to become criminals and to commit atrocities?

Early Christianity made a direct link between the opportunity of free choice with the preliminary, intended, conscious deliberation and discussion of imminent action. This means that if a man has decided to commit intentional homicide, he is prepared in advance for this crime, which means that he

---

weighs everything up, ponders the consequences and possible implementation of his plan. Accordingly, rash actions, i.e. impulsive, affective, accidental, involuntary, spontaneous, are not in fact free. For example, a military officer comes home to find his wife with her lover and immediately shoots them. All of this happens within a few seconds. Conclusion: the actions of the officer are not free. In particular, Nemesius of Emesa wrote: "Voluntary (or spontaneous) action is understood as a conscious, rational activity whose beginning lies in the one acting, that is, the man. Accordingly, involuntary (or not spontaneous) action is understood as an action whose beginning lies beyond human will, and is divided into involuntary by violence and by ignorance."[54]

If all our actions are known and depend on God, why then does He allow a man to commit crimes against his own brethren? John of Damascus in his *An Exact Exposition of the Orthodox Faith* recognises that since God is the beginning and the cause of all good, any good deed is committed with his approval, cooperation and assistance; though God does not wish any perverse deeds to be committed, he "allows it to the free will".[55] According to Augustine, human volition is only possible in relation to sin, to good he can aspire only through divine bliss.[56] D. Dorofeev comments on this position with the suggestion that "this approach led to the need to distinguish terminologically between the voluntary choice of man, made in alienation from God, and the truly free choice which could be made only in God. As to the first negative aspect of 'voluntary choice', the term 'spontaneity' started to be applied to a person as an assessment of his wilfulness as confirmation of his negatively-assessed claim to independence and personal autonomy."[57]

If God knows and anticipates the action of a man, why does He not warn him against committing murder? John of Damascus says: "It is needed to know that God knows everything in advance, but He does not predetermine everything. For He knows beforehand what is in our power, but He does not predetermine it. For He does not wish for defect to be occurred, yet He is not forcing to virtue."[58]

Augustine, criticising the position of Cicero, distinguishes between three kinds of reason in the world: accidental, natural and spontaneous, and acknowledges that human free will is a spontaneous reason for his supposed actions and is positioned in the universal temporal series of cause and effect, which is

---

54 Nemesius of Emesa. *The Nature of Man*, Moscow, 1998, p103.
55 John of Damascus. *An Exact Exposition of the Orthodox Faith*, Rostov-on-Don, 1992, p115.
56 St. Augustine. Op. cit, pp 250–253.
57 Dorofeev, D. *Under the Sign of Philosophical Anthropology*, Moscow; Saint Petersburg, 2012, p86.
58 John of Damascus. Op. cit, p115.

originally known to God as a transcendent and eternal being.[59] Is a man free then in his actions when making spontaneous, unexpected crimes, such as murder? Nemesius of Emesa believed that man in any case was recognised as the beginning of "his own actions and had the ability for self-determination."[60]

Consequently, even committing a crime accidentally, impulsively, i.e. spontaneously, entails responsibility since it is committed upon the man's own will. Anselm of Canterbury believed that spontaneity was a characteristic of intelligent beings. In particular, he noted that man acts spontaneously, as opposed to, say, a stone, which 'acts out of necessity'. A required action is an action that is fully defined by 'nature'.[61] From this statement it follows that all of the actions of human will are spontaneous, unlike animal and organic 'instincts'. The word 'spontaneity' is usually used to describe natural phenomena and human actions. It refers to the special nature of the cause of committed action or a special position of the implemented process.

On the relationship of Islam to this, the Quran clearly and unequivocally affirms the power of Allah over everything that happens in the world, including what happens to people over their actions and behaviour. It follows that the scientists of Islam explain this assertion differently. Some believe in the absolute predestination of all that happens to a man, in other words that all of his actions are the desire of Allah, that the Almighty directs the acts and actions of people. Therefore a man who commits evil or good does it not by choice but by the will of Allah. Then there is the question of man's responsibility for his crime. After all, if the man is not the initiator of his own actions, including crime, and if any committed actions are created by Allah, how can we be held responsible for these actions and deserve punishment? Would this not be injustice caused by Allah if, having created man helpless and directing his actions, depriving him of freedom of choice, He calls on man to be responsible for the crime and to then go to hell for it?

Supporters of the denial of the freedom of human will answer this question in the following way: that human action is merely the epitome of the demiurgic will of Allah. He is the only genuine committer, while man is the committer only in the figurative sense (Ash'arites). This means that apart from the other creations of Allah, man differs only in terms of responsibility for his actions, whether good or bad, kind or criminal, even though they are all dictated by Allah. In other words, Allah creates a kind of action and simultaneously gives people the ability to carry it out, so it is man who should be held responsible.

59   St Augustine. Op. cit, pp 250–253.
60   Nemesius of Emesa. Op. cit, p126.
61   Anselm of Canterbury. *Works*, Moscow, 1995, pp 198–273.

This indicates that prior to a homicide, Allah creates in man the ability to commit the crime. But before that, He must create an action, for without this action it is not possible to carry out the homicide even though Allah has invested man with the ability to carry out the crime. In this case, a reasonable question arises: if Allah is indeed just, and there is no doubt of that because it runs throughout the Quran, then how does He admit punishing someone for a crime, in particular, for a homicide committed by His command? And we know that Allah cannot do anything contrary to justice and fairness. Wise Allah can do only what is good and kind. Allah the Almighty and Just cannot be evil toward his servants, i.e. people, moreover He cannot commit evil deeds, crimes, not can He demand the impossible from His servants. And in any case, why should Allah blame people for the crime they commit against their will but upon the order of the Almighty? Furthermore, if we accept that Allah commands people's actions, this means that He wants something, achieves, needs something. Does Allah, the Lord and Creator of the universe and all living and non-living things, actually *need* something? Desire and criminal desire, therefore, cannot be attributed to Allah.

But why do evil, violence, crime and murder exist? Is Allah powerless before these events that involve negative and harmful acts? If the Almighty has no divine power over evil, in particular over crime, then it shows that He is weak against evil. It also means that Allah has no divine power over evil. On the other hand, if He does have power over evil, crime, then it follows that Allah is not aware of the atrocities and crimes perpetrated on the Earth, otherwise He would not allow it. But if the Almighty is aware of such phenomena, it means that He wants and needs them, otherwise why would He create evil, violence and crime? However, an analysis and deep understanding of the content in particular of many of the ayahs found in the Quran, allow us to assert that Allah gave man free will. But at what point? At birth or before each of his acts?

The justice of Allah means that man must be the creator of his own deeds. For only in this case may he be free and, therefore, responsible for his own actions. In other words, if Allah created man as the author of his own deeds, it means that it is within his will to do good deeds or crimes. However, Allah requires people not to do evil and not to commit crimes. Therefore man is understood as an independent, strong-willed living being whose actions may or may not correspond to divine will. All that Allah needed was to bestow man with free will and choice, then it was enough to grant man reason to guide his actions. As Cleanthes said, "the one willing to go is led by destiny, the one unwilling is dragged".

I have often heard it uttered by people who have committed crimes the words so well known to all: "This is my destiny." Numerous real-life stories told by different individuals lead many to conclude that there is a predestination, an inexorable *Fate*, to which everyone and everything are subject. However, is everything predetermined or can we in some way change the course of events by the force of our will, our desires? This question is of fundamental importance in addressing the problem of human criminal behaviour because, if it is fate that is predetermined from the moment of his birth, the use of punitive measures against the criminal does not make sense. Indian philosophy speaks about *dharman*, the law governing the Universe and all its inhabitants. It also teaches that there is *sadhana*, the meaning of life and a predefined path over which the meaning is shown. It argues that there is *karma*, the law of action and reaction. The ancient Greeks also revered a deity standing above Zeus, the lord of Olympus; he was called Zeus-Zen. Aeschylus spoke of him as the deity of Fate. In the Hebrew Kabbalah, it was called 'Nothing'. It is the one who stands at the top of the crown, who manages all invisible beings. Its impulse comes from the heights to reach our world. In short, all the ancient peoples intuitively felt the existence of a mysterious principle of fate far beyond the manifested, one higher even than a deity. What is fate therefore? Can we change it? What can then be the freedom of choice given to man? How can we understand who of those walking the path of life is to be good, and who is to become a criminal?

The ancient pagans thought that fate was an unfathomable predefined chain of events and human actions. The fate of a pagan was doom. Man is a toy of fate, a slave to circumstances. One cannot escape fate, it cannot be changed, it can only be obeyed as the stoics proclaimed. This notion of fate absolutises only one aspect—the human lack of freedom. We observe the same approach applied by the metaphysicians, who argue that people are guided by higher impersonal forces whose power over them is boundless. What appears to people as a free expression of their will or choice is merely an illusion. There is a mysterious line of destiny unknown to man, and a disposition of providence or doom leads him through it, allowing him to settle for the role of a plaything caught up in someone's immensely powerful will.

In the religious consciousness there is the concept of fate as a theological determination, i.e. of providence. Neither blind fate nor impersonal physical laws, but the All-Wise and Good Creator governs human life. As we can see, religion, unlike pagan belief or the natural science of fatal determination, gives the idea of freedom and the good Providence of God. Personally, man is free to choose between good and evil. So it depends on him alone as to what his fate might be: will he become the well-doer or the criminal? Man carries out his destiny in his lifetime.

The destiny of man in Islam is somewhat different: Muslims have an absolute dependence on the will of Allah. If Allah desires it, a man will be virtuous or, on the contrary, a criminal. It is impossible to predict what precisely needs to be done in order not to become a criminal and then go to heaven. Only one thing is left, obedience to Allah.

We shall proceed from the fact that we all have our own destiny, although nobody knows what that is. Nevertheless we are each responsible for what happens to us at every moment, for not giving up and debasing ourselves. Those who believe in the absolute inevitability of fate allow themselves to be carried throughout life. And life confirms by the facts the way it can be finished. Each person is given the chance, the opportunity to go their way, at their own pace and according to their abilities and willpower; but regardless of their pace and abilities, they should move forward constantly, improving and elevating. Plato said that for their actions, people tend to blame fate, the gods and everything else, but not themselves. People are accustomed to blame fate as an almighty goddess for their helplessness, weakness, disease, birth defects and numerous stupidities. Crime is not destiny but the result of the absence or weakness of willpower. Man is strong-willed in any situation, under any circumstances, except in the heat of passion and under special conditions; in fact, he is never able to commit an act contrary to his own interests.

Psychology and the Origins of Criminal Behaviour

Contrary to the claim of the Scriptures for the divine origin of man, Darwinism demonstrated the indissoluble genetic connection between man and the animal world, demonstrating that man is descended from one of the animal species. This meant that our animal ancestors had a biological essence. The process of their harmonising evolution was a manifestation of unity of the biological and the social. By the time of occurrence of Homo sapiens there was a special genetic programme unique to the species which can be called 'socialised'. Thus, after birth, during the formation of consciousness on the basis of biological preconditions, the human genetic programme does not lose its value; it acquires the properties that ensure the readiness of the newborn for subsequent development in adequate social conditions. In other words, the biological human properties obtain a socialised nature. However, man as a living being still continues to obey basic and fundamental biological laws, and so he has the features and properties inherent in all living things on earth, and especially in animals.

Thus, human development as proven by science is based precisely on the dialectic of interaction between the biological and the social, rather than on their absorption. This is why the natural question arises: what in this case prevails in a human, the biological or the social?

Within the behaviour of highly developed animals and humans there is a significant component of aggression which manifests itself in the tendency to respond to attacks or in hostility to certain types of stimuli. However, as John Crook rightly emphasizes, "there is no reliable evidence in favour of a genetic (hereditary) need for aggressive behaviour",[62] even though aggression is considered the main indicator of the genetic nature of crime. At the same time, medicine claims that aggressive human behaviour is not closed fatally on innate mechanisms of the mind, and hence aggression and emotion can be weakened or strengthened through medicine. Speaking of biological factors in criminal behaviour, some have in mind human physiology, others genetics, still others physical and psychological characteristics of personality. At that, certain human properties are described in a variety of links with criminal behaviour. Ultimately, the conclusion is that none of these sciences is able today to answer the question that has persisted for thousands of years: what pushes a person to commit a crime, what biological properties are the sources of his behaviour, including criminal?

Can man himself oppose these properties? Is it up to his state if he is given the freedom to choose, including the freedom to commit an unlawful act, or rather is man by nature able to choose between criminal and lawful behaviour? There is an opposite argument. For example, Schopenhauer challenged Rousseau's assertion that man is naturally good and that civilisation is to blame for all his moral flaws. He argued that man is in reality like a wild animal that cannot be tamed by civilisation and culture. Indeed, the evil that along with the good is the essence of man has a powerful ability to tempt and entice man in its snares. And if he gives into dark desire, his ability to exercise free will abandons him. He becomes hostage to his passion, the slave of circumstance and a plaything for the forces of fate.

What is this good–evil person? It all depends on our approach. The *natural* man is a collection of innate properties and abilities that ensure his life in nature. He does not know the difference between good and evil, between crime and normal lawful behaviour, because he exists on an unconscious level. The *social* man is a collection of acquired qualities, properties of the psyche, skills, awareness, behaviour and so on. And, finally, the *spiritual* man is the personality, conscious of the intrinsic value of his own inner world, his

---

62   Crook, J. H. 'The Nature and Function of Territorial Aggression', *Man and Aggression*, Oxford, 1968, p154.

uniqueness. In other words, a *man* is a complex being, consisting of innate characteristics (natural man) who has the appropriate political, moral, legal qualities (social man) and is able to navigate in the world of signs, meanings and symbols and reasons from the most simple to the most complex.

What is the role of each of these properties of a man in his actions? Psychology, genetics, psychiatry, biology, sociology, medicine and other sciences have long sought to answer this question. A huge contribution to the development of this comes from psychiatry, which constantly has to deal with phenomena of not only mental illness but also human depravity—as well as crime. Once Darwin drew his conclusion on 'evolutionary' human origin, the concept of a special constant 'substance' constituting 'human nature' proved to be untenable. In this regard, Fromm observed that "new discoveries in human nature can only be expected on the basis of evolutionary theory".[63]

The theory of evolution has enabled psychology to state that science was able to provide an answer to the historical issue of the origins of human behaviour in general and criminal behaviour in particular. This conclusion is based on the fact that psychology studies the mechanisms of stimulation of human behaviour and the way they can be used in order to achieve maximum results. In this regard psychology has made a great deal of discoveries, and there is a spectrum of different theories and trends, although to this day the origins of human behaviour remain a mystery. The reason for this, in my view, as Fromm so rightly puts it, is that "man himself is an imperfect and incomplete being: he is not yet ready and he is full of contradictions. Man may be designated as a being on an active search for optimal ways of his development, and this search often crashes due to the lack of favourable external conditions."[64]

Different approaches and views of psychologists on the issue of aggressive human behaviour have led to different opinions of criminalists on the causes of criminal behaviour. In 1868, an essay came out by Prosper Despine, 'Natural Psychology', devoted to the study of criminals. Familiarity with the facts led the Frenchman to the belief that serious criminals had no moral sense that could distinguish good from evil, prompting the condemnation of criminal desires and causing subsequent remorse. In the early nineteenth century, the French psychiatrist Marraud came to the conclusion that an organism develops and progresses under favourable external influences, and that through heredity it produces more and more sophisticated psychophysical types, while, on the contrary, under the influence of adverse external factors it regresses, spoils, and

63   Fromm, E. *Anatomy of Human Destructiveness*, Moscow, 2012, p300.
64   Ibid, p353.

by the same hereditary transmission produces different constantly deteriorating, sickly varieties that are distinguished by the most evil and vicious inclinations, tendencies and tastes. These types of degeneration not only are unable to promote the mental and moral progress of mankind but represent the greatest obstacle to progress through their contact with the healthy part of society. As D. A. Dril once noted: "Indeed, experience shows that in approximately similar conditions, one of two people falls into crime, while the other deviates from it at the cost of health and even life. On what is such a distinction dependent? It depends on the fact that in the character of the first and, consequently, in its underlying psychophysical organisation at this time, there are some features that predispose him to the crime, while in the character of the second, on the contrary, there are features restraining him from the crime."[65]

Psychiatrists and prison doctors who examine the nature of crime usually indicate the sickly character of this phenomenon. They almost all come to a conclusion about the sickly nature of crime and its analogy with the phenomena of degeneration of the human type on the one hand, and the phenomena of mental illnesses on the other. Thus armed, they point to many mental abnormalities present in criminals: their reduced sensitivity, selfishness and lack of moral sense. For psychoanalysts, the mind is the very starting point from which they begin their studies of the phenomenon of crime, since the mind is considered that which fundamentally distinguishes humans from other animals. Therefore we must look for the cause of this human feature, i.e. the propensity towards crime, within the mind.

Assuming that psychology has to study the mechanisms of the stimulation of human behaviour and the ways in which they can be used in order to achieve maximum results, then psychologists need to answer the question of where the source of human behaviour in general, and criminal behaviour in particular, should be searched for, and what mechanisms encourage this behaviour. According to the instinctivist theory (Freud, Lorenz, Fromm and so on), man lives the past of his kind, and thus his behaviour, including criminal, aggressive and violent, is connected with his ancestors, that is, with the animals. Fromm argues that man's hominid ancestor was a predator endowed with an aggressive reflex towards all living beings, including humans. Consequently, human destructiveness has a genetic (innate) origin, and, therefore, Freud was right.[66] In this respect, it seems appropriate to consider the concepts of the leading proponents of instinctivism on the origins of human behaviour, in particular aggressive behaviour.

65   Dril, D. A. *Criminality and Criminals*, p59.
66   Fromm, E. Op. cit, p175.

We start with Freud as one of the first modern psychologist who examined the richness of human passions: love, hate, vanity, greed, jealousy and envy.[67] The source of all these passions, in his opinion, lies in sexual attraction. Freud artificially squeezed all these passions into the narrow confines of the theoretical scheme, where they received a justification either as sublimation, or as the implementation of sexuality in any form. In short, Freud's basic theoretical message says: a man is possessed by only one passion, the need for destruction of either himself or other people, and this tragic alternative is unlikely to be avoided. From this it follows that crime as a form of aggression (involving violent crimes) is an impulse constantly present in the organism caused by the biological and physiological constitution of the human being, by the very nature of humans. In other words, man is a creature with recurring aggressive criminal energy, which cannot be controlled for long. This energy is either to be used for beneficial purposes, or it will manifest itself through a violent crime such as murder or rape.

Consequently, within man there act forces that he is not aware of, and through rationalisation he protects himself from awareness of them. This means that criminal behaviour is determined by psychic powers which are mainly present on an unconscious level. Therefore the origins of behaviour, including criminal, can be understood by human self-knowledge, through the disclosure of one's unconscious drives. Freud sincerely believed in the mind as the only force capable of saving man from criminal intentions and evil. But what is self-knowledge according to Freud? It means that the person is aware of his being at an unconscious level.

Freud acknowledged this as an extremely difficult process, because the person at the same time meets great resistance that prevents him from realising his unconscious. According to him, knowing oneself means to intellectually and emotionally penetrate into the most secret corners of one's soul. The theory simultaneously pays close attention to the problem of social environment. The Freudian axiom reads: all the negative in the development of patients is the result of harmful influences on them in their early childhood. Consequently, the reasons for the negative psychological factors in a person should be looked for in the child's upbringing and development. At the same time, this means that the origins of criminal behaviour are not genetically related.

The main advance in the views of Freud compared with those of his predecessors was that he distilled all 'desire' into two categories: the instinct of

---

67 See: Freud, S. *Introductory Lectures on Psycho-Analysis*, Saint Petersburg, 2012; *Psychology of the Unconscious*, Saint Petersburg, 2012.

self-preservation and the instinct of sexuality. Therefore Freudian theory can be rightly considered as the last step in the history of the development of the doctrine of instincts.

As his crowning achievement, Freud considered the discovery of the existence of unconscious mental processes rejected by consciousness. What is the Freudian unconscious? Unconscious is an area of deep mental processes that occur beyond the control of consciousness and present themselves in human spiritual activity and social behaviour by diverse manifestations of positive and destructive nature. The unconscious is able to assert itself in the form of crime.

Does the psychoanalytic concept of Freud then hold any value for the criminological and psychological analysis of the motivational prerequisites of crime? In some way it is supposedly so. At least we cannot deny that Freud was able to justify the position that almost always, save for the rational and conscious motives of crime, there are also deep unconscious attitudes that can be the hidden yet leading generator of criminal initiatives. This is confirmed by the fact of many suddenly committed crimes and the science of victimology, i.e. the fault of the victim. Is it possible to smooth out the sharpness of the conflicts between the unconscious and regulatory constraints? In other words, is it possible to make it so that the unconscious does not assert itself in the form of crime? Freud indicates two main means.

The first is sublimation as a method for the transformation of instinctive and sexual energy into social activities. This follows from the statement that the most important motive of human action in society is sexual energy, libido. If this energy does not find its way out, i.e. if it is not spent, then the person becomes either a criminal or mentally ill. What then shall be done with those who are serving long sentences and do not have the means to satisfy their biological, natural sexual needs. They shall either be engaged in debauchery, or meet their needs in unnatural ways. However, based on Freud's theory, another way can be proposed: hard physical work with heavy conditions in order to discharge all of this energy.

The second means is a specially developed psychoanalytic technique, a system of psychotherapeutic agents. Karen Horney, the German-American psychosociologist, held that Freud's classical psychoanalysis shows a clear narrowness and limitation that reduces the causes of all the neuroses to sexual anomalies.

So, according to Freud and neo-Freudianism, aggressive behaviour, including criminal, is a breakthrough of innate drives unimplemented and hidden in the unconscious. On this the American sociologist Edwin Schur notes: "According to some views on crime among psychoanalysts, each of us is a criminal deep inside."[68] In *The So-Called Evil* (1963), Konrad Lorenz sets out to prove that human passion for violence and evil is caused by biological factors that are not subject to human control. Aggression and evil are seen as personal internal tension striving for discharge and expression, regardless of whether there is an external stimulus suitable for this or not. The specific energy required for instinctive actions constantly accumulates in the nerve centres, and when a sufficient amount of energy is accumulated, an explosion may occur—even in the absence of stimuli.

What conclusions may be drawn based on Lorenz's concept when considering the origins of human criminal behaviour? Firstly, according to Lorenz, it appears that criminal behaviour is not a response to external stimulation, i.e. the person commits, for example, murder for no apparent motives and reasons, because it was bound to happen some time, although practice shows that a very large number of violent crimes are committed as a result of the impact caused by external stimuli on the individuals concerned. Secondly, crime, according to this concept, is a kind of a liberator of energy intensity. In fact, the commission of crime results from a long process of tension accumulation in the relationship between the criminal and the victim. This is very common in domestic crimes when the relationship between family members or neighbours are heated to the limit. The result is an explosion for which a small stimulus is enough and the instinct is triggered. According to Lorenz, it turns out that even if the man is not able to commit murder in this case, he certainly would do it at another time, in another place, in relation to other people. However, in many cases, the man in such a situation for whatever reason does not realise his aggressive behaviour, and over time he calms down and does not commit such acts.

Thirdly, the declaration of the criminal conduct of man as his innate trait means the uselessness of struggle with this kind of human aggression. In addition, Lorenz's theory interferes with the understanding of the structure of the personality, individual and social conditions of the emergence and development of crime. What does Lorenz suggest to decrease the number of murders, rapes and other violent offences? He answers with the following: "In contrast to Faust, I know the way and I can teach people how to change themselves for the better. And it seems to me that in this regard I am not exaggerating my capabilities."[69]

His first recommendation is to know thyself, "the requirement to deepen our knowledge about the causal relationships of our own behaviour", i.e. the laws of evolution.[70] It is impossible to disagree with this since all the issues of the solution of the mystery of human behaviour, including criminal, are directly related to the lack of our knowledge of human nature.

The second recommendation is the study of so-called sublimation through the method of psychoanalysis.[71] This is well-known and we have already discussed how Freud has investigated this issue in depth.

The third recommendation is "personal acquaintance between people of different nationalities and parties".[72] Countless examples can be cited where, after considerable communication and friendship, people regardless of their nationality have committed violent acts against one another. Uzbeks and Turks, who for decades lived together in the USSR, at the time of the collapse of the State committed unprecedentedly cruel crimes. The same thing occurred as a result of the Karabakh conflict between Azerbaijanis and Armenians.

The fourth recommendation: "It is necessary to help young people find the true purposes for which it is worth living in the modern world."[73] This is the area of social policy of the state. Would this recommendation be as useful and effective as the previous one if Lorenz himself considered criminal behaviour an innate trait?

Therefore we see that by different routes Freud and Lorenz arrive at an identical view of man as a creature with a recurring aggressive and destructive energy that cannot exist long.

The statement "destructiveness and cruelty are not instinctual drives, but passions which are rooted in the integral structure of human existence"[74] belongs to the equally influential psychologist Fromm. Here he considers human passions in connection with their roles in the life of the whole organism. According to him, their intensity is rooted not in specific physiological needs, but in the needs of the whole organism to live and develop in a bodily and spiritual sense.[75] The psychologist tried to prove that aggression and destructiveness, and hence crime as a form of aggression, are neither biologically driven nor spontaneously occurring impulses, but the result of interaction between different social conditions and existential human needs.

Fromm distinguishes between biologically adaptive aggression that contributes to the maintenance of life—non-malignant aggression (e.g. a person protecting himself from a deadly attack killing the attacker) and malignant aggression not connected with the preservation of life. Biologically adaptive

---

70   Ibid, p374.
71   Ibid, p394.
72   Ibid, p399.
73   Ibid, p401.
74   Fromm, E. Op. cit, p109.
75   Ibid, p23.

aggression is a reaction to a threat to the vital interests of man. It lies in phylogeny, is inherent both in animals and humans, is explosive in nature and arises spontaneously as a reaction to the threat; its consequence being either the elimination of the threat or its causes. The basis of malignant aggressiveness is not instinct but human capacity rooted in the very conditions of human existence.[76]

Consequently, on the basis of this statement, crime should be attributed to malignant aggression as it is not innate, and hence cannot be considered as ineradicable. In this regard, it is assumed that crime is a kind of human potential, from which one can easily liberate oneself. But how? Fromm believes that it is character that determines the choice of behaviour corresponding to the main objectives. This means that by one certain character trait, we can "predict the most probable behaviour of a man. More precisely, we can say the way he *wants* to behave, if he has the opportunity."[77]

Therefore, it can be assumed that it is this character trait that makes man behave accordingly to the image of his character. Hence, the source of criminal behaviour lies in human character. But what does this character mean according to Fromm? He writes: "Character is a relatively-permanent system of non-instinctive drives (aspirations and interests) that connect man with the social and natural world. This is the second nature of man."[78] Based on this definition, Fromm believes that the main fallacy of Lorenz and other researchers of instincts is that they mixed up two types of drives: those caused by instincts and those defined by character.[79] It is remarkable that Fromm reduces all character traits either to sexual roots or to non-sexual passions, meaning that he recommends searching for the causes of crime, i.e. criminal behaviour, in human character, which houses the organisation of human energy aimed at achieving goals. Character determines the choice of behaviour.

Also recognised by many psychologists is the theory of *frustration*, defined as a negative mental state arising from the inability to meet different needs. This condition manifests itself in feelings, frustration, anxiety, irritability, and finally in despair. John Dollard, one of the theory's leading exponents, defines it as follows: "The emergence of aggressive behaviour is always due to the presence of frustration and, conversely, the existence of frustration always leads to some form of aggression."[80] In fact, the inability to meet various needs can lead one to aggressiveness, although this absolutely does not

76 Ibid, pp 255–256.
77 Ibid, p119.
78 Ibid, p310.
79 Ibid, p109.
80 Dollard, Y. et al. *Frustration and Aggression*, New Haven: Yale University Press, 1939.

mean that such aggression will result in violent crime (murder, rape, etc). It all depends on the situation in which the man finds himself and on the relevant circumstances. An understanding of the unconscious as a basic human factor of crime is also found in the works of Schopenhauer and Nietzsche.

Ideas of original human depravity created the prerequisites for the formation of the concept of criminal man. The anthropological model, particularly as proposed by Lombroso, is based on the idea of the person as a primarily biological and psychological, 'natural' being. On the basis of his own in-depth research of prisoners, Lombroso's colleague, Antonio Marro, a psychiatrist and prison doctor, produced a remarkable essay, 'I caratteri dei delinquenti' (1887) in which he leans towards the predominance of the influence of "sickly heredity in the etiology of crime". Noteworthy is the fact that in the matter of the inheritance of physical and mental qualities, Marro refers to the effect of parental age at the moment of conception. He argues that each age is characterised by its physical and mental characteristics—it all affects the propensity towards crime. Incidentally, psychological determinism is characteristic of a number of social and psychological theories of criminality developed by American social psychologists such as E. Sutherland, D. Mats, T. Sykes and E. Gluck.

Thus the results of modern psychiatry cannot explain to us with any precision and clarity the causes of human criminal behaviour, because life shows that the vast majority of the population of the planet copes easily with their own aggressive emotions and successfully suppresses them. Of course, we are not able to explain all human actions, including criminal, nor all mental processes merely through the elucidation of human origin and evolution. Yet some still try to explain and justify heinous deeds such as greed, fraud, lies, violence and even murder by 'human nature'.[81]

Can a man come to know himself at all? Unfortunately, neither Freud, nor Lorenz nor Fromm had the answer to this question. They answered only the question on the meaning of 'self-knowledge'. Lorenz, for example, argues that this is a theoretical knowledge of the facts of evolution and, especially, of the instinctive roots of aggressiveness. In fact, the issue of human essence and nature is considered to be the prerogative of philosophy and religion. We are interested in this issue to the extent to which it helps to understand where to search for the true causes of human criminal behaviour, whether in biological, psychological or social roots. When Darwin's theory of evolution destroyed the image of God as the Supreme Creator, belief in God as the Father Almighty became invalid, though many have managed to keep their

---

81   Fromm, Op. cit, p300.

faith in God together with a recognition of Darwin's theory. Once the 'evolutionary' origin of man was acknowledged, the concept of a singular, unchanging 'substance' comprising 'human nature' became untenable. Therefore, further deepening of the knowledge of man, of the nature and causes of his behaviour is related directly to new discoveries in human nature on the basis of evolution theory. Fromm writes: "A man differs from animals in the fact that he is a killer. He is the only primate that without any biological or economic reasons kills his fellow tribesmen and finds satisfaction in this. This is the biologically-abnormal and phylogenetically non-programmed 'malignant' aggression that is a real problem and a threat to the survival of the human race."[82]

Interestingly, almost all researchers come to the same conclusion: the higher the level of development of a living being, the lesser the role in his life is played by hardwired, phylogenetically-inherent behaviour patterns. However, we are witnessing that a highly developed society with a high level of human development in the broadest sense does not contribute to a sharp decrease in the severity of criminal behaviour.

If we start from the theory of instincts, man has no responsibility for his criminal behaviour, since he does not have any freedom acting as a puppet, i.e. he is controlled by instincts. But then why do the vast majority of people not commit murder, rape and so on? Perhaps man has an anticriminal, antiaggressive instinct? Does man really have no internal barriers against criminal behaviour? Here Lorenz believes that man, unlike the predator, does not have any instinctive barriers against the killing of his own kind. Fromm, in contrast, believes that there is plenty of evidence to suggest that man has an internal sense of 'thou shalt not kill!' and that the act of killing entails remorse.[83]

It seems that the human ability to suppress their passions depends not only on internal factors, but also on the respective live situations and motives of crime—including murder. In explaining the origins of human criminal behaviour, the position diametrically opposed to instinctivism is occupied by the representatives of the theory of environment. According to them, human criminal behaviour is formed exclusively under the influence of the social environment, i.e. it is defined not by 'innate' but by social, cultural, external factors. Philosophical principles of this theory are as follows: a man is born good and reasonable, and if he develops criminal tendencies, the reasons for that are bad circumstances, bad education, bad environmental conditions and so on.

The simplest example of the environmental influence on humans is the

82   Ibid, p17.
83   Ibid, p168.

direct impact of the environment on brain growth. So, B. F. Skinner believes that, regardless of genetic background, human behaviour is completely determined by a set of 'incentives' that are created in two ways: either in the normal course of the cultural process, or according to a prearranged plan.[84] Consequently, by the proper application of positive 'incentives', human behaviour can incredibly be changed from criminal to beneficent. The path to the disappearance of crime, according to Skinner, lies in creating a better, science-based social order, because man is influenced by society and in 'human nature' there is nothing that may drastically impede the establishment of a peaceful and just society. In fact, under certain circumstances, any man can reach any state, including the state of criminal behaviour, contrary to all his notions of morality, contrary to personal decency and all social principles, values and norms. He can often sacrifice everything out of hatred, greed, selfishness, sadism. Therefore, human behaviour cannot be explained if it is considered solely as a consequence of training and education, i.e. of the inoculation of positive 'incentives', as expressed by Skinner.

The theory of environment leaves open very important questions: what do we have to include in environmental conditions that is necessary for the complete development of all human possibilities? Can a correct and just society ensure the formation of a normal person to such an extent that he would not commit murder, rape and other crimes?

Genetics and criminal behaviour

A significant contribution to the explanation of human behaviour has undoubtedly been made by genetics. Modern achievements in this field have produced convincing evidence that many human diseases are either directly inherited or pass on a predisposition towards them. Hereditary traits are passed from parents to children through the sex cells. As geneticist N. P. Dubinin writes: "When recognising the socialised nature of human biological properties, we should not lose sight of the fact that, as a living being, man is subject however to fundamental biological laws and that in this respect he has features inherent in all living beings on Earth."[85]

Genetics is the science of the laws of heredity and variation of organisms. The biological is very important to human life. For man as a social being, the

---

84 See: *The Design of Cultures*, Daedalus, Cambridge, 1961, pp 534–546 (American Association for the Advancement of Science).

85 Dubinin, N. P., Karpets, I. I. & Kudryavtsev, V. N. *Genetics, Behaviour, Responsibility*, Moscow, 1982, p14.

biological serves as a necessary prerequisite for the development of his features that might predominate over the biological. The main question is whether there is any general relationship, even the most remote, between the hereditary properties of the body and human behaviour, including criminal. We should immediately note that every man is genetically unique: he is unique anatomically, biochemically, physiologically, by temperament, character and other features. There is no genetic copy of him on the Earth now, there was none in the past and will be none in the future. Even identical twins differ in sets of somatic mutations. Therefore, this must be taken into account when determining the causes and mechanisms of human criminal behaviour.

The principal conclusion of genetics as the science of heredity is summarised by the following. A reasonable man could not fulfil the role of a thinking active being capable of unlimited social progress if his thoughts and actions were innate and genetically programmed. Nevertheless, science knows a number of facts proving the specific prerequisites that underlie the manifestations of such human phenomena as dementia and crime.[86] This does not mean however that the explanation of human behaviour should be based solely on the study of animal behaviour, because the primary role of culture makes man a unique biological species. As Engels put it: "The very fact of human origin from the animal kingdom leads to the fact that a man is never fully released from the features intrinsic to the animal, and therefore we can only talk about whether these features exist to a greater or lesser extent, we can only talk about the varying degrees of animality and humanity."[87]

It should be noted that the biological is not necessary and not only genetic. Human biology is the structure of his body, the functions of his internal organs, health and illness and so on. Therefore, the relationship between biological and human behaviour, including criminal, is indeed much broader than the role of human hereditary characteristics. In connection with this issue arises a highly interesting question: is it possible to explain the differences in the behaviour of groups, races by genetic characteristics? After all, if genetics indeed plays such an important role in human behaviour, then it stands to reason that it affects the behaviour of entire tribes, races and so on. In other words, if we recognise that human behaviour is affected by genetic properties, then are the genetic properties of different nations similar or different? At least for the moment, science provides us with a negative answer

86 See: Pastushiy, S. A. *Philosophy and Modern Biology*, Moscow, 1973, p195.
87 Marx, K. & Engels, F. *Works*, 2 edn, vol. 20, p102.

in this respect. Another question, then, is whether the human gene pool is subject to change in the process of historical development? If the answer is to be given from the point of view of the issue under consideration, then we should note that over the past twenty years criminality in Azerbaijan has increased, albeit only slightly. This does not mean that during this time the gene pool of our people has changed or that the quantity of 'criminal heredity' has increased. Most likely, this is due to changes in the economic, social, political, and psychological conditions of society, which undoubtedly have a major impact on human behaviour.

Modern genetics makes us think about the formation of a new man. In fact, if we believe the statement that all aspects of human life are determined by his genes, then for the formation of the new man it will be necessary to change human genetic features. Consequently, if it is determined that criminal behaviour is a genetic cause that is linked to heredity then by medical intervention these genes should be changed and man will not commit any evil or criminal actions anymore. So, he will not commit repeated crimes. What of the potential criminals then? One idea comes from Francis Crick who proposes recognising a person only after genetic verification. Based on this, a newborn that could not withstand such a test would be deprived of the right to life.

A genetic surgeon, a character in a Russian novel, says: "Perhaps in the future, in an age of complete humanity, people would find it more humane to destroy not the entire organism of a criminal but the thing in it that makes a person a criminal . . . I mean that life-code record which allows the development of anti-human traits in a human." He continues, addressing the criminal: "I will change not only the colour of your eyes, not just some of the features of your face, but your criminal system of thought. I will redo your nucleic basis."[88]

Of course, if a newborn shows any genetic characteristics that might later become the cause of serious diseases, medical-genetic intervention can be considered valid. However, the determination of future human criminal behaviour by the genetic code on the basis of heredity and the use of surgical methods on this basis is not only unjustified ethically, but is also fraught with serious consequences as regards health.

Before genetics can tackle this, it is necessary to identify *something* in a person that leads to criminal acts. Nevertheless, the question of whether we can 'improve' human nature by medical-biological methods persists.

There is an opinion that the many successes of genetics represent a

---

88   See: Kazantsev, A. *The Ice Comes Back*, Moscow, 1981, pp 387, 430.

scientific basis for the creation of higher races by the selection of people. The Nobel laureate H. Muller, starting from 1929, repeatedly put forward and developed ideas on taking the genes of prominent men, the leaders of the human species, for transmission to their descendants via the artificial insemination of women, even going so far as to offer a list of suitable candidates whose semen was to be used.[89] From this line of thinking it follows that the children born of recidivists will without doubt become criminals. Some even claim that there is no humane person on our planet and that it would only be possible to create one by changing human genetics (Lorenz). Indeed, in the twentieth century and today, the topic of the need for human genetic improvement is highly relevant since it is assumed that human nature is defined by man's genes and that there is nothing to be achieved merely by converting social conditions.

The question of how to make people better, so that they would be beneficent, not villains, has always existed. On this, J. Lengene has the following opinion to offer: "Personally I do not believe that someday 'supermankind' would be created with the use of genetic engineering tricks. In order to create a person that would be more intelligent than we are, we have to be smarter than we can be. Medicine is more modest, but much more effective."[90] This is why I do not believe that there are any medical methods or means capable of making a person non-criminal, because genetics itself still cannot answer the questions concerning the origin of human criminal behaviour and of the role of heredity in this matter.

One thing is clear: in man there is a 'something' that moves, pushes him towards a certain behaviour. Can man regulate and control this behaviour? In other words, can man resist the 'evil' forces which lead him to crime? Does he have these qualities? The secret of human criminal behaviour is concealed in the answers to these questions. If man is by his very nature unable to fight the evil forces acting upon him, then we cannot blame him for his criminal acts. And vice versa: if man himself contributes to or is not opposed to these forces, then he, no doubt, is solely responsible for his actions because it was his choice of behaviour, and moreover, his free choice.

89 Muller, H. 'The Guidance of Human Evolution', in *Studies in Genetics*, 1962, p560.
90 See: Lengene, J. 'Genetics and Mental Health', *Genetics and Welfare of Mankind*, no. 7, 1980, p92.

Philosophy and Free Will

The issue of the causes of human criminal behaviour for philosophy is actually the issue of free will. In other words, the philosophical issue of free will is connected with the determination of whether human behaviour is predestined by anything independent of human consciousness and will, i.e. fate, God, the inner nature of the organism, genes, environment and so on. Depending on the explanation of this question is the resolution of other, more specific tasks, namely whether humans are responsible for their actions and to what extent, and whether they are responsible for their actions in the legal, moral, religious sense. It should be immediately noted that in considering no other issue in the history of philosophy, with the possible exception of the issue of the deity concept, can one meet so many opinions and arguments, mutual accusations and recriminations as in the study of the issue of free will. And this is quite natural, since here intersect the filaments of all the major disciplines of philosophy.

Philosophers tend to associate *freedom* with desire, volition. If the desires are of a carnal nature, man is regarded as an unfree, dependent being. If man is moved by any moral principles, he seeks to suppress these desires and to free himself from their claims, and then he is already regarded as free. It is known that desire bears a carnal nature. A man steals bread simply to survive otherwise he will die, because there are no other options. In this case, is the man not regarded as a free being? After all, he commits theft because he has to. This is a natural need of the body, without whose satisfaction death occurs. In this case, the man knowing it commits an act totally dependent on his free will. If he chooses to die rather than to steal, which is formally considered a crime, then the decision is also deemed free of his will. Sexual intercourse is also a natural human need, it also bears a carnal nature. However, unlike the theft of bread, man is able to suppress his desire and striving to forcibly engage in sexual activity with a woman. He is able to free himself from this claim. Making this decision depends on his will.

But what is 'freedom'? Montesquieu writes: "There is no word that would derive so many different meanings or produce such different impressions on the mind than the word 'freedom'." [91] This is easy to verify by reading the relevant definitions in philosophical literature. According to Spinoza, "a thing is called free when it exists only of one necessity of its own nature and is determined to act only by itself. A thing is called required, or better, forced,

91   Montesquieu. *Selected Works*, Moscow, 1955, p288.

when it is determined to exist and to act by something else in accordance with a known and particular way."[92] Schopenhauer says: "I am free, if I can do what I want."[93] "In the end, freedom is an inner sensation, a subjectively experienced intimate feeling, and a man being in the same conditions can feel free or not free."[94] Pozdnyakov states that freedom is manifested precisely in the phenomenon of desire.[95]

Summarising the many statements and definitions of the concept of freedom, we can conclude that freedom is usually treated as a set of capabilities allowing man to meet his aspirations and to find ways for self-realisation. It is clear that there cannot be absolute freedom. Therefore every time a complete definition of the concept is required, the question will be asked: freedom from what? With regard to human behaviour, freedom is always the ability to follow the requirements of the mind. Man has relative freedom due to his consciousness.

The issue of free will was originally not only a theoretical subject but also a practical one. Through its philosophical consideration, the practical motives of thinking claim their rights as vigorously as the theoretical—and mostly even more vigorously. The first explanation for free will was provided, most likely, in the third book of Aristotle's *Nicomachean Ethics*, which begins by pointing out the value of the voluntariness of actions for their application, especially with regard to criminality. This point emphasizes the correlative concepts of freedom and responsibility. In Socrates' question on the 'voluntary commission of the unfair' there appears the embryo of the issue of free will. In light of this we can hardly agree with Pozdnyakov's belief that ancient philosophy was not interested in the issue of free will.[96]

The ancient sages and philosophers advised on embarking on the study of human affairs with the knowledge of oneself in the first place. This is hardly possible without reasoning, without thinking about the freedom of human will. And so the philosophical debates are reduced to a clash of two concepts: the will is free; the will is not free.

There are some (indeterminists) who proclaim the statement of the unlimited or nearly unlimited freedom of human will. According to them, man can actually make any decisions, he is free to act according to his own choice, regardless and even in spite of external circumstances. As Hegel says: "It is often expressed as: my will was determined by such motives, circumstances,

92 Spinoza, B. *Ethics* (*Selected Works, vol. 1*), Moscow, 1957, p362.
93 Schopenhauer, A. *On the Freedom of the Will*, Moscow, 1992, p48.
94 Sorokina, Y. V. *Introduction to the Philosophy of Right*, Moscow, 2001, p96.
95 See: Pozdnyakov, E. A. *Philosophy of Freedom*, p26.
96 See: Ibid.

temptations and impulses."[97] With this, he is saying that in order to evade responsibility the justification of criminal acts and writing off of all evil as a consequence of social environment and external circumstances, as well as to those anonymous forces creating them, contradicts human nature and essence.

Others (determinists) base their thoughts on the fact that if something depended on free human will, we would have had ample opportunity to escape troubles, not to commit evil and crime. Hereditary and family circumstances lay down in man the initial setting which he carries throughout his life. All this, together with character, is predetermined, and with it many other things on which human life depends are also predetermined. Thus, Montaigne once remarked that feelings were not generated by the mind and reflection, they were caused by circumstances. Therefore, "most surely it would be to explain our actions by the environment, without going into a thorough investigation of the causes and not deducing other conclusions".[98] Paul-Henri d'Holbach wrote about it more specifically: "Nothing in nature can happen by chance, everything follows its definite laws; these laws are only the necessary connection of certain consequences to their causes."[99]

Consequently, man is wholly dependent on two things: heredity and environment. All that he is and all that he has is the product of these two things. And neither of these does a man choose, since they are given to him, and with them and in them he lives his entire life as within fairly rigid boundaries. As Hobbes says: "Nothing starts by itself, but only through the action of any other factor given directly from outside. Thus, when man has the desire or the will to anything concerning which he has no desire or will, then the reason of his will is not the will itself but something beyond his control . . . Every event, no matter how random or spontaneous it may seem, comes with need."[100]

In fact, why is a man, an intelligent being, able to do evil? Perhaps indeed in his nature there are to be found tendencies that push him towards anti-social behaviour. Maybe society itself, his environment, creates conditions and incentives for the implementation of inclinations to commit a crime inherent in human nature (if they are present, of course). All these questions are not just theoretical but, rather, practical since it is impossible to impose on the person responsibility for his crime if it was generated by the biological properties of his organism, if it was rigidly determined by it. Neither can

97   Hegel, G. W. F. *Works over the Years*, Moscow, 1971, vol. 2, pp 26–29.
98   *On Human Nature: Montaigne, La Rochefoucauld, Pascal*, p106.
99   Holbach, P. *Selected Anti-Religious Works*, Moscow, 1994, vol. 1, pp 34–35.
100 Hobbes, T. *Of Liberty and Necessity (Selected Works, Vol. 1)*, Moscow, 1964, pp 556–558.

a man be held responsible for his actions if they were caused only by environmental conditions.

Thus, in recognising the freedom of choice of behaviour we also allow punishment of the criminal. We will only be able to know the essence of crime, and therefore the meaning and significance of punishment, if we are able to reveal human behaviour in general and criminal behaviour in particular. Man, endowed with great vitality, is capable of creating and destroying, of making both good and evil. However, he knows what to avoid and what to wish for, because of his ability of reasoning and comparison of different things. Therefore, when a person commits a crime he knows what he is doing, since this choice is the result of his mental reasoning and his comparing the benefits and possible losses resulting from his actions. Hegel frames this as follows: "If a man refers to the fact that he was warped from the true path due to circumstances, temptations, etc, then he wants to remove himself from the act, but in doing so he only demeans himself to an unfree being, a being of nature, whereas in fact his act is always the act of his own, and not the act of someone else, i.e. it is not a consequence of anything external to this man. Circumstances or motives prevail over the man only to the extent that he allows them to."[101]

Normally everyone looks for the source of their weaknesses and vices not in their own life or in themselves but in circumstances beyond their own life. Dostoevsky encapsulates it succinctly: "The doctrine of the environment, when making the man in all dependent on each error in the social organisation, leads the man to absolute impersonality, to his absolute release from all moral personal debt, from all independence, it brings him to the most awful slavery imaginable."[102]

The usual argument, by which public consciousness justifies punishment for a criminal act committed by a man, is to ensure that the man has free will, i.e. if he chooses a crime, he is responsible for his choice and, of course, he has to bear the punishment for it. This is also discussed by traditional philosophy, followed by the classical branch of the science of criminal law. According to the religious concept, man has an autonomous area where his conscience remains the autocratic master, because good or evil ultimately depend on free will. Thus, depending on whether man is free or not and depending on the degree of his freedom of choice, we can define his responsibility and degree of blameworthiness. There is no rational creature lacking free will. Man is naturally endowed with a powerful mind, he has the ability

101   Hegel, G. W. F. *Works over the Years*, Moscow, 1971. Vol. 2, p26.
102   Dostoevsky, F. M. *Diary of a Writer, (Complete Works: 30 Volumes)*, Leningrad, 1980, vol. 21, p16.

88   *The Philosophy of Crime and Punishment*

to reason and to distinguish good from evil, lawful conduct from unlawful. So he knows what he wants and what to avoid. The choice is up to him. Based on this, we cannot agree with L. Feuerbach, who claimed that "often the culprit of the act cannot explain it by self-examination, exclaiming in astonishment: 'How was it possible that I was willing to act like this? How could I besmirch my honour so dear to me? How could I sacrifice my nobility, for example, for the sake of a girl and my wellbeing for the sake of some trifle?' "[103]

This *seems* to be correct. There is hardly a man who would not commit an act that he later regretted. This is perfectly natural. Regretting doing things is evidence that man is an intelligent creature, that his act is his own wilful decision. The committed crime appears before his eyes in all its abomination when the crime is already beyond human reach, when he can no longer make it invalid. But this is not always the case. Typically, this refers to those crimes that are committed without preparation, that is, unexpectedly, spontaneously, due to certain circumstances. However, in this situation, man is able to suppress or turn aggressive instincts into non-violent forms of the discharge of psychic energy. Everything depends, again, on the strength of human will. The feature of the 'cultural man', as emphasized by Freud, is the ability of willpower to suppress instinct. The choice of behaviour as a consequence of willpower often happens unconsciously, automatically, without focusing on it, out of habit, but nevertheless it always happens.

In this respect, I would like to argue with Pozdnyakov, who believes that freedom of choice "does not give man anything but a painful conflict of motives and arguments, confusion of mind, determination and extinction of impulses."[104] In elaboration and clarification of his thought, he goes on to say: "The possibility of choice not only does not increase freedom of action, but, on the contrary, reduces it to a minimum. The more degrees of freedom, the less a being is free—this is the law, at least in the case of man. There is nothing worse and more painful for man than the freedom to choose between different alternatives of behaviour and action, between different opportunities, between different paths."[105] Choice is the process of evaluating, comparing, weighing different alternatives. Therefore, the more choices, the more the man can carefully consider and weigh everything to make the right decision. A minimum alternative is the basis for the wrong choice.

Always, in any situation, the broad possibility of choice indicates freedom of action. I was convinced of this when faced with different cases of criminal

103 See: *Legal Thought: Anthology*, Moscow, 2011, p275.
104 Pozdnyakov, E. A. *Philosophy of Crime*, p104.
105 Ibid.

life as the head of the Institute of Forensic Science of Azerbaijan. In one of the districts of the republic, a 72-year-old man shot his own 30-year-old daughter with a hunting rifle. She was married, had a family and two children, but moved to Baku where she led an 'immoral life'. On hearing this, the father, who in his village enjoyed great prestige among his fellow villagers, was greatly disappointed. After a while, the daughter returned home unexpectedly and between her and her father there took place a conversation in which the father asked the daughter to return to the city and keep out of people's eyes, for he had already been disgraced because of her behaviour. This encounter took place in the father's home where on the wall hung a rifle. The daughter cynically refused this request of her father's and said that she lived the way that she wanted. The father grabbed the rifle from the wall and killed her with a single shot.

What compelled him to do this? Could he keep himself from doing it? After a long conversation during a psychological examination, it was found that her words, "I will live the way I want to", became the incitement to murder his own daughter. What then was decisive and determined the choice of criminal behaviour in this case? Man is known to act not on the basis of instinct, but of his thinking mind, or of the mechanism that mainly determines his wilful behaviour. But what is this mechanism? Does it exist in the man or outside him? Some scientists believe that human *desire* is a part of his conscious volitional life.[106] And human desire is always manifested, albeit imperceptibly, even when it is slowed down by other volitional activity. Man, being already conscious, is always able to control the desires that are neutralised by other desires. Therefore, desires mutually control each other. As a result of the adjustment of desires there arises choice. However, in this case, as it turned out, the father had no desire to kill his own daughter. So, this mechanism could not be decisive in the volitional choice of behaviour.

Other scientists believe that the primary and main trigger in man, as in animals, is *selfishness*, i.e. the attraction to being and wealth.[107] Need is the sense of insufficiency in every living organic being which interacts with the outside world and draws from it the means to sustain its life. Meeting the needs and desires gives man pleasure, frustration causes him pain. Therefore, man is naturally committed to meeting his needs and avoiding suffering. In order to meet his needs and desires, man, when it is impossible to do so in a lawful way, continually breaks the law and commits crimes. And as these needs and desires are given to him at birth, then we can say that he has the

106 See: Windelband, W. *On Free Will*, Moscow, 2000, p16.
107 See: Schopenhauer, A. *On the Basis of Morality: Free Will and Morals*, Moscow, 1992, p196.

natural desire to sin. Hence, there is a struggle between evil occurring in him, i.e. between the desire to commit a crime and consciousness resisting against law-breaking.

Inborn needs can only be considered as the natural human needs to eat, drink and so on. As for drives, these are not inborn but acquired throughout life, such as the drives to drugs, alcohol and prostitution. Therefore, we can hardly agree with the fact that the father killed his daughter as the result of a drive. This appears to be more correct if we turn to mental forces, which play a crucial role in the mechanism of selection of a particular behaviour in a given situation. I believe that the above example of a particular type of criminal behaviour confirms this argument. As a result of the psychological analysis of the elderly father, the killer, it was clearly seen that during the commission of the crime, his behaviour constituted the implementation and identification of mental experiences that had long been accumulating in him and strongly impacted him. They were connected with the immoral life of his daughter. If the father was himself an immoral and unworthy man not respected among the villagers, then of course he would never have felt those experiences that led to the commission of the murder of his own daughter. According to Freud (psychoanalysis, the unconscious), the unconscious can come to the surface at any given time and with weak psychoanalytic control it can cause irrational, strange acts and painfully perverted behaviour.

We should note that Freud's theory was consistent with traditional philosophical, legal and psychological concepts of free will, considering which the possibilities of the mental and rational regulation of human behaviour seemed truly unlimited. On this Maltsev writes: "As the key idea, Freud considers the idea that human behaviour is ruled by irrational psychic forces and not by the laws of social development, that the intellect is the device of masking these forces, not a means of active reflection of reality, the deeper understanding of it, and that the individual and the social environment are in a state of eternal and secret war."[108]

In the example we have seen, the satisfaction of selfishness also contributed to the commission of crime by the father, the killer, for he put his personal dignity and honour above the life of his daughter. In this case, selfishness played the part of the trigger in the man as in the animal. However, this would not have happened if there were not relevant external factors independent of the criminal: the father and the daughter were alone; the rifle was at hand; everybody was asleep as it was late. If one of these external conditions was missing, the crime could not have happened. For example, if

108 Maltsev, G. V. *Social Foundations of Law*, Moscow, 2011, p150.

there was a third person in the room who was trying to defuse the situation, could the old man have contained himself and chosen a different line of behaviour, i.e. not to commit murder but, for example, to strike her or spit in her face and leave the room? To help answer this, I am able to offer another example from personal experience.

A police officer, unexpectedly for his wife, found her with another man 'in a warm bed'. Carrying his duty weapon with him at the time, he was able to freely use it. However, when he took in the scene, he quietly went into the kitchen and asked the couple to get dressed, and then he saw his wife's lover off. Having calmly discussed the situation, the couple decided to separate. Why did the police officer contain himself, although the conditions and circumstances contributed to assuming that the unconscious would cause irrational behaviour? Why did his thinking mind direct his wilful decision not to commit a crime?

Given virtually the same conditions and circumstances that contribute to the commission of crime, some do it and others do not. Hence the human factor, psychological attitudes, i.e. everything connected with the personality, play a crucial role and are the causes of criminal behaviour in murder, as well as in violent crimes without intent of profit. Not everyone is able to contain himself from committing a crime because of the humiliation of his honour and dignity. This is not revenge for humiliation and insult, but it is the *inability* to control oneself due to his natural and human features. It is another thing when a man especially prepares for some time to kill his wife's lover. This is called revenge. When we talk about the reasons of acquisitive or acquisitive and violent crimes, then to the foreground of course comes the social, external factor, although in the profit motive there is also the human factor: greed, desire for enrichment, profit and so on.

We have discovered that crime is a product of free individual choice; it is the implementation of will and *not the result* of enslavement of will by individual patterns. But why does a man having a choice of behaviour on the basis of freedom of will commit a crime regardless? What pushes him to it? In fact, man by nature is passionately attracted not to something within his reach but to something distant and prohibited. It can be hedonism, longing for possession and the will to power and so on. The analysis of specific crimes always proves this. By revealing the causes of crime or, more precisely, of human criminal behaviour, we thereby reveal the essence of the nature of the individual and his actions, his psychology, sociology, character, inclinations and interests, his level of development and education.

Being one of the forms of action, crime tends to put man to the test, to make him open up completely, to find those qualities which in other circumstances would have remained hidden, undetected. For example, the essence, nature and properties of a briber can be discovered after he acquires the appropriate authority. Rape gives us the opportunity to discover in a rapist such qualities that we would never have noticed if he had not committed this crime. Where should we search for the causes of criminal behaviour? David Abrahamsen believes that they should not be searched for somewhere 'on the side', in the process coming up with theories and identifying the action of external factors, but in ourselves, in basic human characteristics, in the mental psychic human constitution.[109]

For psychoanalysts, the mind is the very starting point from which they began their studies of the phenomenon of crime, because the mind is considered that which fundamentally distinguishes humans from other animals. Therefore we must look for the cause of this human attribute, i.e. the propensity towards crime, in the mind. The twentieth century has made us take a new look at the old on the world issue of crime. For example, Camus argued that this would be done best through the prism of the category of the absurd. In his understanding, absurd is a state in which higher meaning cannot be seen in anything, where everything gets mixed up and the difference between for and against, virtue and crime vanishes. As a result of the disappearance of boundaries, hierarchies and rules, everything becomes acceptable and permissible. It seems that a search for the common causes of all crime does not make sense because they simply do not exist. There are no similar crimes and there cannot be any. Additionally, there are no completely similar causes of crime. Each specific crime, taking into account the peculiarities of the individual, has its cause.

In his novella *The Kreutzer Sonata* (1889), Tolstoy depicted sexual passion as a terrible, destructive force leading man to the path of crime. In this case, sexual passion may be the cause of rape. Some may suppress this passion by will power, others cannot. Sex murder is a different thing. It is not sexual passion, rather a biological phenomenon. It is clear that the search for the common causes of crimes such as robbery, bribery or rape does not make sense. It should be noted that none of the fields of science today has been able to prove any genetic connection between a man and his criminal act, of which Lombroso spoke so persuasively at the time.

At the same time, there is no reason to doubt that the actions of a man in general and criminal actions in particular are largely dependent on his psychophysiological features. Social environment should rather be regarded

---

109 See: Abrahamsen, D. *Who Are the Guilty? A Study of Education and Crime*, Westport, Connecticut, 1972, p16.

not as the cause of criminal behaviour but as the condition under which human psychophysiological features manifest themselves. Most people living in very difficult conditions do not rob, do not rape, do not kill. This means that the causes of specific criminal behaviour are not in the social context but in the criminal himself. As we know, in many European countries the conditions we are talking about are almost absent. However, it is a fact that serious crimes are committed that are absolutely unrelated to the conditions of social life. As a result we cannot agree with Karpets' statement that the causes of specific crimes, due to the presence of common causes, "are provoked by certain shortcomings at each stage of social development, by negative phenomena still existing in public life, they are associated with conditions that impede overcoming them".[110] The contrary opinion of Pozdnyakov, where society as a whole does not contain the causes of criminal behaviour, is also incorrect. Society creates only the best or the worst, more favourable or less favourable conditions for development of the evil inherent in humans and inclination towards anti-social behaviour as the true germ from which grows the whimsical flower called 'crime'.[111]

So Pozdnyakov, the philosopher, believes that evil qualities and propensity towards crime are laid in any person. This depends on the surrounding conditions whether the man will go from potential criminal to a real one. In this case, it is problematic to explain the percentage ratio between persons who have committed crimes and law-abiding citizens. If we recognise as proven the fact that in every man are laid criminal qualities and evil, it is impossible to explain annual fluctuations in crime growth, the nature of crime and so on.

G. A. Avanesov's view is also unsubstantiated and unfounded where he says: "A man . . . has certain innate features. Some of them may, in our opinion, under appropriate conditions, facilitate the commission of a crime or even to act as one of the causes of a particular criminal offence."[112] We can agree that certain human psychophysiological qualities may be the causes of criminal behaviour under appropriate conditions but we cannot believe that these qualities are innate. In addition, a person being the victim of this terrible inclination sometimes still retains the ability to defeat it or give it the wrong direction. But the power to win weakens in such a person in proportion to the degree of the faults of education and lesser development of organs and capabilities of the highest order. Thus, although the features Avanesov

---

110 Karpets, I. I. *Modern Issues of Criminal Law and Criminology*, Moscow, 1976, p69.
111 Pozdnyakov, E. A. *Philosophy of Crime*, p141.
112 Avanesov, G. A. *Criminology, Prognostics, Management*, Gorkiy, 1975, p91.

mentions are innate, they are still controlled by man himself. It all depends on the power of human will. It is quite possible of course that the most decent, law-abiding person, having a strong character and will, under the influence of hunger can reach a degree of bitterness which can lead to all sorts of crimes, including the theft of bread. In this case, his character and will can hardly be considered as definitively changed.

We must not forget either that every nation has its own features of psychology and character. This fact is important in determining a particular behaviour as criminal. Over the centuries, every nation developed its ideas, culture, psychology and, therefore, all the motives of behaviour. Under the same circumstances, a Caucasian is capable of making, by his character, psychological condition, emotion and so on, a move that would surprise a European. At the same time, the ordinary act of a European may be perceived by a Caucasian as not only immoral but criminal. And so national and human fate is 'supervised' by our ancestors, their customs, traditions, character and morals. At times we bear the burden of their errors. For example, blood vengeance as a crime is what we inherited from them, and unfortunately we still cannot completely get rid of this relic of times past, because the dead generations pass us not only their physical organisation but their thoughts too. Gustave Le Bon notes: "Never has it been so clear to me that people of each race possess, despite the difference in their social status, an indestructible stock of ideas, traditions, feelings and ways of thinking that make up the unconscious heritage from their ancestors, against which any arguments are completely powerless."[113]

Currently many are wondering why, unlike us Caucasians, Europeans tend to be law-abiding. Will we ever be like them? Whatever a man would do, he is always the first and foremost representative of his nation with its soul. The soul is that stock of ideas, feelings and psychological characteristics brought into being by all individuals of every nation from birth. The soul actually directs behaviour or at least has a significant impact on the choice of behaviour.

The soul of every nation has a set of moral and intellectual characteristics. The anatomical features and psychological characteristics of each nation are reproduced by heredity. The unit of general psychological features is that which is reasonably called national character. Even murderers of different nations differ in their psychological characteristics before the crime and in the course of its commission. It should be noted that the idea of lawfulness begins to exert its effect only when, after a very slow processing, it is

---

113   Le Bon, G. *The Crowd: A Study of the Popular Mind*, Moscow, 2012, p8.

converted to senses and penetrates into the unconscious, where our thoughts are generated. Unfortunately, unlike Europeans, we still have this feeling unformed. This explains why we still feel the need to resort to harsh measures of criminal punishment, and it follows that it remains too early to adjust our criminal legislation to the European model.

Of course, it should be noted that the history of every nation is determined by various factors. It is full of special events, accidents that occurred but might not have occurred. In order that a nation, a people, might transform their attitude to the law and become law-abiding, they must first 'remake' their soul. It follows that this issue cannot be solved by legal education alone, because under the influence of legal education can only the level of intellectual development can be raised in this area. The quality of character almost completely eludes its actions. Today, as we all know, Europe, out of benevolent intentions, is trying to make other less civilised nations accept its conditions in the application of criminal punishment for criminals, i.e. to reconsider the role and importance of punishment in the fight against crime. Is this possible?

At this moment it would be a mistake. We are not ready for this. Do not forget that there is a gap between the psychological make-up of the peoples of Europe and the former Soviet Union. Nations that are very similar in appearance may be very different in their own way of feeling and acting, their beliefs, culture and art. These qualities affect people's behaviour, including criminal, and not climate, race, skin colour, i.e. the anatomical factors pointed out by Lombroso.

The character of a nation is formed by the combination of different elements, which is referred to by psychologists as feelings (perseverance, energy, ability to self-control, morality)—as Le Bon points out, "the greatness of nations depends mainly on the level of their morality".[114] In relation to the law-abiding, morality means hereditary respect for the norms of the law, which is the basis for the existence of the rule of law, and hence of the society. To have morality for a nation means to possess known firm rules of conduct and not to commit crimes, as there would be less of them when various nations would comply with the laws upon conviction and not upon coercion, as they honour their good customs and traditions.

Thus, the causes of human criminal behaviour must be sought in the psychophysiological features that are not of genetic inheritance, they appear under certain environmental conditions and circumstances, resulting in that a person freely accepts this or that decision on their own. Therefore, neither

114 Ibid, p24.

the social conditions of society or economic factors (beggary, poverty, wealth, luxury), nor, moreover, inheritance, can serve as the causes of crime.

In summary, we can conclude that the philosophical essence of crime is a free volitional form of human behaviour, the origins of which are the psychophysiological features of an individual resulting from the impact on him of external negative socio-economic conditions and circumstances.

*

3

The Criminal Personality

The culprit of crime, no matter what value is attached to external factors, is always an individual. It is impossible therefore to ignore the position of personality in crime. Classical lawyers proceeded and continue to proceed from the fact that a criminal, except for obvious and exceptional qualities (age, intoxication, illness, etc), is the same person as others. However, it is obvious that such an approach does not allow for bringing criminal law to a truly scientific method of studying the causes of criminal human behaviour.

In his day, S. K. Gogel noted: "And to this legal castle of criminal law dogma, with its medieval legends and traditions, to the world closed from any contact with real life, came scientists of a new direction . . . they stated to the dogmatists that they forgot about a living person, and by breaking the general algebraic formula of the concept of a criminal demonstrated first-hand that there is not just one criminal, but many: innate and occasional, murderers, and thieves, and that they have nothing in common, and that it is inadmissible to lump them into one general concept of rule-breakers."

The foundations of the study of the criminal personality were laid mainly by the research of English prison doctors and other professionals. The question was whether the criminal is to be viewed, as in ancient Greece and Rome, as a slave, as a creature of a special different breed, not like the others. It may be that anyone who commits a crime is a madman or a savage. Perhaps he is a degenerate, as believed by Ferri. Or an epileptic, according to Lombroso. Perhaps the criminal has a specific psychology. It should be noted that as a result of the development of mental teachings which have had the strongest influence on the correctness of the development of human behaviour, it was possible to study the person who committed a criminal act and his attributes. So, for example, B. Moritz, based on twenty-two cases observational cases, suggested that the criminal's brain is a particular type deviating from the 'normal' brain.[1] A year after releasing his findings, Moritz announced that "the organic failure or basic element in psychology of a professional criminal is 'neurasthenia' or nervous exhaustion, nervous weakness in the physical, moral and mental sense, and, moreover, weakness either innate or acquired in early childhood".[2] He eventually reached the conclusion that a professional incorrigible criminal is actually a deviation from the generic 'homo' concept. As we have seen, familiarity with the facts led Despine to the conclusion that hardened criminals had no moral sense with which they were able to distinguish good from evil that would prompt condemnation of criminal desires and cause subsequent remorse.

Anthropologists, after studying around 2,000 individuals in prisons and asylums, indicated that they could distinguish natural-born killers from other criminals by physical signs, especially in the most severe cases. Lombroso, one of the leading exponents of this trend, actually developed F. I. Gall's ideas concerning the fact that criminals or, at least, their majority, bear a specific external type and that the task of research is precisely to discover those specific external signs peculiar to criminals.

The idea that the criminal, especially in cases of the most prominent criminal type, is none other than a savage caught up in our civilisation was expressed before Lombroso, in particular by Despine. However, Lombroso first used the term 'born criminal', which in his opinion is both the result of painful deviations and *atavism*. A born criminal is "a wild and at the same time a sick man". Lombroso saw the possibility of reconciling these two views on the criminal in the theory of the delay in the development of some organs and, most importantly, in the development of malnourished psychic centres. On the one hand this makes such organs 'places of least resistance', i.e. predisposes them to a variety of disorders, and on the other hand, it relegates them to a type of lower development. He also claimed that the body fluids of a born criminal differ from those of an accidental criminal and ordinary law-abiding people, as if a born criminal excreted less urea and more phosphates than those set by norms.[3] Lombroso identified a huge range of features, especially in the skulls of born criminals, in almost every bone of the skull as well as in its general structure and shape. For example, criminals, particularly thieves, often have small skulls and one rarely encounters skulls of maximum capacity. In Lombroso's laboratory, the objects of detailed

---

1   See: Report at the Congress in Antwerp in 1885.
2   *Gazette des tribunaux*, 1852.
3   Lombroso, C. *Recent Advances of the Science of the Criminal*, 1892, p66.

scientific study covered not only the skulls but also other physical features such as the ears and noses.

Analysing the data collected by Lombroso in order to establish this special 'type', Manouvrier insisted that only one thing can be argued on their basis, namely that criminals on average display more deviation than so-called honest people. He also pointed out the incorrectness of Lombroso's method, consisting in the fact that for the formation of the type, the latter combined in one unit the features found in very different criminals. In fact, there is no general type of an ugly or 'pathological' person, there are merely different types of malformations. These are simple observations made by Manouvrier on the existence of a special anatomical and physiological 'criminal type'.

At the Fourth Congress of Criminal Anthropology, Ferri, who was Lombroso's student and colleague, reported on 'criminal temperament', seeking to abandon the concept of 'criminal person' earlier used by the followers of Lombroso with its specific and 'criminal type', with the phenomena of crime reduced to their source, the phenomena of mental degeneration. S. V. Poznyshev also referred to criminals as possessing a specific type, with the explanation: "A criminal type is not a simple sum of known psychic personality properties but a known personality pattern, a known combination of mental properties, creating, so to speak, a slope for an individual towards crime, prompting him either to look right for an occasion to commit a crime, or not to miss such an opportunity once it appears, or at least not to resist well enough the temptations of this case dictated by known sensual drives."[4] Modern legal scholars "allow themselves to talk about the criminal personality as a separate, independent social and psychological type",[5] although they clarify that the concept of 'criminal personality' is a conventional terminological designation. The phrase 'identity of the person (the individual) who committed the crime' would be more correct."[6]

What distinguishes the identities of criminals and ordinary people in the opinion of these writers? By way of answer, Y. M. Antonyan and V. E. Eminov offer the following: "Comparative psychological study of the identity of large groups of criminals and law-abiding citizens showed that the former differ from the latter by a significantly higher level of impulsivity, i.e. the tendency to act upon the first impulse, and aggressiveness combined with high sensitivity and vulnerability in interpersonal relationships."[7]

---

4   Poznyshev, S. V. *Criminal Psychology, Criminal Types*, Moscow, 2007, p31.
5   Antonyan, Y. M. & Eminov, V. E. *Identity of the Criminal: Criminological and Psychological Research*, Moscow, 2010, p12.
6   Ibid.
7   Ibid, p9.

Antonyan and Eminov even see in the criminal a "genetically-determined predisposition and inclinations".[8] In psychology, there is a chapter entitled 'Identity', which means that the term 'identity' is so difficult to define and it has such a wide range of use that it can be can freely written about without assuming any responsibility for the definition. Nowadays, a few dozen definitions of the term can be listed, maybe more even: the theory of types (the Hippocratic theory of the four basic temperaments: choleric, melancholic, sanguine and phlegmatic); the theory of features (human personality as a set of features or characteristic ways of behaviour, thinking, feeling, responding, etc). There are also psychodynamic and psychoanalytic theories (Freud, Jung, Fromm, Horn). Personality in them is characterised by the concept of integration. To which definition would it be correct to refer the identity of the criminal?

As previously noted, anthropologists have most often spoken of the 'criminal type' as a known 'external' type, i.e. as a combination of certain external features that distinguish criminals from other people and are able to serve for their classification and recognition, as the anatomic and physiological or anthropological type. Thus, in the 'type', the leading and critical position belongs to external features. Hence those who support the point of view of the 'criminal type' focus primarily on human appearance. Hardly anyone today believes that a criminal can be distinguished from a law-abiding person by their appearance.

A criminal is not a special type with specific external features. It is a perfectly normal human physically. Maybe criminals have a special psychology? But the science of psychology has not come to this conclusion. The psychology of a killer is, in fact, the psychology of any human which in appropriate life circumstances may also become a killer. The criminal, like all people, is the sum of his individual features. Everyone possesses known constant physical and mental features that form their physical and mental constitution, and both of them consist of the innate part and the part of acquired features. Therefore, it makes little sense to allocate criminals to a special category, to a particular 'type' and to consider them as special identities in a negative sense.

The concept of the 'identity of the criminal' also provokes a negative attitude among the population. Indeed, can we relate the concept of the 'identity of the criminal' to a person who has committed a crime out of negligence? Thus, *identity* is a stable system of ideological, psychological and behavioural traits that characterise a person. Can we identify a special system

8   Ibid, p10.

of these traits in criminals? Nowadays, science does not give a positive answer to this question.

Identity type is an abstract model of personal characteristics inherent in a particular set of people. There are people with strong features deviating from the characteristics, structures and levels of development of the individual typical for this particular socio-cultural system. However, this does not mean that they constitute a special type. It merely emphasizes the low level of development of these people for whatever reasons. For example, a man who lived his entire life in the mountains and then found himself in a civilised country in Europe. Needless to say, such a man would be sharply distinguished from the rest in his behaviour, communication and so on. However, this does not mean that he may commit a crime and become a criminal.

Everyone is a personality that has a unique set of features of character and psychological makeup that distinguish one person from another. This applies to the criminal as well. However, there are no such qualities that could unite all the criminals in any group and create a special 'type' of identity. Therefore, we should abandon the concept of the 'identity of the criminal' and use the concept of 'the person who committed a crime'.

*

4

The Future of Criminality

The classics of Marxism-Leninism considered the task of eliminating criminality as completely solvable and linked it with the destruction of the exploitation of man by man. Following this doctrine, the authors of textbooks on criminology, in particular, wrote: "In the process of the development of socialist society the basic social roots of criminality are undetermined, but some of its causes are retained. They are not associated with the nature of socialism and are caused by the particular historical context in which socialism is built, overcoming a number of contradictions and difficulties within the country and leading to an acute class struggle in the international arena. In communist society, criminality will completely wither away as a social phenomenon."[1]

This was the position of almost all the scientists and experts of the Soviet period. On this basis, criminologists set the tasks of the 'liquidation', 'eradication', even 'destruction' of criminality, while Western scholars believed that 'socialism had not coped with criminality'. The temporary nature of crime however was spoken about long before the Soviet scientists. For example, the utopian R. Owen wrote: "Seek to raise the level of general wellbeing persistently and systematically, resort to measures of lesser severity for the protection of public order against crime, and gradually crime will disappear, for even the most vicious and established inclinations cannot fight persistent benevolence for long."[2]

As Antonyan so rightly points out, "no one nowadays is making such

---

1   *Criminology: A Textbook*, ed. by A. A. Gertsenzon, I. I. Karpets & V. N. Kudryavtsev, Moscow, 1966, p54.
2   Cit.: Chubinskiy, M. P. *The Course of Criminal Policy*, 2nd edn, Saint Petersburg, 1912, p178.

utopian plans because it is clear that it [i.e. criminality—*I. R.*] is an inevitable and natural companion of mankind for all time, like sickness and death."[3] In this respect, I would like to share Karpets' sincere confession: "A historically retrospective look at the whole process of criminality knowledge slowly but inexorably reveals our mistakes, delusions and illusions."[4]

Nowadays, many scientists speak about the eternity of criminality. For example Antonyan writes: "There should be almost no doubt that criminality has always existed. This finding is of great importance, since it inherently contains the statement that it will never disappear as the inevitable companion of mankind, no matter what different makers of the 'City of the Sun' might think about it."[5] E. Pozdnyakov, a philosopher, also states that criminality is "an essential element of the great and multilateral human nature, and, hence, the whole being of the human race".[6] Consequently crime will not disappear so long as there is a person. Alexandrov addresses this in another way: "Complete victory over criminality and its elimination are practically unacceptable, at least in the known socio-economic formations—this is only an ideal to aspire to."[7]

The theory of criminal eternity was born in the West. E. Durkheim, W. Landen, C. Breytel and many others wrote about it. For example, Durkheim believed that "criminality is normal because a society is quite impossible without criminality. Criminality is needed: it is firmly connected with the basic conditions of social life, and precisely because of this it is useful because the conditions, of which it is itself a part, are inseparable from the true evolution of morality and law."[8] From his point of view, if criminality was an element of a healthy society, this meant that it could not be a negative, harmful phenomenon. In other words, it is useful. Schur also argues that it is "pointless to think of the elimination of all crimes".[9]

So the reality is that no sociopolitical system has solved the problem of criminality yet. In the words of Tagantsev, "the life of all nations shows us that whenever and wherever there were and are committed acts for various reasons not recognised as non-permitted but also provoking the known actions of society or the state against the persons committing them. The acts are recognised as criminal—that whenever and wherever there existed

3   Antonyan, Y. M. *The Causes of Criminality*, Moscow, 2006, p16.
4   Karpets, I. I. *Criminality: Illusions and Reality*, Moscow, 1992, p73.
5   Antonyan, Y. M. Op. cit, p14.
6   Pozdnyakov, E. *Philosophy of Crime*, Moscow, 2001, p502.
7   Alexandrov, A. I. *Philosophy of Evil and Philosophy of Criminality*, Saint Petersburg, 2013, p148.
8   Durkheim, E. *Norms and Pathologies, Sociology of Crime, Modern Bourgeois Theories*, Moscow, 1966, pp 40–42.
9   Schur, E. *Our Criminal Society*, Moscow, 1979, p15.

persons who to some extent have stubbornly not complied with the requirements of the legal order and the dictates of the authorities protecting it."[10]

Medicine teaches us the following: in order to find a remedy for any disease, one must first discover and examine the causes of this disease. It appears that the issue of criminal eternity or temporality cannot be resolved outside the context of the causes of human criminal behaviour. Assuming that the causes of crime are only social in nature, then the eternity of criminality is in question, because a society that would not have these social conditions is quite possible. If the causes of criminal behaviour are directly related to human nature out of connection with the external social conditions, then criminality will exist until we find the sources of this evil and the means of their eradication.

And finally, the causes of crime can be both social conditions and the physiological characteristics of a person. In this case, criminality will disappear under the condition of elimination of both social conditions and human 'defects'. Nowadays, unfortunately, we are unable to answer the question of the causes of human criminal behaviour. Therefore, crime is an eternal evil for us. What shall we do? Could it be that the fight against criminality is not worth it? Antonyan answers these questions as follows: "Fighting criminality is well within human capabilities, but the absurd task of eradicating it shall not be set."[11] V. N. Kudryavtsev also acknowledges the difficult nature of this struggle: "Fighting crime has a long and unending nature; seemingly defeated and destroyed criminal forces are 'reborn from the ashes', they 'spring up like mushrooms', new criminal forms and new methods of criminal behaviour arise, in criminality are involved new and mostly more educated people."[12]

Recently the term 'control' has been used more often in relation to criminality than the usual words 'war', 'struggle', 'eradication' and 'overcoming.' Even an attempt to combine all forms of the treatment of criminals into one term, 'the response to crime', has been made. Kudryavtsev believes that the replacement of the word 'struggle' can be understood only as the inability to overcome criminality: we can supposedly only 'control' it, i.e. just watch the situation.[13] He is right that the expression 'to control' shows the helplessness, passivity, ineffectiveness of society in the struggle against criminality. But in our opinion, it is more relevant to use the expression 'crime prevention' because it is more democratic and progressive than 'struggle'.

If we are not able to eradicate criminality, then what task should be assigned

---

10   Kudryavtsev, V. N. *Strategies of the Struggle against Criminality*, Moscow, 2003, p9.
11   Antonyan, Y. M. Op. cit, p7.
12   Kudryavtsev, V. N. Op. cit, p29.
13   Ibid, p36.

to society? According to Antonyan, "the urgent task remains its maintenance on a so-called civilised level".[14] For us, the issue of the future of criminality is interesting. And we are speaking not only about the eternity or temporality of this phenomenon but also about its immediate future. This interest, of course, is connected to the need to be prepared for its prevention. However, in order to even imagine the state of criminality in the future, in three to five years, we need relevant information about the condition and its quantitative characteristics, the dynamics of a more-or-less extended period of time, i.e. information about the past and present state of criminality. And this is, as we know, the issue of criminal prediction that requires us to learn to anticipate changes in criminality.[15] Avanesov emphasizes: "Prediction becomes a tool making it possible to know the trends and patterns of change in criminality in the future, it has acquired the feature of a method to study criminality."[16]

Is such a form of prediction possible? Mathematicians managed to prove that it is impossible to establish with predetermined accuracy the future state of a nonlinear non-uniform system, i.e. a system in which small deviations can cause significant changes, and that is far from the state of stabilisation. Any trend that has become apparent in such a system can instantly change and the further process becomes fundamentally random. It can be argued that criminality refers to the considered class of systems. Therefore, it is impossible to predict the future of criminality, i.e. to determine precisely the state of criminality even in two to three years, because as a mass antisocial phenomenon it is largely an amorphous, chaotic, spontaneous formation, "like a conglomerate of various micro-organisms corrosive to a highly-organised living being."[17]

In other words, the elusiveness, the unpredictability of criminality in the set of randomness, which is prevalent in this area, is of a spontaneous, unexpected, hardly predictable character. We do not know when, why, who is going to commit a crime and what crime is it going to be, just as we cannot explain the existence of criminality at all times of humanity. Therefore, so long as we cannot answer the question of why crime is an inevitable and ineradicable companion of mankind, we are not ready to predict the future of criminality. It is also important to take into account the fact that criminality is a statistical system, obeying the laws of probability, the actions of both objective and subjective factors.

14   Antonyan, Y. M. Op. cit, p17.
15   For more information on the possibility of predicting criminality, see: Avanesov, G. A., *Theory and Methodology of Criminological Prediction*, Moscow, 1972; Ragimov, I. M. *The Theory of Criminological Prediction*, Baku, 1987.
16   Avanesov, G. A. Op. cit, p27.
17   Kudryavtsev, V. N. Op. cit, p27.

So, the purpose of criminality prediction is to establish the most common indicators that characterise the development (change) of criminality in the future, to identify on this basis any undesirable trends and patterns and to find ways of changing these trends and patterns in the right direction. From this position, we shall attempt to determine the probable state of crime in Azerbaijan over the next five years. Let us start with an analysis of the state of crime in the past and trace its dynamics for a fifty-year period, which shall be divided into two parts: the state and dynamics of crime in Soviet Azerbaijan and then in the sovereign independent state.

In fact, it can be reported that, regardless of the political system, the crime rate in Azerbaijan over the past fifty years has grown. For example, if the average crime rate in 1961–1970 amounted to 13,600 crimes, then in 1971–1980 it was 14,650, and in 1981–1990, 15,850. It should be noted that for a country with a small population, this increasing trend of criminality is quite noticeable. Since 1981, there has been growth in ordinary crimes: 1981, 42%; 1985, 45%; 1990, 58%. The level of grave and other violent crimes is gradually increasing. If in 1981 of the total number of crimes 390 were murders, then in 10 years, in 1991, this figure was 489. In 1981, there were committed 222 grievous bodily injuries, and in 1991, 397; armed assaults 169, robberies 186 (1981), and in 1991, accordingly, 295, 213. At the same time, the number of rapes dropped: 1981, 119; and in 1991, 48. Since 1986 there has been a trend towards rapid growth in the theft of state and public property.

Therefore, despite the tough and harsh criminal policy on the application of penalties in the period of Soviet Azerbaijan, an increase in criminality was recorded, including serious and very serious crimes. By 1970, the average annual sentence to imprisonment was made for 28-32% of criminals, and since 1970, this percentage has not fallen below 52%. Quite often the death penalty was imposed for a variety of serious crimes, including economic crimes. So, starting from 1971 to 1991, i.e. for two decades, 400 people in Azerbaijan were sentenced to death: 20 persons a year. Such, in general terms, are the state and dynamics of criminality in Soviet Azerbaijan.

Now, crime statistics in modern Azerbaijan over the past twelve years also suggests that there is a trend towards growth. The picture is as follows: 2000, 13,958 crimes; 2001, 14,607; 2002, 15,520; 2003, 15,206; 2004, 16,810; 2005, 18,049; 2006, 18,667; 2007, 19,045; 2008, 20,185; 2009, 21,250; 2010, 23,000; 2011, 24,000; 2012, 24,320 crimes.

Since crimes such as murder, theft, rape, robbery and drug addiction are at the core of criminality, criminality and its condition should be evaluated based not only on statistical data but also on the nature and proportion of grave and dangerous crimes. It should be borne in mind that the above crimes remain unchanged for decades and needs therefore to be taken into account when determining and predicting future crime rates.

What conclusions may be drawn from an analysis of the state, dynamics and nature of crime in Azerbaijan?

Firstly, from the objective point of view, criminality varies from formation to formation, inside of it, depending on socio-political and economic conflicts, and transformation. Before the collapse of the Communist regime, in Azerbaijan each year between 6 and 10% of the total number of convicts were sentenced to imprisonment for profiteering from agricultural products and the same amount for cheating customers. Of course, this affects the -overall picture of crime in the country. Meanwhile nowadays, our legislation provides responsibility for crimes that did not exist in the period of Soviet Azerbaijan. Therefore, we must bear in mind that, in addition to objective changes in crime, there are also subjective factors which depend on changes in legislation and law enforcement practices.

Secondly, since criminality is a dynamically developing phenomenon, it should be considered in the context of the processes taking place in the community. Crime then makes itself felt with particular force when a society is struggling in the grip of economic, social and political problems and contradictions. And no sociopolitical system is free from this pattern. It is safe to say that the Karabakh conflict, which resulted in around a million refugees, had a serious impact on the state of crime in 1989–1992. Hence this growth was naturally facilitated by the collapse of the Soviet Union, which resulted in the political, economic and legal crisis in all the republics of the USSR. A sharp increase in murders and serious crimes took place. For example, in 1988, 285 murders were committed in Azerbaijan, in 1990 it was 482 and in 1991, 489. In general, the average level of homicides in the period from 1992 to 1998 was 450. Since 1999, there has been a process of decline in this type of crime to an average of 200. There is no doubt that this is directly associated with the establishment of stability in the country, especially political.

Therefore, the future of crime, namely its core components—being murders, particularly grave violent crimes, robberies and burglaries—no doubt depends on the economic, social, political and spiritual life of the society. Much also depends on the activity of the bodies involved in crime prevention. Unfortunately, we are not able to demonstrate at least some progress in this matter, although we do have powerful practical means. For example, we all know that corruption is one of the most dangerous trends in crime in Azerbaijan. It inevitably leads to the degradation of society. Our legislation provides severe penalties for corruption and bribery, and yet due to the fact that this kind of punishment exists only in the Criminal Code and is not actually applied properly, it becomes an object of mockery. And this leads to the fact that people's attitudes towards corruption along with other economic crimes as money laundering, tax evasion and illegal privatisation, attest nowadays to the fall of public morality because there is no negative attitude of the population towards such acts, events. In the public mind, these crimes are no longer harmful, dangerous, immoral, and they are regarded as perfectly normal phenomena. In fact, since 1992, there has been a trend towards a constant decrease in the number of identified cases of bribery—it turns out that bribes in the country are almost non-existent. Needless to say, this does not match reality. In 1997, there were 68 bribery cases, in 1998, 66; in 1999, 68; 2001, 54; in 2004, 5; and in 2007 there were 8.

Based on the above and taking into account the state of crime in the past and today, we can conclude that in the next five years it will be impossible to stop the increase in crime in the country, unless of course adequate measures of a social and legal nature are taken. The existing social injustice that people psychologically cannot perceive yet, the gap between rich and poor, the uneven distribution of material wealth, the impossibility in many cases of solving many problems in life by legal means, will have a strong influence on the psyche of the people, which in some cases will lead to the commission of violent crimes. Therefore crimes such as murder, grievous bodily harm and disorderly conduct will, at best, remain at the current level. The unresolved Karabakh conflict will also have a negative impact on this category of criminals. The economic condition of a certain part of the population will contribute to the growth of such categories of crime as theft, robbery, fraud, tax evasion. For example, theft now accounts for more than 16% of all crimes.

It should also be noted that more than 90% of thieves, robbers, swindlers are the able-bodied unemployed. It is expected that the proportion of crimes related to drugs will increase. On average, each year in the country approximately 2,500 crimes of this nature take place, representing 15% of the total number of recorded crimes. The lack of proper efficiency on the part of the relevant bodies allows us to come to this conclusion.

Thus, predictions about the future of the state and dynamics of crime, both in territorial and temporal breakdowns, are highly inaccurate and approximate, because no one can anticipate where, when and who will be committing another crime. At the same time, when implementing statistical forecasts, it is reasonable to assume that every year a certain type of crime will be repeated with some changes in indicators.

*

II
Punishment

I

The Concept and Essence of Punishment

The Philosophical and Religious Basis of Punishment

For centuries, the concept and essence of punishment has been a subject of disputes and discussions, resulting in numerous models, theories and doctrines. Even the word 'punishment' itself has never been treated as unambiguous. Several centuries ago, the word meant atonement, compensation, and before that, punishment was equated with the idea of revenge. The classical school views it as retribution and misery brought upon a person, the positivists view punishment as a preventive and repressive defence measure, while religious dogmas tell us that punishment is a form of divine retribution. It seems that Nietzsche was right in saying 'as for that other, fluctuating, element of punishment, its 'meaning', in the latter cultural stage (e.g. modern Europe), the concept of punishment indeed has not had one meaning within it, but rather a whole fusion of 'meanings'; all previous punishment history, the history of its application for the most various purposes, has jelled into a unity of some sort, indecomposable, hardly analysable, and, I want to stress this, completely unsurmountable."[1]

At times authors, especially those of a philosophical bent, make no distinction between the concept, essence and substance of punishment—these include Plato, Aristotle and Hugo Grotius. For when one wants to define punishment, he has to ask himself what it really is. And so we conclude that punishment is a specific means of government to achieve a certain goal. It becomes a wholly different matter however if one wants to find the essence of these means. Then we have to say that the essence of punishment is

[1]   Ref.: *Legal Notion: The Anthology*, Moscow, 2011, p309.

atonement. And then, when one strives to understand what punishment is comprised of, we might answer: of different elements of penance and judgment. Understanding and defining punishment is possible only through understanding its essence and substance, and this is why initially we should tend to consider its essence and substance. And yet we should take into account the fact that 'essence' and 'matter' are philosophical concepts not legal.

Democritus wrote: "I shall talk of the essence of the things." So 'essence' is an answer to the question: what is the subject of being? It means that essence is the core entity of all things and facts in all their possible diversity of variants and forms. In logic, essence is an inseparable quality without which the object is unthinkable and thus non-existent. Kerimov noted that "essence is an internal thing as opposed to external, generalised as 'phenomenon.' It is a consistent approach, something unified in diversity of facts and things."[2] V. V. Sorokina understands the subject of essence in the following manner: "The philosophical category of essence means the source of understanding of all the things in existence. Essence is the internal meaning of an object expressed in the unity of all the diversified and contradictory forms of existence."[3]

Consequently, in order to understand the essence of the subject of punishment, we need to find its core, identifying meaning and understand its purpose. Alternatively speaking, the essence of inflicting punishment implies the indication (definition) of those internal and binding, general and basic, main and fundamental characteristics, properties and features, whose unity and interdependence define their specifics, their genesis and their influence upon human behaviour. The essence of punishment is objective; it is not an objective-subjective phenomenon, but rather a truth that remains the core meaning of punishment since its first occurrence in human history. This truth is retribution.

It appears that analysis of the historical genesis of punitive measures is the key to understanding the essence of punishment. We have to analyse the social response to dangerous or objectionable behaviour that has had to be terminated or suppressed to a certain extent. That said, we must also bear in mind that the essence of punishment, as well as the doctrine of punishment itself, can never provide us with positive results solely on the basis of juridical concepts and practical data concerning the effectiveness of criminal penalty. It is a more complex issue, its study falling far beyond the scope of criminal law. The study of the issue of punishment shall remain shallow without

2   Kerimov, D. A. *The Methods of Law*, p155.
3   Sorokina, V. V. *Introduction to the Philosophy of Law*, p289.

philosophy, psychology and sociology, among other things, taken into account. And today we owe our scientific knowledge of punishment not to criminologists but rather to brilliant philosophers and other scientists.

A man has always thought and still thinks of punishment as retribution. The thought of punishment as retribution is rooted so deep within the human mind that one can simply not see anything but retribution in it. At any rate, punishment is aimed at the satisfaction and recovery of the victim, in other words at bringing retribution upon the guilty for the damage done. So the main purpose of punishment is indeed retribution for the crime committed. But what is retribution in truth? It is surely not retribution in terms of revenge, but rather an absolute justice, a claim for punishment to become an expression of moral, social judgment for committing crime. As S. P. Mokrinskiy notes: "The modern penalty, originating from age-old feud and collective revenge, has little to do with its historical prototypes. Revenge for oneself or for the sake of others implies a strong emotional response, an exasperation against the subject of revenge. Quite the contrary, retribution is absolutely compatible with compassion for the guilty, being based not on the fact of damage done, but on an abstract moment of misdeed, of breaking the moral rules."[4]

Our attitude towards the person guilty of a crime—to the criminal—is based on our own understanding of retribution. Punishment is justified retribution not because it is a manifestation of power or because it is a form of administrative coercion that causes suffering to a person for committing a crime, but rather because this reaction is awaited and endorsed by society, because it satisfies their civic sense of justice, being anticipated as a penalty for what they consider a socially harmful deed.

In his day, B. N. Chicherin expressed a very reasonable thought: "The true punishment theory is one that rests upon the very heart of law—upon the truth that gives everyone his due."[5] Ancient philosophers also agreed that punishment is fundamentally retribution. Aristotle, admitting that punishment is retribution, wrote that people tried to return evil for evil, and if such a form of retribution was impossible then this state of events was considered a slave-owning one. Such ideas could also be found in the works of Plato, Cicero and Seneca. This philosophy of punishment was one of the first legal concepts in the ancient world and the most relevant to the dominant opinion on the right to give punishment as one of the features of the vengeance instinct.

4   Mokrinskiy, S. P. *Punishment, Its Purposes and Postulates: In 3 Parts*, Moscow, 1902, pp 82-83.
5   Chicherin, B. N. *Philosophy of Law*, Saint Petersburg: Nauka, 1998, p127.

It seems impossible to find any doctrines on the revengeful essence of punishment in the writings of Greek and Roman philosophers, though they postulated certain aphorisms and statements on criminal law issues. It was not until Hugo Grotius that the 'punishment-vengeance' doctrine received a more or less clear interpretation.[6] Here he identified punishment as talion, a reciprocity, while backing up his views mainly with examples from history. This theory however only later finally matured and became popular in German philosophy when Kant was the first to acknowledge the vengeance concept as the sole essence of punishment, postulating that "evil calls for an evil payback, so only an equality-based retribution can define the measure and extent of punishment, or rather an equally efficient action brought upon the guilty as such".[7] Meanwhile, Hegel's theory of retribution had a special meaning for the development of philosophical ideas as well as for criminal law doctrine. According to his theory, the law is to be restored by retribution for its violation, through the subjection of private opposing will to self-existent sapient free will, i.e. law. He claims that "punishment is retribution, but not retribution of equal value between the damage done by the criminal and the damage brought upon him by punishment".[8]

Thus, the absolute punishment theory as detailed by Kant and Hegel comprises a retribution for the committed action and a payback for it: crime is a sin, and *punishment becomes an act of atonement.* The only difference being that Kant developed a theory of material retribution while Hegel stood for a dialectical one. Thus Kant's view of retribution demanded arithmetic equality while Hegel's demanded geometrical commensurability, equivalence. Punishment-retribution doctrine originates from religion, so it is no wonder that religious texts contain the very first attempts of punishment interpretation. If one proceeds from sacred texts, it can be found there that punishment was a divine influence tool originally established by God to control the human being created by Him. It is believed that the first theological theories on punishment were based on the Old Testament dogmas: punishment was a retribution for evil doings, an intimidation by the *lex talionis* rules—"an eye for an eye" (Deuteronomy 19-21).

In making His first covenant with Adam, the Lord warned him not to eat the fruits of the "tree of knowledge of good and evil", otherwise "thou shalt surely die" (Genesis 2: 17). So it is possible that criminal legislation originated from the *jus divinum*, and that the first human, Adam, was the very first

6   Hugo Grotius. *De jure belli ac pacis*, 1625.
7   Kant, I. *Metaphysische Anfangsgrunde der Rechtslenze*, 1797; ref.: Oizerman, T. I. *Kant's Philosophy and Modern Times*, Moscow, 1974, pp 187-191.
8   Hegel, G. W. F. *Philosophy of Law*, Moscow, 1977, pp 49-51.

criminal, who can also be considered the first person ever to incur the ultimate punishment—the death penalty. It is also important to understand the essence of punishment as it was defined by God. Punishment is retribution: "I will render vengeance to mine enemies, and will reward them that hate me" (Deuteronomy 32, 41). The question on the matter of the expression "thou shalt surely die", i.e. on the death penalty, is ambiguous. But in any interpretation, it cannot be ignored that the matter at hand is punishment for disobedience, for the violation of a ban, of the first law ever, and that this penalty is capital, and that it comes from God Himself. It was ordered to prevent the sin committed by Adam (a 'crime' from the juridical point of view) from perpetuating, from beginning to "live forever" (Genesis 3: 22).

Now Islam, as a world religion, also associates punishment with the concept of retribution (vengeance). The Quran admonishes people from breaking the law, for Allah does not care for those who do not observe borders (Surah 5: Al-Ma'ida [The Table Spread], ayah 87). This is a major basic principle for crime and punishment concepts. The Almighty admonishes people from breaking the laws established by Him, for He does not love those who are not subject to His will. This message, or rather this warning from Allah, also may serve as a guarantee for retribution (vengeance) for those who disobey. In what follows, the Quran becomes more specific and explains this principle to people. "And leave what is apparent of sin and what is concealed thereof. Indeed, those who earn [blame for] sin will be recompensed for that which they used to commit" (Surah 6: Al-An'am [The Cattle], ayah 120). In this case, the Quran text takes 'sin' in a generalised sense that comprises different possible criminal deeds. The essence of punishment, according to the Quran, is not only retribution but also a correction that brings kindness, compassion and cure while creating conditions preventing the commission of new crime: "Whoever comes with a good deed will have ten times the like thereof. And whoever comes with an evil deed will not be recompensed except with the like thereof; and they will not be wronged" (Surah 6, ayah 160).

According to the Quran, retribution as an essence of punishment is characterised by the following features. Firstly, retribution should be just, i.e. equivalent. "And the retribution for an evil act is an evil one like it" (Surah 42: Ash-Shura [Council], ayah 40). Ayah 45 of Surah 5 specifies the principle of retribution: "And We ordained for them therein a life for a life, an eye for an eye, a nose for a nose, an ear for an ear, a tooth for a tooth, and for wounds is legal retribution." Secondly, the Almighty expressed the great benefit that was brought to people through the Quran's prescription to bring vengeance. For it saves many people's lives by refraining them from committing crimes: "And there is for you in legal retribution [saving of] life, O you [people] of understanding, that you may become righteous" (Surah 2: Al-Baqarah [The Cow], ayah 179). Thirdly, the Quran encourages and endorses the deeds of those who are able to forgive and settle the matter, as well as to bring peace, so Allah does not want retribution, He favours peaceful settlement if it is possible. "And the retribution for an evil act is an evil one like it, but whoever pardons and makes reconciliation—his reward is [due] from Allah. Indeed, He does not like wrongdoers!" (Surah 42, ayah 40). Fourthly, the Quran, as is the case with other sacred texts, warns people of retribution (vengeance) not only in this life, but in the afterlife as well.

The Quran has a clear answer for the ultimate question: what happens to those who do not receive their retribution during their mortal life both for the good and evil deeds they have committed? Mortal life is short, and in the afterlife we shall be judged by how we have overcome the challenges in our earthly course. Those who disagree that every punishment in the afterlife is deserved are asked by the Quran: should we treat those who committed violence, murder, fraud and torture to others equally with those who took care of the sick, supported widows and orphans, spent their wealth to help the poor and did their best to follow the guidance of Allah?

The descriptions of the tortures of the damned that can be found in the Quran are so horrifying and persuasive that they serve believers as a truly forceful motivation. "Indeed, the penalty for those who wage war against Allah and His Messenger and strive upon earth [to cause] corruption is none but that they be killed or crucified or that their hands and feet be cut off from opposite sides or that they be exiled from the land. That is for them a disgrace in this world; and for them in the Hereafter is a great punishment" (Surah 5, ayah 33).

But what is this great punishment, this torturing punishment that is so often mentioned in the Quran? "Those are the companions of the Fire; they will abide therein eternally" (Surah 7: Al-A'raf [The Heights], ayah 36). The Gospel claims almost the same: "But if ye do not forgive, neither will your Father which is in heaven forgive your trespasses" (Mark. 11: 24-26). "The Fire is your residence, wherein you will abide eternally, except for what Allah wills" (Surah 6, ayah 128). Even more awful is the punishment mentioned in Surah 10: Yunus [Jonah], ayah 4: "But those who disbelieved will have a drink of scalding water and a painful punishment for what they used to deny."

Allah also created Jahannam (Gehenna) to be one of the punishments mentioned in the Quran as retribution in the afterlife. It is worth mentioning that the Quran not only warns people of severe punishments in the afterlife for their crimes in their mortal life, but also reminds them of the rewards that may be earned by the faithful and people in general for good deeds. "So give them tidings of a painful punishment, except for those who believe and do righteous deeds. For them is a reward uninterrupted" (Surah 84: Al-Inshiqaq [The Sundering], ayahs 24-25).

But what is that reward? "But they who believe and do righteous deeds— those are the companions of Paradise; they will abide therein eternally' (Surah 2, ayah 82). The Quran also explains what Paradise is: "Indeed, Allah will admit those who believe and do righteous deeds to gardens beneath which rivers flow. They will be adorned therein with bracelets of gold and pearl, and their garments therein will be silk" (Surah 22: Al-Hajj [The Pilgrimage], ayah 23).

But why does Allah not punish the people who commit evil in this life? The Quran has a very wise answer to that question: "And if Allah were to impose blame on the people for their wrongdoing, He would not have left upon the earth any creature, but He defers them for a specified term. And when their term has come, they will not remain behind an hour, nor will they precede [it]' (Surah 16: An-Nahl [The Bees], ayahs 61-62). So only Allah is entitled to decide whom, when and what to punish, for Allah strives to make people live without evil, hatred and crimes toward each other not only in their mortal life, but in the afterlife as well. "And We will remove whatever is in their breasts of resentment, [so they will be] brothers, on thrones facing each other. No fatigue will touch them therein, nor from it will they [ever] be removed" (Surah 15: Al-Hijr [The Stoneland], ayahs 47-48).

Thus, religion legitimises people's right to take revenge and retribution on people who shed blood and stain their human soul, through the principle of "whoso sheddeth man's blood, by man shall his blood be shed". At the same time, God imposes man with a part of this burden of retribution, as though receding from His own principle: "Vengeance is mine; I will repay." An analysis of Biblical and Quranic concepts of vengeance, retribution, revenge, judgment and other punitive categories shows us how deep and comprehensive the views of ancient people could be, how many meanings they had and how well they hitherto preserved their meanings.

In summary, therefore, through learning the Quran and Bible we can find concepts and ideas that express the very essence of ancient man's views on life and death, murder and crime, revenge, judgment and punishment.

Anticipating Freud and Skinner by several centuries, the Quran has presented people with important doctrines on the afterlife regarding a maximally pleasant experience, called *sa'id*, which means 'blessed' or 'happy', as well as the most terrible ordeal, the state of *shaqi*, which means 'damned' or 'unhappy'. According to the Quran, the people who reach *sa'id* deserve to be sent to paradise while those who experience *shaqi* are doomed. There is hardly a person to be found who would deny the great importance of religion in the matter of the upbringing of people through the principles of inclination for good and reprobation of evil.

It is also worth noting that belief in retribution (revenge) in the afterlife for evil (crime) is found in all human tribes, nations and communities in the form of revival of the dead victim of the crime. Hindu doctrine on the afterlife, and the Buddhist philosophy that has to a great extent derived from it, postulated that metempsychosis is as important as direct reward or punishment, every form of which is perishable and impermanent. Whether a man becomes a plant, a reptile, a woman, a Brahman or a wiseman totally depends on him and his behaviour in this life. Which means that in case a person dies without wiping out his sins through repentance, he will be reborn as a foul creature; but if he dies with a quiet conscience, it is possible for him to become a perfect human being.

The *Manusmriti* and *Vishnu Purana* can therefore be classified as legal texts, as they comprise highly accurate codes of conduct, as well as a list of punishments for breaking these codes. Ultimate criminals are reborn from one plant species into another, thus passing through the whole circle of vegetation. Persons that commit a mortal sin are reborn as worms and insects. Persons that committed minor crimes are reborn as different kinds of animals. Criminals of the fourth rank turn into aquatic animals. Those who commit crimes punishable by banishment from caste are reborn as amphibians (*Vishnu Purana*, XLIV: 2). According to this law, a person that misappropriated a beaten track will be reborn as a cave-dwelling snake. Those who misappropriate grain turn into rats. Those who misappropriate water are turned into aquatic game.

Horrification through afterlife retribution by transmigration of the soul from one creature into another had a strong influence on the rules used in common life, and which were afterwards included in the statute books. The violation of rules, commission of crimes, evil deeds that contravene existing laws spatter the soul of the violator with blots that can only be extinguished by self-imposed repentance, otherwise those blots will persist after the person's death and can then be purified only with an even harsher reprisal. According to Hindu law, if a Brahman is killed, then the number of dust flecks stained with his blood on the hot Indian soil shall mark the number of millennia to be spent by the murderer in hell, i.e. in the afterlife (*Manusmriti*, XI: 20).

Also worthy of mention is the fact that Muslim and Christian jurists have always paid much attention to the concept of punishment. At that, all of them have definitely thought that punishment is retribution. Abdel Kader Auda writes: "Punishment is retribution for disobedience, imposed *pro bono publico*."[9] Ahmad Fahti Bahnasi shares almost the same point of view, noting that punishment is a retribution preset by the state for the violation of bans and for the purposes of crime prevention, both for the convict and for other persons.[10] Al-Mavardi defines punishment as follows: "*Hudud* [punishment stipulated in the Quran—*I. R.*] is a punishment set by Allah for the violation of bans; as human nature comprises both lust for pleasures and consciousness of the punishment promised in the afterlife for the violation of bans, so *hudud* as a promise of pain is provided to withhold the thoughtless from misdoings."[11]

This deep and complete definition of al-Mavardi's contains a number of particularly interesting aspects. Firstly, the definition he provides clearly has an obvious religious context, for it justifies and substantiates crime prevention not only by protection of social interests, but also by fear of the tortures promised by Allah in the afterlife. This is a truly fundamental aspect. Besides, al-Mavardi, unlike other lawyers, highlights the fact that the punishment, as well as bans, are established and provided not by legislators but by Allah himself. Secondly, he postulates reasons for human criminal conduct, connecting them with internal, psychological features of personality. Thus, he somewhat inclines toward the fact that the main reasons for crime are human features of a biological nature. Thirdly, this definition marks the role of punishment in the prevention of misdoings that contradict the objectives set forth in the Quran, through horrification and the promise of pain. Hence religion sets punishment as retribution as well as correction, a counsel comprising kindness, sympathy and cure.

It is easy to see that philosophers regarded punishment as a philosophical concept and that clergymen regarded it as a phenomenon of divine nature. In fact, we are unable to know the truth of punishment through philosophical and sacred writings alone, although they are methodologically versatile means, tools, methods and grounds for understanding social nature and mind. But in seeking to define punishment, a jurist cannot do without concepts of a purely juridical nature. The main point to remember is that we will never be able to grasp the concept of punishment if we start separating law from the real world of facts and phenomena that are its basis.

9   Auda, Abdel Kader. *Muslim Criminal Law*, Beirut, 1987, vol. 1, p609.
10 See: Fahti Bahnasi, Ahmad. *Punishment in Muslim Law*, Cairo, 1989, p13.
11 See: Ibid.

Retribution, according to Maltsev, is a form of satisfaction of the indemnitee through the penalty imposed on the person that caused the suffering.[12] As defined by S. N. Timoshev, retribution is a consequence occurring for a deed that can be treated as positive or negative by some legal framework, a destiny of the deed's performer that is equivalent to the intrinsic value of the deed.[13] The plain English of this is that retribution is vengeance, repayment, indemnification of either good or evil to the person that committed either a bad or a good deed. By using philosophical categories, one can define retribution as a way and means of achieving *justice*. Therefore, inequivalent retribution is unjust.

Where then did retribution come from? Montaigne writes that "revenge is a most delightful passion, it has a certain dignity, and it is quite natural".[14] It appears that this passion is associated with an urge to equalise, for it is human to wish that evil is returned for evil deeds. That is why we regard retribution with satisfaction and consider it right. Of course, we are talking about just, fair retribution and vengeance. The origins of blood vengeance lie in the ancient concept of retributive justice concerning that part of it which demands the establishment of commensuration between an evil, dark deed and the response, bringing vengeance for it.[15]

A widely-held opinion states that the first expression of the punishment concept, retribution, was blood vengeance. It was later that the custom of repayment for guilt was established. This process ended when the state abrogated the authority of retribution to itself. By way of example, we can look to A. M. Bogdanovskiy's opinion: "Everywhere in the world, the first form of punishment as vengeance for evil was so-called *revenge*, or, in a broader sense, arrogation. Sooner or later, this form was replaced by another, more righteous, less ambiguous form, the so-called *repayment system*. The idea of punishment in this form tends to exist in public law for very long time, and is only changed upon the appearance of the notion of the state as an integrated living being, and on crime as an action hostile to this being. As of this period, a supreme punishment concept is developed as retribution for crime, for abusing the concept of law, the most comprehensive body of whose expression is the state."[16]

According to I. Y. Foinitskiy, in the initial stages of the history of punishment, punitive actions were undertaken by the individuals suffering

12 Maltsev, G. V. *Revenge and Vengeance in Ancient Law*, p228.
13 Timoshev, S. N. *Conditional Sentence*, Saint Petersburg, 1914, pp 303–304.
14 *On Human Nature: Montaigne, La Rochefoucauld, Pascal*, Moscow, 2009, p151.
15 See: Maltsev, G. V. Op. cit, p129.
16 Bogdanovskiy, A. M. *The Development of Crime and Punishment Concepts in Russian Law before Peter the Great*, Moscow, 1857, pp 5–6.

from criminal deeds themselves. There was no punishment save for revenge. Gradually, social groups began to claim punitive powers for themselves and deal with criminals unassisted. Personal revenge and the personality of the victim thus faded into insignificance. Foinitskiy considers that in the modern law structure of civilised nations, the amalgamation of social groups led to a situation where the final entitlement of handing out punishment belonged solely to the state as a legal subject.[17]

Ferri for his part states that punishment, from its origin to the present day, has undergone four stages of evolution: from the *elementary*, i.e. defence reaction and revenge, it evolved into the *religious* stage (divine power manifestation), then to the *ethical* stage (Middle Ages atonement) and, finally to the *juridical* stage. In the present day, he believes it is necessary to begin and implement a *social* stage, in which, by virtue of the newest anthropological and criminal statistics on crime data, punishment ceases to be a commensurable retribution for moral guilt (ethical juridical stage), but rather comprises a set of proactive and repressive social measures. The latter, echoing the nature and origins of crime, prove to be a much better and humane way of safeguarding society from criminal offences.[18] On this account, the evolution of pure revenge into public criminal penalty should be associated with the time of state formation. Hegel also wrote on this.[19]

The idea that private blood vengeance is the source of public penalty is based on supposition of the reasons for a person's (victim's) reaction to such harmful and hazardous actions as murder, pillage, robbery and so on, at the early stages of human development. This reaction corresponded to the custom of blood vengeance and was private. In other words, the essence of revenge was in the return of evil for evil done by someone or something, that every offence was followed up by vengeance. If the offence was a deadly one, such as murder, then the vengeance had to be deadly as well—blood for blood. This was not only a matter of retribution, but a matter of obligation as well, a sacred duty, a right, a satisfaction of possessiveness. In this context, one should highlight that above all other things, only in *revenge* does a man reveal his *right*, i.e. not only recognising the physical, bodily pain or material loss but also understanding and recognising the fact that he is humiliated and offended.

Therefore it is only through blood vengeance that a man can wash out this insult and consequently satisfy his inner sense of justice. We cannot forget

17   Foinitskiy, I. Y. *Punishment Doctrine in Relation to Prison Administration*, Saint Petersburg, 1889, p18.
18   See: Ferri, E. Op. cit, pp 363–364.
19   See: Hegel, G. W. F. *Philosophy of Law*, Moscow, 1953, p146.

also that revenge, however wild it is by nature, has a certain preventive meaning. But is it possible to postulate that private blood vengeance is the social background for punishment? Was it not before private vengeance that deeds dangerous to the commune, tribe or group were punished?

Kistyakovskiy was completely right in noting that "before the first rays of understanding of the grounds for punishment dawned upon humans, it had long existed and functioned".[20] And the first rudiments of what we now call punishment can be found in social and natural phenomena—in people's reaction, being the basis of self-preservation, in external hazards and dangers for the community. In all primitive communes, even in the wildest of tribes, people were punished for deeds that had no connection with private vengeance: treason, sacrilege, witchcraft and so on. So can one regard the community's reaction as private vengeance if the punishment was viewed as the organised expression of social discontent, as consensual resentment, but not as universal revenge? This really is social punishment, since treason was one of the crimes concerning every member of the community.

The most frequently noted primitive socially hazardous crime was witchcraft, in other words the belief in certain community members' ability to control or have supernatural powers. If a sorcerer prevented the rain from falling, he became the archenemy of the community and was subject to unavoidable punishment because he had presented a threat to the others, to the society. This was no personal blood vengeance but the elimination, prevention of a great social danger. Murder committed in a plainly physical way, i.e. a community member killing another community member, was something else again. In that case, society did not interfere with these relations, for that was not a matter of social interest, but rather a completely private matter. That was private blood vengeance.

In summary, if we assume that the history of punishment began with *private vengeance*, then we must also agree that public reaction to those deeds discussed is not punishment and that those deeds cannot be treated as socially dangerous.

Primitive punishment did not pursue the objective of revenge on the traitor or the sorcerer. It was imposed for the purposes of atonement—not for the criminal himself but rather for his society, to prevent revenge from a supernatural being brought against the whole society. Therefore, this punishment is to be regarded not as retribution but as sacrifice. Consequently, one might say that the source of punishment is directly connected with

20   Kistyakovskiy, A. F. *Elementary Book on General Criminal Law*, Kiev, 1890, p764.

grasping the idea of originating and developing the concept of punishment.

In principle, not only the history of the origin of punishment but all fundamental issues of the institution of criminal punishment are impossible to explain and understand beyond crime and the context of its reasons. Whichever issue of criminal penalty we bring into the picture, we always end up facing issues of crime. Therefore to find the source of punishment, it is necessary to track down the process of development of the crime concept. For it is known that before these concepts, people's deeds existed that actually or presumably endangered society. So, society had to react accordingly. Oppenheimer believes that crimes punished in primitive societies or deeds regarded as dangerous by communities, tribes and so on, and consequently leading to a necessary reaction, are the following: witchcraft, unnatural vices, treason, sacrilege, different kinds of crime.[21]

In summary, punishment originated not along with personal blood vengeance, but out of the fear of danger coming from supernatural beings arising from the deeds of some of the community's members. To prevent vengeance from this supernatural being, it was necessary to banish the dangerous person from the society. Hence Oppenheimer is undoubtedly right in stating that the "idea of public crimes originated from magical and religious notions".[22]

Punishment emerged when community or tribe authorities imposed true public penalties such as the death penalty or exile. It was these penalties that were the true means of deliverance from public nuisance. But the concept of private blood vengeance can be considered the true source of the retribution principle. Primitive practices graphically and persuasively associated vengeance with the concept of retribution. Blood vengeance currently exists in societies where family and ancestral connections remain in traditional force, as well as in countries where the state authorities have little credibility among the population. Incidentally, some tribes—most notably the Alaskan Tlingits—have never had blood vengeance procedures for murder when both the victim and the murderer belonged to one family within the tribe. It must be emphasized that blood vengeance cannot be regarded as a prototype of the death penalty.

Blood vengeance therefore is the initial form of returning the action performed by a person to another person or persons, i.e. *retribution* that gradually recedes into the background, yielding to a repayment system. We

21 Oppenheimer, H. *Historical Research on Punishment Origins*, Moscow, 2012, p6.
22 Ibid, p29.

may suppose that this fact was due to the introduction of money into social life. There are different forms of equivalent retribution. The simplest is *lex talionis* (return with equal action in similar degree), where the classical talion formula is stipulated in sacred texts such as the Bible and the Quran: "And if any mischief follow, then thou shalt give life for life, an eye for an eye, a tooth for a tooth, a hand for a hand, a foot for a foot, burning for burning, wound for wound, stripe for stripe" (Exodus 21: 23–25). "And We ordained for them therein a life for a life, an eye for an eye, a nose for a nose, an ear for an ear, a tooth for a tooth, and for wounds is legal retribution" (Surah 45: Al-Jathiya [Crouching]). In these divine instructions, talion is filled with horrification, i.e. God wants to prevent human aggression through talion and end the violence that can perspectively lead to the extirpation of entire peoples. *Lex talionis* was also stipulated in the Roman Law of the Twelve Tables (451–450 B. C.), which states: "If anyone has broken another's limb there shall be retaliation in kind unless he compounds for compensation with him."

Eventually talion complexified, changing beyond recognition into a system of retributive principles that later became the basis for the criminal policy of modern states. In practice, by talion people sought to put blood vengeance under restraint, for they well understood the dangers of reckless slaughter. Hence talion is actually a step towards the doctrine of punishment, its meaning being to make people learn that they commit evil and violence at their own cost. In other words, talion was an intermediate step between blood vengeance and criminal punishment, and the introduction of talion into blood vengeance practices initiated the process of the transformation of indiscriminate penalties into punishment for a specific crime.

It is practically undeniable that talion originated from blood vengeance practices and then evolved into the criminal law of some ancient states. As Maltsev notes: "The unobvious relation of modern law to talion is discovered every time we strive to find the logical and historical origins of the punishment system or discuss the justification of imprisonment or the death penalty."[23] This is the theory of vengeance as the only basis and essence of criminal punishment. Legal punishment—retribution—is at the same time the most feasible. But above all, it also has to remain an actual act of retribution, i.e. a justified evil action, sufferings brought upon the criminal in an act of repayment for his misdoings. Justice is the moral basis of the essence of punishment: retribution.

Thus, the internal concept of punishment, its essence as expressed in

23   Maltsev, G. V. Op. cit, p249.

criminal law, allow us to notice that the doctrine of punishment's distinctive feature as compared to other legal measures is its intrinsic element of retribution. Furthermore, it is necessary to underline that retribution is not a legislator's invention or an element that can be withdrawn from the system at the sole discretion of any punishment system members. For retribution is a phenomenon that lies at the heart of punishment's objective nature. *We understand retribution not as an aim of punishment, but as a moment characterising the very essence of it.* It is impossible to imagine punishment without it. Retribution is based on a strong feeling resulting from the commission of crime. This is why retribution is a way of satisfying the social sense of justice.

Society will only be able to put retribution aside when the need for punishment itself is eliminated, for retribution is the essence of punishment. Retribution theory as the essence of punishment has always been seriously disputed. It was repudiated by various famous scientists and the Socialist revolution rejected it altogether, which is why in Communist doctrine the issue was not even considered as the subject of serious research or discussion. Known counter-arguments against retribution as the essence of punishment in literature vary greatly in their original points of view.

The Russian philosopher V. Solovyev in his 1897 treatise *Justification of the Good* shows the basic pointlessness of the punishment doctrine or 'vengeful justice', following from the fact that vengeance and horrification are mitigated relics of the 'animalistic stage' of humankind, historically aiming at entering the 'divine stage'. In his other writings, Solovyev notes that the criminal legal doctrine of retribution, deprived completely of logical and moral sense, is but a remnant of the wild prehistoric state, and that criminal punishments still in use merely because they aim reaction to the crime at the intentional causing of physical suffering to the criminal are but a historical transformation of primitive blood vengeance. The immoral nature of retribution is also indicated here. For instance, Poznyshev notes that this concept (the concept of retribution), as suggested by the brute urge for vengeance, is immoral in and of itself.

There are those who point to the poorness of retribution theories because they are indeed deprived of a stable punishment measure criterion of any kind. Firstly, when it is claimed that the essence of punishment is retribution, this means retribution only (retaliation). If retribution goes beyond the crime, if it is not equal to the evil deed committed, then it is not punishment but rather persecution, for here the justice principle is broken. If retribution (retaliation) is too lenient as compared to the evil deed it reacts to, then it is not punishment but rather impunity. Therefore, only those means of reacting to a crime may be considered punishment whose essence is just retribution (retaliation). Secondly, one should not deny the meaning of the word 'retribution' (retaliation), for it does not express the negative reaction that was provoked by strong feelings. The concept of retribution has changed greatly since the Age of Enlightenment. Now, punishment is merely a *reaction* to a crime voluntarily committed by a person, in accordance with the principle of retributive justice.

Retribution is indisputably the basis of revenge, as well as the basis of punishment but that does not undermine the meaning of retribution as the essence of punishment. The similarity of the bases for revenge and punishment cannot by itself bring into discredit the view that acknowledges retribution as the essence of punishment. The concept of retribution is not the concept of talion, i.e. formal, qualitative or merely quantitative equality. It is not revenge which is marked by the brutality, instinct, unbounded and senseless reaction of the victim. It does not mean the satisfaction of the latter, recovery or moral vengeance indistinguishable to the naked eye. It is the idea of how crime as a disturbance of the public peace should provoke a backlash adequate to its negative meaning. It is the core of punishment.

The Moral Background of the Essence of Punishment

Kant enunciated the immortal words: "If justice ever disappears, life on Earth will cease to have any value at all." The issue of punishment is above all a moral issue. This is why humanity has been wondering if it is moral to punish when the death penalty and lengthy imprisonment are involved. Even today, we ask the same question: can we, people living in the twenty-first century, continue to doom criminals to suffering through criminal punishment which does not even achieve the set goal of preventing crime? Should we not instead find an equally effective yet non-punitive measure characterised by humanity?

One thing is clear: whether we are talking about legislative activities or the commensurability of punishment and crime in certain cases, we cannot ignore the demands of justice and humanism. Modern civilised society simply does not have the right to it. People always want a just punishment. A wise legislator in a proper civil lawful state understands this and tries to base his activity on the moral foundation of punishment, while judges search for elements and criteria of the gravity of the offence to find the appropriate gravity of punishment.

Hugo Meyer pointed out that "not only in private relations, but in legislation as well, there is the question of whether a person receives too grave or too lenient a punishment, if an individual receives his due."[24] But is this even possible? It is a question that has been asked since man began to understand the meaning and purpose of punishment, and the evil, harmful essence of crime. Everyone decides this for himself, relying on whatever moral standards are prompted to him by his conscience. Of course, this attitude towards justice is subjective. For instance, a person believes that abolition of the death penalty is unfair, because the legislator would be compelled by political ideas, while ignoring the victim's interests and social legal conscience that match precisely with the victim's personal opinion. This person can be argued with, but cannot be ignored, since a rather large number of the members of society hold the same opinion.

At the same time, there are moral standards that enjoy a broader recognition and thus may be denied by no reasonable man. Therefore, when we try to convince death penalty advocates of the justice of abolition we must among other arguments mention the humanism principle that protects justice. Consequently, a legislator, while defining the type and amount of penalty for certain deeds in the law, must rely upon those moral standards that have received universal recognition even if they contradict his (the legislator's) understanding of justice. Otherwise, the society in practice, in real life, would face unjust punishment and corresponding negative consequences. If it is true that only God himself can be just for he can learn all the secret thoughts of man, their motives and causes of their behaviour, which is beyond our understanding these days, then the legislator is not able to assess a just penalty, for he does not possess a gift similar to God's. Therefore, there never can be true equality between crime and punishment. It is impossible both from the moral as well as from the juridical (legal) point of view.

But this positively does not mean that the state, represented by the legislator, is able to violate justice when defining the type and amount of penalty for the purposes of achieving his political goals, which can often be noted in the history of many countries. Just retribution, i.e. visible equality between crime and punishment, should be a kind of border, a line that the legislator is not entitled to cross. For example, when the state authority fixes a criminal penalty for non-authorised picketing, meetings, assemblies, then it is certainly a violation of this border of justice between the deed and its punishment, since the legislator does not have the basis for the certain and solid moral criterion of the public assessment of criminal gravity.

In making a decision on punishment for certain deeds, the legislator

---

24 Meyer, H. *Die Gerechtigkeit im Strafrecht*, Abdruck aus dem Gerichtssaal, vol. xxxii, p101.

understands that upon breaking the law, the criminal is subject to a definite suffering, moral distress or restraint as a necessary and sensible consequence. A legislator acts immorally if he knows beforehand that this suffering does not correspond to the deed and that retribution does not serve the idea of law and justice. It is obvious that the more important the law, i.e. the subject that is guarded by it and violated by crime, the more important the crime itself. The importance, value of the subject of infringement defines the gravity of punishment. But which subject is more important?

This is a relative concept since it is the state's prerogative, i.e. it is the individual view of every state. And this is quite just and right, for every nation has its own moral-value assessment criteria and its own view on the importance of particular values. Consequently, every nation has its own view on the gravity of particular crimes. This means that there are in general different punishments for the same crime in different states. Surely it was totally pointless, unjust and immoral to impose the death penalty for stealing state and public property in the times of the Soviet government. In that case, the state by imposing a penalty of such gravity was led not by moral standards, humane principles or the concept of justice, but by ideological guidelines and false ideas on criminal policy for the prevention of crime.

The importance of every deed is defined by the legislator in every epoch comprising the interests of dominating power and in accordance with the position occupied by the individual in society, as well as with the individual's interests. Therefore, the development of a punishment system suitable for every epoch and every nation is as impossible as regarding certain deeds criminal in the different historical periods of different nations. Consequently, the development of an ideal punishment system, as well as ideal explicit punishments, is impossible both in form and in matter. Types and amounts of punishment are constantly subject to change, since every epoch draws its own criteria for assessing the gravity of crime. For instance, today we find the punishments of the Middle Ages incompatible with humane principles, even though they were considered completely reasonable by Middle Ages legislators. And little wonder, for every epoch develops its own types of punishment, its own corrective reactions for crime, which may be considered unsatisfactory and unreasonable in another, future epoch.

But what then is justice? What does it mean for punishment? The concept of justice as one of the expressions of moral conscience and man's social essence emerged from a certain stage of the development of human society and therefore is of a historical nature. Z. A. Berebeshkina notes that "justice as a value, concept, ideal, standard with certain historical characteristics emerged from a certain stage of the development of human society".[25] It is strange that today the concept of justice still provokes dispute, although this ethical category has a rather long history. Kant wrote: "A man of natural simplicity obtains a sense of justice very early, but very late or never understands the concept of justice."[26] This however never proved an obstacle to knowing just from unjust. As the Swedish legal theorist Per Olof Ekelöf once said: "The general concept of justice is similar to the image of God—everyone talks about Him, but none know what He actually is."[27]

Justice, being a moral category, finds its application in every aspect of human life. In the history of ethical doctrines, justice is often regarded as a measure of ethical consciousness and demand. In principle, this understanding is right. For there is good reason why the symbol of justice is a pair of scales. As Paul Lafargue put it: "Blow for blow, repayment equal to the damage done, equal shares when distributing food and land—those were the only concepts of justice known to the first people, the concepts that the Pythagoreans expressed in the axiom of scales."[28]

Since the beginning of time, the concept of truth has been associated with equality. Something equally applied to everyone was considered just. This notion evolves from the nature and essence of human identity: "All people are sensible beings with free will, all of them created after the image and likeness of God and as such are equal. Admission of this basic equality is the supreme demand of truth, that from this point of view is called an equalising truth."[29]

Philosophers and scientists from all times starting from Confucius, Plato, Aristotle, the Roman legislators and up to the experts of today regard the essence of the justice phenomenon in a philosophical legal context, which includes: a) equality of everyone in similar conditions; b) interrelation of deeds and retribution; c) equality between loss and acquisition. Everyone acknowledges justice as the basis and guiding principle of law, and considers its essence to be 'paying everyone his due'. This means that punishment for crime should correlate with justice principles both in criminal law, i.e. in criminal legal sanctions, and in law enforcement activities while imposing the penalty. As it is said in the Book of Proverbs: "Dishonest scales are an abomination to the Lord, but a just weight is His delight."

According to Aristotle, a just thing is above all a thing that corresponds to

25 Berebeshkina, Z. A. *Justice as Social Philosophical Category*, Moscow, 1983, p30.
26 Kant, I. *Works*, Moscow: Nauka, 1964. vol. 2, p196.
27 See: Bondeson, W. 'The Concept of Justice in the Ideas of the Public and Judges', *Criminology and Criminal Policy*, Moscow, 1985, p44.
28 Lafargue, P. *Works*, vol. 3, Moscow/Leningrad, 1931, p82.
29 Chicherin, B. N. *Philosophy of Law*, p96.

legislation. But what if the legislation itself is unjust? After all, the legislator may impose any penalty for any deeds at his sole discretion. For instance, in Soviet times, as we have previously noted, the legislation in all its republics provided the death penalty for stealing ten or more thousand rubles. One can hardly call this law just. Therefore, it is impossible to agree with Hobbes the single justice criterion is the law itself and that whatever standards are stipulated in it are just.

The Ancient Greeks obeyed state law even when they considered it to be wrong or immoral. Socrates voluntarily took poison even though he understood how unjust his sentence was. He believed obedience to the state to be the moral duty of each citizen. The ancient Greek philosopher Antiphon wrote: "Justice involves keeping within the law of the state you are citizen of."[30] Contrarily, the ancient Jews believed that it was necessary only to obey state laws when they did not contradict divine laws. The Caucasian nations have a special respect for customs, which is why such peoples have often obeyed not laws but rather customs and traditions. It is understood that law cannot be absolutely to everyone, for justice demands an individual approach to a person and law is not able to take into account all of the personal features relevant to moral attitude.[31]

Every society has its own life with its own standards and a limit that marks intolerable extremities. That means that all the laws in these different societies differ significantly and are simultaneously accepted there as appropriate standards of justice. The concept of the justice of punishment was crafted in accordance with the historical development of peoples, customs, traditions and so on. The ancient Chinese philosopher Mozi wrote: "In olden times, when people had just come into existence, there were no punishments, but at the same time everyone had his own concept of justice. One person has one concept while two have two, ten have ten concepts of justice. The more people there are, the more different concepts of justice they have. Everyone believed that his views were right and ignored other views, and the result was that there was a great feud between people."[32] At the same time, humanity always strove to develop a generally-accepted concept of justice. Of course, the first to try solving this task were the philosophers.

In philosophical literature, justice is defined as the virtue that is the essence of moral beauty, and as harmony with reality, and as equality before law, and as the correspondence of retribution with the deed, and so on. But how can it be defined that life imprisonment is more just than the death

30   See: *Legal Notion: The Anthology*, p75.
31   See: Romanets, Y. V. Op. cit, p237.
32   See: *Legal Notion: The Anthology*, p44.

penalty? Are the twenty-one years of imprisonment for the intentional homicide of seventy-seven people imposed by Norwegian legislation just? Is the death penalty for the intentional homicide or rape of one person set by the legislation of some Asian countries just? Every society develops a just penalty on the basis of moral standards, customs and ethics, as well as on the criminal situation in the country. According to Democritus, every state considers it necessary to impose severe punishment *pro bono publico* for the violation of justice: "Any that do wrong and wish to do so may be killed with impunity, and it conduces to wellbeing to do so rather than not do so. One must punish wrong-doers to the best of one's ability, and not neglect it. Such conduct is just and good, but the neglect of it is unjust and bad."[33]

It is the lack of a unified concept of justice that makes it practically impossible to define a correspondence between punishment and the committed deed. The Norwegian legislator considers twenty-one years of imprisonment in a two-room cell complete with every comfort for a terrorist that killed seventy-seven people just from the point of view of applicable law. But that does not mean that this punishment is just from the point of view of the international community and the legal conscience of the Norwegian people. The death penalty for the rape of minors set forth in the legislation of some countries, including Central Asia, is an unjust punishment from the European point of view and badly characterises these peoples' development level as a whole. But that is the European understanding of justice, while the society of the countries mentioned as well as their legislators consider this kind of punishment to be quite just for certain crimes.

The fact that every crime deserves punishment and that every punishment must be just has been adopted since ancient times, because all conscious people understood the usefulness of just punishment both for society and for the criminal. For otherwise, punishment loses its meaning. But how can we balance crime and punishment without allowing excessive leniency or extreme severity, but strictly observing the demands of retributive justice? As A. Frank wrote: "When punishment exceeds or falls short of the amount of flesh to be cut out of the body of our enemy, when punishment is not imposed with strict observation of absolute equality, then it turns into injustice and iniquity."[34]

For thousands of years, thinkers have tried to reveal the formula of just and adequate retribution. Plato wrote of the necessity of just punishment, both during the setting and imposing of it. Representatives of the classical

---

33   See: *Ancient Greek Materialists*, Moscow, 1955, p170.
34   Frank, A. *Criminal Law Philosophy*, Saint Petersburg, 1868, p133.

law school that was founded one hundred years after Beccaria published his work based their opinions on the fact that punishment must be an unavoidable and just repayment for the crime committed. In the nineteenth century, Bentham, both lawyer and economist, developed a practical punishment theory that postulated three conditions for the setting and imposing of punishment: that it shall not be imposed if it will not prevent the harm done by the crime; that punishment shall not be too grave, i.e. graver than the harm done by the criminal; that punishment is not needed when the harm done by the crime may be prevented not by punishment, but rather by another, less grave way. Franz von Liszt believed that "we must attach more value to the internal state of the criminal than to the external consequences of his deed while defining the type and amount of punishment in law and sentence".[35] In conclusion, the consequences of crime are the measure of the gravity of punishment for the classical school, while the internal state of the criminal is the measure of such for the positivists.

According to N. Khavronyuk, a contemporary lawyer, in order to provide an absolutely just and adequate punishment that corresponds exactly to the crime committed, one needs to develop and adopt general standards of criminal statistics, and to carry out questionnaires and surveys. Official statistical data, however accurate they might be, are to be elaborated with social victimisation survey data, mathematisation of criminal law, and expert support of criminal procedures. Khavronyuk concludes that "the actual social hazard of a particular deed should be above all considered as the severity (lenience) criteria of sanctions".[36]

In my opinion, in order to turn punishment into just retribution for a deed, it must satisfy the following basic requirements. Firstly, punishment must correlate with and depend on the moral, religious, historical and cultural foundations of a certain people, certain nation. Secondly, it must be commensurable with the evil done by the crime. These conditions are of a critical nature to the development and definition of punishment by the legislator during lawmaking activities. The third condition is associated with court activities on imposing punishment. During this stage of the practical implementation of the punishment, all attention should be driven towards the personality of the criminal, i.e. the subject of the punishment; his attributes and his state of mind should play a significant role in imposing a just punishment.

Now, if justice as a principle has an essential meaning in the definition of

35   von Liszt, F. *Strafrechtliche Aufsätze und Vorträge*, vol. 2, p377.
36   Khavronyuk, N. 'What Should Criminal Penalty Be, or Why Does Jurisprudence Lag Behind Physics?', *Beijing Science Conference Proceedings*, December 1–3, 2012, pp 14–15.

punishment by the legislator, then humanism as an ethical, philosophical category is essential to imposing and executing punishment. Humanism as a principle of law-enforcement activity should above all be comprised of the general concepts of the theory of humanism. One of the tenets of its principles is the recognition of a human being as an absolute value. Therefore everything that concerns a human being and his most advantageous development is defined by the general concept of 'humanism'. "Humanism is a moral position that expresses the recognition of human value as an individual, respect for his dignity, dedication to human benefit as a social improvement goal."[37]

Humanism therefore is the relationship between society (the state) and the individual. Thus one can talk about the dual nature of humanism. One aspect of it is exhibited through society and involves the protection of state, social and personal interests from criminal infringement. Put this way, humanism corresponds quite well with strict measures of criminal punishment. As E. A. Sarkisov notes: "The humane concepts of socialist society and the protection of Soviet citizens from criminal activities demand severity and intransigence towards criminals, especially those of them who arrogate objects protected by the law."[38] The other aspect deals with criminals and denotes a humane attitude towards personality, the repudiation of severe punishment methods, and account for mitigating circumstances, and so on. Jean-Paul Marat, in drawing up his *Plan de législation criminelle*, sought to achieve his goal "to bring together leniency of penalty with its efficiency, to balance humanity with the safety of civil society without affecting justice or freedom".[39] Beccaria added that "one should only impose the punishment that . . . would make the strongest impression on human souls and would be less tormenting for the criminal's body".[40]

According to Karpets, severe penalty imposed on criminals in favour of social safety from criminal infringement is not humanism for society, but rather a forced departure from consistency in the implementation of this principle.[41] This position reduces humanism to one of its aspects: humanity towards the criminal. In general, the term 'humanism' means the recognition of human value as an individual, the acceptance of the benefit for the human being as a criterion in the assessment of social relations. Consequently,

37 Kelina, S. G. & Kudryavtsev, V. N. *Principles of Soviet Criminal Law*, Moscow, 1988, p147.
38 Sarkisov, E. A. *Humanism in Soviet Criminal Law*, Minsk, 1968, p23.
39 Marat, J. P. *Selected Works*, Moscow, 1956, vol. 1, p213.
40 Beccaria, C. *On Crimes and Punishments*, Moscow, 1939, p244.
41 Karpets, I. I. *Punishment: Social, Legal and Criminological Issues*, Moscow, 1973, p87.

humanism may only relate to one particular person and is understood in the modern sense as humanity, mercy. Social protection through inflicting harm on one particular person, even if it is necessary and conforms to social benefits, cannot be considered humane, since harm and humanism are incompatible concepts. The humanism principle in criminal law is associated only with the personality of a criminal and involves a humane attitude towards him. This raises the common-sense question of whether it is right to reduce humanism to imposing the minimum possible punishment on a criminal. A. S. Gorelik notes that "imposing even the minimum possible punishment can only nominally be called humane. Any punishment is a penalty, and penalty is opposite to humanism. Punishment cannot be more or less humane; to be more specific, one should talk about more or less inhumane punishment. In other words, not about the degree of humanity but about the degree of departure from it, and meaning only that while using the term."[42] In short, the principle of humanism is necessary to explain the commensurability of a certain punishment to a crime, taking into account all the of the criminal's personality characteristics. Therefore, humanism can only be regarded as a means of achieving justice. The understanding of legislators and judges of criminal law categories of justice and humanism, which surely should not be abstracted or even opposed to the concepts of justice and humanity developed by philosophy, is of immense importance.

Justice becomes an assessment measure of activity, people's deeds, provided that everyone is assured of their rightness. This especially concerns judges. A judge convinced of the rightness of his attitude towards crime must be direct and confident in defending the justice of punishment through the prism of humanism, forgetting all of himself, despising timid qualifications and ambiguous hints, caring only for the truth, not for what people might say of him. It is also necessary to understand that one of the essential conditions of a judge's justice is the incorruptibility and self-forgetfulness of the judge. As Cicero said, "it is a crime to take bribes for fixing sentences, and even a worse crime to take bribes from a person for justification", while Democritus noted that "a corruptible person cannot be just". Bacon added to this thought, saying: "Judges are to be more learned than witted, more respectful than skilled in argumentation, more prudent than self-reliant. But their major virtue is incorruptibility."[43]

One cannot do without justice and humanism while dealing with matters that rely upon the personality characteristics of the guilty. The sheer variety of characteristics that distinguish people from one other does not allow for

42 Gorelik, A. S. *Accumulative Sentencing*, Krasnoyarsk: Krasnoyarsk University Publishing, 1991, p83.
43 Bacon, F. *Works*, vol. 2, Moscow, 1978, p473.

their expression as standardised, exact criteria. Therefore when using this kind of standard, it is especially important to take into account the moral aspects of justice and humanism that should be relied upon when assessing character and personality danger level. Foremost among these standards are those that define the rules of imposing punishment.

Subjectivity in the application of punishment is unavoidable. In this respect, we face issues of the individual judge's opinion and judicial discretion. Both of these mean a state of mind that allows a judge to regard the imposed punishment as the most just, tailored and undeniable option. Personal opinion as a state occurs not as a result of instantaneous impressions but comprises an analysis of the gravity and nature of the social danger of the crime, the personality of the guilty, and the circumstances that mitigate and aggravate the punishment. In Azerbaijan, judicial practice demonstrates that crimes equal by nature and gravity are often imposed with different kinds and terms of punishment solely under judicial discretion. What is this judicial discretion?

A. Barak defines judicial discretion as "the power granted to the judge by the law to choose from different alternatives of equal legitimacy". However, this is "neither an emotional nor an intellectual state. It is rather a juridical condition upon which the judge is entitled to choose from several alternatives."[44] This is hardly agreeable, since the juridical condition for choosing a certain punishment is defined by the law. And this means that the judge is not entitled to step outside these bounds, even when he is unable to make a just decision within the law. Juridical discretion is, rather, a compilation of the moral, practical, psychological and pedagogical conditions upon which the judge makes a particular decision. Therefore, the rightness of such a decision depends upon the judge's quality development in each case. At that, it goes without saying that along with professional qualities, the judge's ability to think in panhuman terms is of almost equal importance. Consequently, we suppose that juridical discretion is a moral certainty in fixing a just sentence while imposing a penalty for a criminal. It is clear that juridical discretion cannot be limitless. We are talking about the most effective variant of discretion. However opposed some authors might be to juridical discretion, it should be recognised that wherever there is a right to do so, there will be an opportunity for choosing at the judiciary's discretion.

In this sense, we share the same apprehension as V. P. Nazhimov when he warns that "trial participants, especially the accused and the defender, are almost helpless before the judges' discretion in choosing a certain punitive

---

44 Barak, A. *Judicial Discretion*, Moscow, 1999, pp 13–14.

measure. Judges may introduce any kind of aspect into this matter, however subjective it might be—for instance, a bad mood, intuitive antipathy towards the accused and so on."[45] Apparently this depends on the judge's personal characteristics, not on the limits on juridical discretion. We are not sure if the limitation of juridical discretion may affect the rightness and justice of decisions. Therefore the question at hand is not whether we should give up on juridical discretion, but what the limits of such discretion should be.

Certainly, along with other necessary preconditions, mental activity, comprising reflections, inter-comparison, the pondering of certain evidence, the overall critical assessment of a possible sentence model, and, finally, a check-up of the whole system of conclusions and the logical, cause-effect relationships between the data providing the basis for the decision, there are also elements of developing moral beliefs.[46] The background for a rational, moral judge's belief lies in the fact that the judge practises constant self-restraint while regarding all the possible 'draft' decisions and amounts of punishment as models created by his conscience. Doubt is the key element of self-restraint. Every judge relies upon his own moral principles while choosing the type and amount of punishment. At that, it is worth noticing that the judge's philosophical, legal and panhuman belief system plays an exceedingly important role in setting just and reasonable punishment. Any political or ideological principles should be ignored by the judge.

Therefore, the law places certain limits on the discretion of law-enforcement bodies and officials, with the aim of making the right decision based on justice and humanism concepts. For instance, the following dialogue took place between Muhammad, the Messenger of Allah, and Mauz, appointed as a judge in Yemen: "How will you judge?" asked Muhammad. "According to the Writings of Allah," answered Mauz. "And what if you are not able to find the answer there?" asked the Prophet. "According to the Sunnah of the Messenger," said Mauz. "And what if you are not able to find the answer even there?" asked Muhammad. "Then I shall judge according to my own opinion, and I shall not spare myself in finding the right decision," answered Mauz. "Praise Allah, for He put you on the right path!" exclaimed the Prophet.

*

45 Nazhimov, V. P. 'Justice of Punishment as an Essential Term of Its Efficiency', *Court Organisation Issues and Administration of Justice in the USSR*, Kaliningrad, 1973, vol. 2, p3.
46 Nad, L. *Sentence in Criminal Procedures*, Moscow, 1982, p92.

2

The Substance and Attributes of Punishment

Juridical literature boasts few who use the term 'essence of punishment' differently from the term 'substance of punishment'. Most of its exponents either assign these terms the same meaning, or use only one of them. Let us therefore provide several opinions on the concept of the essence of punishment.

Russian criminal scientists in pre-revolutionary times considered the causing of suffering to criminals to be the essence of punishment.[1] For instance, N. D. Sergievskiy believed the essence of punishment to be judgment and reproof "in the form of certain physical or moral harm".[2] And the Soviet specialist P. P. Osipov noted the dual nature of punishments that comprise both education and nurturing.[3] I. A. Tarkhanov defined the essence of punishment as "reproof for the person that committed a crime, expressed by the authorities in terms of lawful limitations".[4] Often enough, the essence of punishment is considered to be penalty.[5]

---

1   See: Tagantsev, N. S. *Russian Criminal Law, Lecturing Course: General*, pp 91–93; Spasovich, V. D. *Criminal Law Textbook*, vol. 1, issue 2, Saint Petersburg, 1863, p180; Poznyshev, S. V. *General Issues of Punishment Doctrine*, Moscow, 1904, p335.

2   Sergievskiy, N. D. *Russian Criminal Law, General: Lectures Guidebook*, issue 2, 1915, p84.

3   See: Osipov, P. P. *Theoretical Backgrounds for Drafting and Imposing Criminal Law Sanctions*, Leningrad, 1976, p68.

4   Tarkhanov, I. A. *Punishment Replacement in Accordance with Soviet Criminal Law*, Kazan, 1982, p9.

5   See: *Punishment Doctrine in Russian Criminal Law*, Moscow, 2011, p58; Natashev, A. E. & Struchkov, N. A. *Backgrounds for Correctional Labour Law*, p17.

The reality is that it is an extremely challenging task to reveal the true essence of punishment, to define it and distinguish it from the logically and historically close concept of penalty that is associated with the substance of punishment. Kerimov backs this up, saying: "The gap between the essence and substance of law cannot be justified: not only the substance but the essence of law as well are objective categories that are subjectively reflected in legislation."[6]

Unlike its essence, the substance of punishment is transient, variable and dubious. The substance of punishment is constantly developing by its nature, this development reflecting movement and changes in the material, spiritual and social political life of the society, which is why the identification of the essence and substance of punishment is inadmissible, because punishment's essence is a deeper and broader category than that of substance. The former as the grounds and basis for punishment is a phenomenon, while the latter is its expression through various manifestations of the essence of punishment.

Essence reveals punishment's intrinsic nature, while the substance of punishment expresses exactly certain deprivations and punishments of this essence though criminal law sanctions. That is why the substance of punishment does not go beyond *penalty*, with all of its attributes, characteristics and so on. By the substance of punishment, one is able to define which media and methods the state uses to implement the essence of punishment. And this implies that state authority is not capable of affecting the essence of punishment, which is objective and permanent by nature, while the substance of punishment, broadly speaking, changes constantly along with society's development level.

Penalty is not a goal of punishment, but rather its substance. It is objectively inherent to it and does not depend on a legislator who can feasibly use this medium or misuse it to his own ends. The complexity of the punitive substance of punishment is due not only to different scientific approaches to the definition of penalty's role in punishment, but also to different views of experts on the origins of penalty itself. For instance, B. S. Utevskiy defined penalty as coercion.[7] B. S. Nikiforov, criticising this definition, assumed that penalty suggests suffering,[8] therefore he understood penalty not just as a general coercion but rather a coercion to suffering, indeed a suffering commensurable with the crime committed.

6   Kerimov, D. A. *Methodology of Law*, p167.
7   Utevskiy, B. S. 'Issues of Correctional Labour Law Theory and Its Practical Implementation', *Theoretical Conference Proceedings on Issues of Soviet Correctional Labour Law*, Moscow, 1957, p37.
8   *Theoretical Conference Proceedings on Issues of Soviet Correctional Labour Law*, p128.

I. S. Noy also expresses his attitude towards the definition of penalty: "Penalty is a coercion aimed at causing suffering. Only this understanding of penalty allows us to tell it apart from other kinds of coercion that comprise punishment but make no penalty."[9] S. V. Polubinskaya sees penalty as the essence, the integral feature of punishment. Penalty in this regard involves the deprivation of criminals of the opportunity to commit new crimes. In this respect, penalty is the necessary prerequisite for achieving the goals of crime prevention by punishment.[10] And finally, according to V. K. Duyunov, "penalty is always a reaction of judgment, reproof, reproach for the guilty for the crime he committed, whatever facet of social life this concept is used in".[11]

In a great many languages, both European and Asian, there is no special analogue for the Russian word *kara* ('penalty, penance'), as distinct from the word *nakazanie* ('punishment'). In Russian, *kara* has a special hint to it. According to V. Dahl's dictionary, the meaning of the word is not just a general punishment, but a highly severe one, associated with execution. This penalty feature sets punishment apart from other state coercive measures. Therefore, since crimes have different gravity levels, so punishments differ from each other both qualitatively and quantitatively, by the extent of penalty.

The specific expression of penalty forms the substance of specific punishment. In the process of punishment-system analysis, one cannot fail to see that it comprises different kinds of punishment, which differ greatly from each other while having the same essence. This is testimony to the fact that the substance of punishment, unlike its essence, can change very rapidly. A legislator can affect the substance of a certain punishment by defining the 'dose' of penalty in it. For instance, the dose of penalty in imprisonment differs qualitatively from that in a fine. And that is quite natural, for there are situations where the maximum penalty dose is required to achieve the goal—and then there are situations where only the minimum penalty seems fit.

The execution of punishment doles out a certain amount of suffering to the convicted. This property is an integral feature of penalty as a component of punishment substance. It is worth noting here that suffering is not a punishment goal but rather a property of penalty, i.e. the intrinsic basis, characteristic and property of penalty. And the fact that moral suffering

---

9   Noy, I. S. *Essence and Functions of Criminal Punishment*, p31.
10   Polubinskaya, S. V. 'On the Question of Punishment Objectives', *Issues of Criminal Legislation Improvement*, Moscow, 1984, p100.
11   Duyunov, V. K. *Is Punishment in Russian Criminal Law a Coercion or a Penalty?*, p65.

has to come jointly with physical suffering is totally just, because the crime's commission itself dishonours the criminal. Criminal punishment then as a fact of material life is an act of coercion to suffering. If not, the concept of punishment would have vanished from juridical vocabulary as obsolete. Mokrinskiy wrote: "Should we take away this identifying feature of punishment, its purposive infliction of suffering, or suppose that this act in general cannot induce the required effect, then everyone would be able to understand that this act no longer conforms to the concept of punishment, that it can be regarded as an authoritative rehabilitation measure, an act of contempt, of isolation, but not as punishment."[12] At the same time, pain and humiliation should not run to extremes and turn into causeless and aimless torment. In the meantime, we should take into account Ferri's warning: "We vigorously oppose the overthrow of social justice, when jails become more cosy and comforting than the dwellings of honest but poor people."[13]

Suffering is among those concepts with a real meaning so clear that even the simple mind is able to understand it. But it has a contradictory, complex substance. In the *psychological* sense, suffering is a special emotion associated with the feeling of displeasure. In the *social* sense, suffering is a result of alienation from society, rejection. According to religious concepts, suffering is a purely religious doctrine that stays within the framework of religion and does not interfere with everyday life. It is associated purely with the relationship between a person and God, not merely between people. This means that suffering is a form of sacrifice to the supreme powers—to God, to the Holy Spirit. Suffering can also be deemed endurance, while from the *juridical* point of view, suffering is understood as a result of the evil committed by a person, as a consequence of crime.

Suffering comprises the unpleasant, depressing or agonising experiences of a living being, giving it physical or emotional discomfort, pain, stress, torment and so on. It is understood that different circumstances may cause suffering (love, illness and so forth). This kind of suffering does not possess a coercive authoritative basis, i.e. it is not a coercive suffering, but rather a natural human feeling. Suffering as an attribute or property of penalty, is notable for its coercive nature, for it is caused regardless of the will and wishes of man himself, under special conditions. Therefore, this suffering should be distinguished from moral torments, the qualms of conscience felt by the criminal, even when they are so great that he would

12   Mokrinskiy, S. P. *Punishment, Its Purposes and Postulates, Parts 1–3*, Moscow, 1902, p3.
13   Ferri, E. Op. cit, pp 270–271.

rather surrender to authority so as to work out his guilt through torment. It is owing to suffering that a person committing evil should wash away his guilt, acknowledge how wrong his behaviour was and how beautiful life out of prison is. At the same time, it is worth noting that suffering is dangerous for human health, causing neuroses and psychoses. Punishment loses its original meaning in case of the total loss of the penalty component, the latter being inconceivable without deprivation, suffering and limitations. Maltsev was right to state that "pure punishment without penalty elements are nothing but a dream of modern liberal characters and an illusion capable of turning the social reaction to crime into a feeble, insignificant act".[14]

Therefore, if penalty is withdrawn from punishment, thus leaving it without the elements of suffering, stress and so on, then this phenomenon (punishment) will not work for the concept of criminal punishment. In principle, even if one tries to do that, it would turn out in vain, for penalty is an objective and integral property of punishment. The idea of divine punishment had a radical impact on the criminal law concept of punishment. According to religious dogma, it is impossible to do purely cerebral penance for it is senseless and ineffective. That is why true religious penance comprises suffering and pain, and agonising panic for committing a crime, a sin, an evil deed—everything that is a part of punishment imposed as penalty.

The issue of the pedagogical capabilities of penalty has frequently arisen in literature. For instance, A. Loeffler thought that when the best among citizens loathe the very idea of most of the deeds deemed crimes by the state, than this feeling is the result of social education, and criminal punishment plays the most significant role in it.[15] If penance comprises pedagogical elements along with sufferings, deprivations and so forth, then punishment, apart from its punitive essence, has pedagogical features and thus cannot merely impose suffering but also educate and rehabilitate. State identification of a rehabilitation objective during the imposition of punishment does not at all mean that punitive elements comprise those of rehabilitation. The purpose of corrective rehabilitation cannot be set before punishment, but rather before the bodies that impose punishment, which is not the same thing.

In imposing punitive measures of punishment it is understood that it is impossible to positively affect the personality of the convicted, since

---

14 Maltsev, G. V. Op. cit, p524.
15 Loeffler, A. *Der Begriff der Verantworlichkeit*, Mitt. D. I. K. V. VI, p388.

penalty—i.e. causing deprivation, introducing law limitations, the overall infliction of harm against the private interests of the convicted—cannot be considered a means of rehabilitation. Just as no one can force a man into patriotism, or respect for property, into neighbourly charity, so punishment cannot reform or improve that man's inner self, since punishment is coercion not persuasion. Therefore, it is wrong to centre hopes on punishment as an instrument of the rehabilitation and correction of people, criminals in particular. Issues of the improvement of people's inner qualities are beyond the compass of punishment.

Penalty does not rehabilitate, it depresses and horrifies, and, if one is fortunate, forms law-obedient behaviour.[16] The imminence of penalty cannot rehabilitate, or change one's mind, or fix moral standards. Penalty, when regarded as leverage for affecting the personality of the convicted, can help in achieving a preventive, but not a rehabilitation objective. Therefore, punitive and rehabilitative impact are relatively different phenomena with a different legal basis. Rehabilitation measures do not belong with the substance of penalty, but rather are unified with it in the single process of punitive rehabilitation impact on the convicted in order to achieve a crime prevention objective. The unity of punitive and correctional elements in achieving a set goal is especially obvious when it comes to imprisonment. Integrated in a comprehensive system, they form a qualitatively new phenomenon: punitive correctional impact comprising elements of penalty and rehabilitation. Imposing punishment carries out two separate yet very relevant tasks: realisation of penalty elements and organisation of the rehabilitative influence that accompanies punishment.

The difference between penalty and retribution should also be highlighted. Though both are elements of punishment, their difference lies in the fact that penalty is expressed through causing suffering to the condemned, while retribution characterises a certain repayment for the person that committed an evil deed. This repayment comprises equalisation, redemption, and thus restoration of the thing that was infringed. However, this repayment is not revenge for the crime. Moreover, penalty as a component of punishment is implemented in the process of imposing punishment, and retribution is implemented in the process of fixing the sentence.

16 Osipov, P. P. *Theoretical Backgrounds for Drafting and Imposing Criminal Law Sanctions*, p68.

Interpreting Retribution and Deterrence through Punishment

Any activity, including an authoritative one, has a definite purpose, otherwise this activity is pointless. In principle, purpose is not a criminal law category, but a philosophical one. In philosophy, purpose is the conscious anticipation of the result the action is aimed at. In the context of law, "purpose as a philosophical category forms the basis of research on legal phenomena and processes, determines law-making activities, law itself, legislation and its implementation, improvement and development of the legal system."[17]

Every purpose is itself subjective, for it is formed (defined) by people, and is expressed in legislation and accomplished through the subjective activity of people. At the same time, if and when it is necessary, purpose is accomplished in either material or spiritual form, which basically is the result of realisation of the need. As Hegel puts it: "Purpose is above all something that exists inside me, something subjective, but at the same time it must be objective as well. It is able to leave that demerit behind, becoming not only subjective."[18]

It is worth noting that punishment pursues no goals, all the more so because it is impossible to set a goal before it, because goals can only be set by society, i.e. the subject, taking into account the objective capabilities of punishment and fixing it all in law. Consequently, punishment should be regarded as a means of achieving goals. That being said, it is important for the goal to be real and based on the essence of punishment, otherwise it would be of a purely declarative and senseless nature with no direct relation to punishment.

Of course, the state may use other media and possibilities to achieve this set goal. They would be delegated not to punishment, but to other subjects. Criminal law science goals are those that lead to the ideal desirable result of imposing punishment. What are those goals, those purposes that the state sets before itself using criminal punishment as leverage? Perhaps the most disputable question here is the issue of retribution and penalty. It is a widely held opinion that retribution is the purpose of punishment. Firstly, as previously noted, punishment sets no purposes, while secondly, the state itself cannot set the goal of retribution. Retribution is a phenomenon that lies at the heart of punishment's objective nature. It characterises, as previously noted, the essence of punishment and is realised in the process of utilisation

17 Kerimov, D. A. *Methodology of Law*, pp 270–271.
18 Hegel, G. W. F. *Works*, vol. vii, p39.

of this medium by the state to achieve a self-set goal. The abandonment of retribution means the abandonment of punishment as a whole, which is hardly possible in the present day. Retribution cannot play both the roles of the goal and essence of punishment.

This also covers penalty, which characterises the substance of punishment and cannot be regarded as a social objective. As for the goal of rehabilitation, the state surely sets this goal itself. But punishment here is nothing but secondary leverage, for punishment comprises no elements of the correction through which any rehabilitative impact could be made upon a person. Therefore, the state utilises other media and methods to achieve this goal, these media being outside the framework of punishment.

As for special (personal) deterrence, there are two views of this in literature. Some believe that the task of special deterrence comprises the creation of special conditions of enduring the punishment, conditions that would make impossible the commission of new crimes by the convicted, the formation of such a state of mind that would eliminate even the very thought of committing new crime.[19] This means that the purpose of rehabilitation is comprised of the function of special deterrence, and that the reference to it in legislation merely supports the necessity of applying corrective measures to the convicted.

Others believe this broad definition of the special deterrence concept cannot be justified, since it engulfs the purpose of rehabilitation of the convicted. They understand special deterrence as the creation of conditions that eliminate the possibility of committing crimes during imprisonment.[20] By committing a crime, a person declares himself dangerous to society. Therefore, as was noted by A. S. Chervotkin, one of the manifestations of special deterrence is the prevention of the committing of new crime by the convicted, not through personality modification or its elimination, but rather through the elimination of possibilities, conditions for the committing of crime.[21]

Literature contains another point of view, differing from others, where the special deterrence orientation of criminal law does not provide an efficient criminal enforcement system in itself. It evades diagnostics, and one must truly be endowed with a highly active imagination to suppose that a person who spent five years in prison becomes a better individual and more useful

19   Efimov, M. A. 'Imprisonment as a Type of Criminal Punishment', *Scientific Work Book*, issue 1, Sverdlovsk, 1964, p200.
20   Belyaev, N. A. *Purposes and Media of Punishment*, p21.
21   Chervotkin, A. S. 'Special Crime Deterrence Purpose and Means of Its Achievement for Application in Criminal Punishment', *Topical Questions of Crime Prevention*, Tomsk, 1984, p156.

to society, "because the leverage used in correctional purposes nowadays is far from perfect".[22] We rely upon the fact that the concept of special deterrence falls within the domain of punishment execution. Supposing that the purpose of special deterrence influence during the execution of punishment is to prevent the committing of new crimes by the convicted during the imprisonment period, then we should admit that *special deterrence is only creating specific conditions to prevent crimes during imprisonment.*

This form of deterrence is a part of the general crime prevention system. Therefore, the so-called special deterrence is nothing but a *condition* for achieving the only purpose of punishment: the prevention of crimes. On this basis, it seems feasible to use the term 'special crime prevention conditions' instead of 'special deterrence'. The modern criminal legislation of the post-Soviet states above all names the restoration of social justice among the purposes of punishment, with other purposes deemed less significant. V. D. Filimonov has "modifications of penalty purpose" as the basis for the goal of the "restoration of social justice".[23] V. K. Duyunov is of the same opinion, noting that "proclaiming the purpose of 'restoration of social justice' in legislation is simultaneously the legislative recognition of penalty as one of the purposes of criminal punishment, though in a disguised and subtilised form".[24]

It is worth noting that in the 1960s, N. A. Belyaev wrote on the restoration of social justice as the purpose of criminal punishment. But this legislator's position cannot be supported for a variety of reasons. Firstly, social justice is not a legal nor juridical but rather a philosophical, ethical category. Therefore its proclamation in law is purely declarative and thus lacks definiteness. Why do we not then simply stipulate that one of the social goals is the elimination of crime? Secondly, criminal legislation does not disclose a definition for the 'restoration of social justice'. It is a matter of judgment. Thirdly, achievement of the goal of restoring social justice is possible not through criminal punishment but via the social policy of the state. The problem of social justice falls far beyond the borders of criminal punishment. If the legislator understands social justice as a just punishment imposed against the person who committed the crime, taking into consideration the gravity of a crime, its circumstances and the personality of the guilty, then it is better to use the term 'recompense'.

Though justice is assessed and understood as an ethical category, it can be

22   Korobeev, A. I., Uss, A. V., & Golik, Y. V. *Criminal Law Policy: Tendencies and Prospects*, Krasnoyarsk, 1991, pp 139–141.
23   See: *New Criminal Law of Russia: General Part*, Moscow, 1996, p96.
24   Duyunov, V. K. Op. cit, p152.

juridically viewed and characterised as 'recompense', and, moreover, its attributes and criteria should be of a criminal law nature. Such categories as 'justice' and 'humanism' should be used by the legislator as principles for the drafting and fixing of punishment, not as the purpose of criminal punishment.

In conclusion, the state strives to prevent criminal manifestations, and to achieve this goal it uses different forms, methods, ways and media, one of which is criminal punishment. In what manner does this happen? In other words, how does the state as a legal subject use this unique medium to achieve the set goal? The whole process can be divided into three inter-related and interdependent stages: the definition and adoption of separate punishment types and the punishment system as a whole, the fixing of punishment for certain crimes, and the execution of punishment. Therefore, punishment as a preventive measure manifests itself in two directions, though it consists of three stages. It is utilised for the purposes of general influence on social consciousness, acting as a protection and horrification measure, while at the same time in regard to a particular person it serves as an admonition that prevents him from committing new crimes. This means that crime prevention through punishment is possible both via psychological crime prevention and physical deterrence from criminal activities for a certain period of time.

As of the moment when the law enters into force, the process of realisation of the protective and horrification influence of punishment is commenced. It is already 'in use', exercising its functions. This is why we cannot agree with the opinion by which punishment in the beginning—i.e. after the law's commencement—works as an impersonal threat.[25] The protective horrification influence of punishment reveals itself in two directions. It generally influences social consciousness acting as a precautionary measure, i.e. punishment serves as a kind of reminder of its existence, of its 'work', but does so relatively leniently. At the same time, it informs the citizens of the consequences of misbehaviour and criminal actions. It is the realisation of the horrification influence of punishment, which is objective regardless of the demands of the government. In this case, horrification is effected through psychological countermeasures to crime, and not physical deterrence from criminal intentions.

Due to the preventive qualities of punishment, it affects the intellectual facet of human existence, the associations rooted in the subconsciousness, thus creating a constant link between the idea of crime and its punishment. Horrification affects the human mind directly, i.e. provokes fear and makes

---

25   See: Korobeev, A. I., Uss, A. V. & Golik, Y. V. *Criminal Law Policy*, p157.

people behave in accordance with the set requirements. In this respect, criminal punishment suggests a psychological impact on society. But which part of society is affected? According to Feuerbach's theory, it is not aimed at society as a whole but at potential criminals, forcing them as dangerous individuals towards more prudent behaviour or the conscious abandonment of crime. But how can we define a potential criminal? If we had such an opportunity, we would be able to isolate him from society even before the crime was committed.

Threat of punishment is aimed at society at large for the purposes of crime prevention. There is a point of view that punishment immoralises people through horrification, that carnal fear plays the most significant role among the deterrent motives of punishment. This may well be true, but unfortunately we currently know no other medium of deterrence. The fear of physical and moral suffering is the basis of horrification, the repressive psychological impact of the punishment threat. And so logic says that the mitigation of punishment, i.e. the decrease of penalty's dose in punishment, as well as the reduction of punishments with a large dose of penalty elements, should lead to an increase in moral, and not physical, suffering.

But in practice social embarrassment gradually disappears, in other words people cease to regard being convicted as something embarrassing. Therefore, moral suffering ceases to be the basis for the repressive, preventive force of the punishment threat. It goes without saying that the psychological impact of the punishment threat is more dramatic the more it conforms with the moral beliefs of the society. The higher the development level of the nation, civil society and culture, the higher the personal self-esteem, the more effective is the preventive power of punishment. Therefore, when a nation's development level rises, the 'gravity centre' of the psychological impact of punishment moves from horrification to moral pressure. To what extent punishment affects citizens is still unclear, but one should hardly doubt that its influence is great or can be great under certain conditions. Therefore, all society has to do is to consciously use punishment to achieve the set goal.

By horrification, punishment essentially opposes those qualities, demands, wishes that seduce a person into crime, warning him of all the unfortunate consequences. B. S. Volkov writes: "The thought of punishment, if it does not totally eliminate the notion of committing crime, at least serves as a strong opposing motivation, a background for a persistent and active sociopathic position, for the strength and speed of dominating intentions."[26]

26   Volkov, B. S. *Criminal Motives*, Kazan, 1982, p119.

Through its protective qualities of horrification, punishment expresses an order to behave properly. Therefore, recognition of the blameworthiness of a deed constitutes a large part of the psychological discretionary process, serving as a counter motivation for sociopathic behaviour. And this leads us to the fact that the image of punishment's gravity, i.e. horrification strength, is of vital importance for the creation of a dampening effect in crime commission, and consequently belongs to factors that often affect the choice of behaviour pattern. It is important for the legislator to remember the following principle statement: for punishment to create the dampening effect that deters people from crime, on the one hand it must not be too grave, and on the other, taking into account the development level of citizens, must be impressive enough with the help of the necessary horrification methods.

For instance, if the historical experience of mankind shows that it is pointless to fight murder with the death penalty or imprisonment, this does not necessarily mean that you have to bend over backwards to fix a very lenient punishment for that crime. Punishment is to be intrinsically wise and reasonable. In recent years, there have been several articles on the negative, adverse nature of horrification by punishment, because it is immoral and ineffective for civilised society, and it is high time to deprive punishment of its 'iron fists' and to cease holding society in a state of fear. It is worth mentioning that these comments are not new, such opinions have always existed. As H. Aschaffenburg wrote: "We should confine ourselves to the thought that the horrification influence of punishment is not strong enough to successfully prevent evolving social dangers."[27]

This comment may be answered by the words of Cesare Beccaria: "Power close to gravity makes us reach for personal wellbeing, and is limited only by the obstruction opposite to it. This power manifests itself through a complex variety of human actions, and punishments which I myself would call political obstacles, prevents various negative consequences from the collision of these actions, without destroying the reason for their existence, which is the sensibility truly intrinsic to all humans. By acting that way, the legislator acts as a skilful architect whose duty it is to eliminate the harmful impact of gravity and make it useful whenever possible for building up the ruggedness of this construction."[28]

The role and meaning of criminal punishment absolutely cannot be understood as if the impact of horrification is aimed at the common good and interests of individuals. Therefore, it would be completely wrong to say that

---

27 Aschaffenburg, H. *Crime and Its Prevention*, Moscow, 2010, p204.
28 Beccaria, C. Op. cit, p95.

punishment is unjust by its essence through the grounds of general deterrence. For if a man is punished just to motivate others and deter them from criminal deeds, then the punished suffers not for what he has done but for the inclination of other people to do the same.[29] Society often treats its members like this, in order for it to contribute to the common good at the expense of individuals. This is possible during natural disasters, in *force majeure* situations and so on. But it is inadmissible for society to use a person who has committed a crime for the purposes of crime prevention on the basis of the fact that this person is currently at the full disposal of the state.

We are not casting doubt on the fact that even the most draconian laws— executions by fire and sword, breaking on the wheel and hanging—did not eliminate crime. But we think the idea of punishment that appears in the mind next to the idea of crime is itself capable of preventing, eliminating or deterring the urge to do the opposite. Of course, punishment cannot achieve one hundred per cent of this goal, but it is perfectly clear that it is capable of certain countermeasures with the help of horrification. As fairly noted by Johannes Andenaes, "we know even less about how many people would have committed crime if there were no threat of punishment".[30]

Of course, anyone would want to live in a society without punishment, but according to the words of the Polish humanist Andrzej Frycz Modrzewski, "human degeneracy is so great and people are so shameless and inclined to commit crimes that only the most severe and harsh laws can prevent malice, interdict forwardness and keep a tight rein on inhumanity. This appears to be so, and it means the following: numerous and severe laws serve as proof that the people of this state received poor education, have bad character and manifest even worse qualities one day after another. If rulers strive to prevent this, they need to create more accurate laws and fix more grave punishments."[31] In assessing the horrification power of punishment, Feuerbach writes: "I want to make it impossible to steal with the help of law, i.e. I believe in the possibility of the existence of such a thing as the antithesis of theft. I believe that theft is casual and that the thief is free and may as well not steal. Therefore, the law, in its vile belief in its all-powerfulness does not want anything from the thief except recognition of the fact that theft is prohibited, to sentence him to be hanged right away."[32]

The state has fixed certain rules of our behaviour, forbidding actions that

---

29   See: Buttur & Platt. 'The Meaning of Punishment', *Issues in Criminology*, 1966, no. 2, pp 79, 93.
30   Andenaes, J. *Punishment and Crime Prevention*, Moscow, 1979, p31.
31   See: *Legal Notion: The Anthology*, p133.
32   See: Ibid, p277.

contradict social and individual interests. Interdiction is a source of interaction between a man and the law. Therefore, the system of 'man–threat of punishment' features an assessment of man's capacity to recognise, understand the *interdiction*, for it is necessary to determine if man is capable of understanding the regulating role of the basic norms and standards of society, to acknowledge him as competent enough to receive retribution (punishment) for violating the interdiction. And for that, he has to have access to information on interdictions, he has to understand what is forbidden and what is allowed. Only after that is a man capable of taking their existence into account and finding the relevant solution, following them or rejecting them in simple choice situations. In other words, a person who wishes or intends to commit a wrongful act has to understand the interdictions and be able to assess the act itself and its consequences. At that, it is enough to assess the capability of understanding the norms and values that control behaviour in criminal-pertinent situations, and take them into account when choosing a behaviour pattern. Therefore, if a subject understands the harmfulness of his act and its consequences for others, if he recognises the fact of breaking criminal law norms, it is enough for liability to be incurred.[33]

Recognition of the harmfulness of consequences in case of an offence against individual or social wellbeing is present even if the criminal is relatively ignorant. In regard to that, one may deem Hegel's opinion interesting: he believed that the capability of forecasting the consequences of selective behaviour is enough for punishment, for only their knowledge can be incriminated. Plus, a person must understand the 'general nature' of his act, i.e. be capable of rendering it with the guidelines set by society, which should also be known by him.[34]

Legal science traditionally relies upon the fact that punishment suggests recognition of both the actual and juridical characteristics of a criminally-punishable act. This approach also corresponds with the general theoretical characteristic of law as a regulative tool of social relations, which has to penetrate the mind and will of the people. An idea from V. P. Salnikov seems appropriate: orientation towards moral standards that form the basis of legal principles is enough by itself, especially towards the essential juridical concepts, e.g. 'crime', that manifest those principles.[35]

This gives us the opportunity to decide what is wrong or right regarding

33   Sitkovskaya, O. D. *Criminal Liability Psychology*, Moscow, 1998, p84.
34   Piontkovskiy, A. A. *Hegel's Doctrine of Law and State, and His Criminal Law Theory*, Moscow, 1993, pp 245–249.
35   Salnikov, V. P. *Socialistic Legal Culture*, Saratov, 1989, pp 46–47.

behaviour in circumstances where no information on the exact legal standard is available, when one has to rely upon an understanding of general legislative direction and its functions, on the moral demands expressed in it. For after the words that set *punishment* follow the words that set *interdiction*, and everyone who is sane understands what this means. While interdiction allows desire to appear, the words of punishment provoke horrifying images.

According to religious philosophy, *fear* before punishment while alive or shortly and surely after death for the sins or wrongdoings committed was a fundamental factor and motive supporting the divine foundations of official order. This fear was most successfully developed where it was based upon persistent faith in the immortal soul and afterlife judgment of the gods. B. Malinovskiy wrote: "A savage conformed with his taboos not out of fear of social punishment or reproof. He abstained from them partly because he was afraid of the consequences that directly arise from divine will or the actions of divine powers, but mainly because his personal responsibility and consciousness did now allow him to commit them."[36] This is also backed up by Freud: "Taboos have somehow emerged and have to be conformed with due to overwhelming fear. External threat of punishment is not necessary, because there is an internal belief (consciousness) that a violation will surely lead to an impossible disaster."[37]

"And the Lord God commanded man, saying . . . But of the tree of knowledge of good and evil, thou shalt not eat of it: for on the day that thou eatest thereof thou shalt surely die" (Genesis 2: 16–17). While committing his sin, Adam understood that he had violated the ban, God's Law, and that he would be punished for that. Nevertheless, he was unable to help himself. On the one hand this ban provoked a demand of him, and on the other it horrified him because it gave him the possibility of freedom. Therefore, the nature of original sin should be interpreted through the category of fear that is a part of every punishment. The threat of impact provokes fear before punishment and thus often deters people from committing crimes. This fear appears even before the ensuing of the harmful consequences of wrongful acts, which can trigger punishment.

Walter Bradford Cannon, a Harvard physiologist, investigated the physiology of emotions back in 1927 and came to the conclusion that "fear, anger, pain and hunger are elementary feelings that can be rightly referred

36 Malinovskiy, B. *Magic, Science and Religion*, URL: http://malinovskii-magia.ofilosofii.ru
37 Freud, S. *Totem and Taboo: Resemblances Between the Mental Lives of Savages and Neurotics*, 1918 (1913).

to as the most mighty factors that define the behaviour of men and animals."[38] Fear arises at the very moment a man feels the need to commit a crime, for from that moment the instinct of self-preservation comes to life, which is the basis of fear. In other words, fear is an internal state based on real or expected disaster. As psychologists say, fear is the desire for something that you are afraid of, sympathetic antipathy. A man breaks the law willingly, but at the same time he is afraid, for he remembers that there is a punishment set for that.

Fear is an alien power that engulfs the individual and holds him hard, all the more so that the individual does not want to break free, and remains afraid of what he desires. This is why all potential criminals are familiar with fear. This concerns people that repeatedly commit crimes—habitual offenders, recidivists—hence the claim that the "psychology of so-called recidivists and professional criminals is commonly known: the fact that the threat of repression is inoperative for them is a proven matter"[39] is completely untenable and unreasonable. This view was supported by A. F. Zelinskiy, who believed that one of the conditions of recidivism is an emotional deafness not only towards other people, but to one's own destiny, which makes recidivists indifferent to the threat of punishment.[40] One can only talk about the amount of fear. Fear is instinctive, it is biologically framed and is intrinsic not only to people, but to animals as well. The fact that there allegedly are people who feel no fear should be understood in the context that Adam too would have felt nothing when breaking the law if he were a mere animal. Therefore the inability to fear is proof that the individual concerned is either an animal or an angel—and both are less perfect than human in accordance with the divine texts. Consequently, fear is a manifestation of the perfection of human nature.

Recidivists have a somewhat numbed sense of apprehension, but they still have it. Therefore, committing another crime is not of major consequence for them, because the threat of punishment does not have the proper deterrent impact on them. And vice versa, a man that commits his first crime has a deep sense of apprehension which may deter him from the wrongful act. If that happens, it may be deemed a successful result of the influence of criminal punishment.

Everyone knows that women commit much less crime than men, and in Azerbaijan, women commit only ten per cent of all crimes. One of the main

---

38 Cannon, W. *Physiology of Emotions: Physical Changes in Pain, Hunger, Fear and Anger*, Leningrad, 1927, p15.
39 Krylenko, N. V. *Court and Law in the USSR*, Moscow, 1930, vol. 3, p68.
40 Zelinskiy, A. F. *Recidivism: Structure, Associations, Forecasting*, Kharkov, 1980, p44.

reasons for this is that fear is more common among women than men, since women are more sensible and have more fear of criminal punishment. Therefore, the deeper the fear the greater is the man who feels it, if not in the sense that we are used to, when a fear arises from something external. Here, it is the man himself that creates that fear. And this fear prevents him from committing a wrongful act.

Psychologists have analysed fear and its causes and divided it into four types: biological, social, moral and disintegration. This classification is based on the situation that causes fear. Situations related to a direct hazard to life cause a biological fear that is a primal type arising in case of the deprivation of basic vital needs. For instance, oxygen deprivation (e.g. in the case of heart failure) causes an acute panic attack. Social fear arises from cases of the violation of behavioural patterns in society (fear of being rejected by the family, fear of punishment, fear of the teacher and so on). Accordingly, the fear of criminal punishment arises from the violation of certain social life rules. By this process, the individual understands that he will receive the relevant punishment for this. Therefore, the fear of punishment arises, accompanied with the corresponding intensive physical symptoms such as anxiety, tremor and palpitation.

Fear influences psychological processes, including impaired mindfulness and difficulties with concentration. Fear can have different impacts on brainwork. There are those who experience increased intelligence which they use in search of a way out. In that case, a man who intends to commit a crime finds it easier to make decisions, i.e. to determine the feasibility of the wrongful behaviour. Others experience a decrease in brainwork efficiency, i.e. they barely understand the consequences of the crime to the full extent. Therefore, threat of punishment has little influence on them. According to a survey by A. Naumov, when asked the question "why do you think people don't commit crimes?", out of 400 respondents 17.4 per cent gave the answer "out of fear of punishment".[41]

Some writers, while not completely denying horrification by punishment, do not rely on the redemptive influence of fear. For instance, Dril wrote: "Fear cannot and does not last forever. Bad personalities are easily involved in actions inherent to their nature, and then the time comes when the image of danger and sense of apprehension cease to exist in them, and they run into crime again. It is necessary for internal deterring elements to exist inside every man on their own."[42] The influence of the fear of punishment is also

---

41 See: Naumov, A. V. *Implementation of Criminal Law*, Volgograd, 1983, p28.
42 Dril, D. A. Op. cit, p75.

denied by Bekhterev, who believes that fear cannot affect crime prevention because a man who commits crime on purpose first and foremost thinks of the ways of escaping justice.[43]

One thing is clear: until criminal law exists as a reflection of social development conditions, the fear of punishment persists, for while it is not the only component of preventative measures, it surely is an inherent one. There is a Buddhist tale from the *Jataka*, 'The Mosquito', which informs us that "a smart enemy is better than a simple friend, for a smart enemy would never commit homicide, having a dread of punishment". Risk in the 'man threat of punishment' system plays a rather specific role. Linguistics defines risk as "a haphazard action with a view to a successful result".[44] The most common definition of risk in psychology is a situational characteristic involving the uncertainty of its result and the possibility of unfavourable consequences for failure. Risk is a defining factor preserving the elements of threat that are taken into account by a potential criminal, because many people do not break the law because they are deterred by an exaggerated idea of risk. As Andenaes notes, "even common sense tells us that the amount of discovery and condemnation risk is of primary importance to the preventive influence of criminal punishment".[45] Therefore, by threat of punishment we try to convince people that crime is not feasible because of the greatness of risk. 'Signals' sent by sanctions of criminal law on the one hand contain actual information on what is associated with the risk of disobedience, and on the other claim that disobedience is evil.

Generally the threat of punishment is psychologically connected with understanding of the sanction, i.e. the amount of risk in case of wrongful behaviour. In this regard, account for the psychological attitude of potential criminals to the threat of punishment has a supreme meaning for the efficiency of the general preventive impact mechanism and thus for the development of effective criminal law sanctions. The potential criminal has to understand that the risk that he takes via committing crime is so great and the punishment for it is so severe that he might well lose more than he gained through committing crime in the end. And this means that the potential criminal must recognise the following factors: amount of risk, severity of punishment, and a settlement system for committing crimes.

Research on the psychology of potential criminals allows us to claim that the defining factors in creating the deterring effect of criminal punishment are: inevitability of punishment, and increase in the threat of punishment for

43   Bekhterev, B. M. Op. cit, p716.
44   Ozhegov, S. I. *Russian Language Dictionary*, Moscow, 1988, p848.
45   Andenaes, J. *Punishment and Crime Prevention*, Moscow, 1979, p69.

certain crime categories. Now if the first of these factors is obligatory for all crimes, then an increase in the threat of punishment might create a general preventive impact for those potential criminals who, due to the specific nature of the crime, have plenty of time and an opportunity to understand the consequences of discovery and weigh the benefit of crime against the threat of punishment. The psychological attitude of potential criminals towards this category of punishment threat is distinguished by the opportunity to compare the benefit of crime against the liability for it, before or during the committing of the crime. Eventually, they make the decision as to whether the crime is worth committing or not. In this case, one may note the meagre efficiency of the general preventive impact of criminal punishment. Therefore, it is expedient to increase liability for these kinds of crime to the extent that they become not worth committing.

It cannot be doubted that the efficiency of punishments depends on their severity. If punishments cannot provoke fear in potential criminals, then it means they are pointless. When people are not afraid of breaking the law, when they hope for impunity, it is a sign of weakness and crisis in criminal policy on crime prevention. Dostoevsky sums this up with the following: "I would not want that my words are mistaken for cruelty. But I still will take the liberty of saying this. I will say unequivocally: severe punishment, prison and forced labour would have saved half of them. Served them right, not wrong. Self-purification through punishment is much easier than the destiny to which you condemn them through justification in court. You only put cynicism in their souls, leaving them tempted and able to mock you. You don't believe it? They mock you, your judgement, the judgement of the whole country. For what you put in their souls is disbelief in the common truth, in the truth of God, you are leaving them confused . . . Such a man leaves, thinking, 'There is no severity in that. Maybe they thought better of it. Maybe they are afraid. Maybe it will turn out this way the next time. Sure—I was in need and I was bound to steal.' "[46] At the same time, one cannot go to the other extreme. One should always bear in mind that all punishments that numb the moral sense, that make the criminal or society even worse, should be abandoned. Victor Hugo noted: "The peculiarity of this sort of mostly severe punishments that numb the mind is the fact that they change the man, gradually turning him through some senseless transformation into a savage beast."[47]

It should first be taken into account that the system and nature of

46 See: *Legal Notion: The Anthology*, p428.
47 Hugo, V. *Collected Works*, 15 vols, vol 6, Moscow, 1954, pp 109–112.

punishment depend directly on the state of the society. The less developed that society is, the more absolute is the power and the more severe are the punishments. And vice versa. Secondly, the higher the cultural level of the man, the more significant are his objective reasons. Therefore, a society with citizens of a high cultural level does not need very severe punishments. And vice versa. Thirdly, the more power the authority has, the more severe the punishments. In the process of setting punishments, the legislator should pay special attention to attaching special qualities that would guarantee both the justice and usefulness of their imposition. Only those punishments that have such qualities may be deemed as punitive measures and accepted in the punishment system.[48]

The main horrification power of criminal punishment is its publicity, i.e. the fact that it directly affects the other citizens. Therefore, the people must be well informed about this. It should also be noted that the same punishment often affects different people's behaviour in different ways. The closer it is to the moment of committing, the greater its influence on human behaviour. A very lenient yet immediate punishment might be as effective as a severe one. For instance, a punishment in the afterlife is a distant one, and so to have the proper impact on human behaviour, it is compensated for with an abundance of horror and severity in all the divine texts.

There is a category of crime where the subject of the crime has no time to calculate the benefit he receives as a result of such antisocial behaviour, or the punishment. For instance, when committing some instantaneous hooliganism, a person understands that he is committing a wrongful act, but he has neither the time nor the opportunity to think about the amount and type of punishment set for this act. Therefore, the threat of punishment cannot fulfil its functions properly, and this is why we do not need to make the punishment for this kind of wrongdoing more severe. Sanction, or, to be more specific, the threat of it, might be called a 'motivation', but this motivation is of another kind, as implicit in its indirect regard for behaviour and various other emotional, psychological, evaluative and other points. The deterrent impact of horrification is not as simple as thought by many. Many criminals are so tense in the process of committing crime (especially when it happens for the first time) that they are barely able to understand the consequences of their behaviour. Others pretend to themselves that they will escape unpunished.

Any threat of punishment, even the most strict, is unable to prevent the

48   Berner, A. *On the Death Penalty*, Saint Petersburg, 1865, p59.

person from his criminal intentions if this person is unable to assess the profit and loss of such a wrongful act. Therefore, the threat of punishment must be exactly set in the sanction of criminal law to outweigh the losses associated with deterrence from crime. Every criminal intent arises from the image of pleasure, the benefit that the man hopes to gain as a result of committing the crime. A person intending to commit a crime has his own reasons for it. One scale measures the benefit that awaits him, and the other measures the threat of incurring suffering and loss. Therefore, if the threat outweighs the profit, then the will of the potential criminal will be paralyzed, and he will be able to abandon the criminal idea.

Threat of retribution is increased by the effective actions of law enforcement bodies on the discovery and punishment of criminals. Therefore, the fact of the imposition of a penalty against certain persons, the realisation of chances and the imminence of punishment are effective preventive means that deter the majority of people from committing crimes. This is the horrification function of punishment. The amount of horrification therefore depends directly on the amount of conviction in the imminence of punishment. Since the times of Beccaria, it has been considered common knowledge that the imminence of discovery and punishment plays a more significant role in deterring people from committing crimes than the severity of punitive measures. Even common sense tells us that the amount of discovery and condemnation risk is of primary importance to the preventive influence of criminal punishment. As Beccaria writes: "Assurance of the imminence of even the most moderate punishment always has a greater impact than the fear of another one, more severe, but accompanied with the hope of impunity."[49]

This important point was also noted by representatives of the Russian pre-revolutionary criminal law school. In respect of this, it is worthwhile to say that the concept of 'impunity' comprises not only the fact of non-discovery of a criminal, but also the opportunity to escape liability during investigation and trial, and also the hope for pardon and amnesty. In principle, one should agree that in modern days, the idea of escaping liability has spread widely among the population. This distrust in law enforcement bodies has surely affected the existing level of crime in the country. An average of 8–10 per cent of crimes a year remain unsolved in Azerbaijan, with 10–14 per cent for grave and extremely grave crimes, and about 10 per cent for homicides.

In *On Crimes and Punishments*, in his chapter 'On Pardon', Beccaria warns:

49 Beccaria, C. Op. cit, p124.

"Showing people that a crime might be pardoned, that punishment is not always the necessary form of repayment, means to give them hope of impunity and makes them think that if a pardon might be given, then the execution of punishment for those who are not pardoned is an abuse of powers rather than a manifestation of justice."[50]

In the period between 1996 and 2010, 53,558 people were pardoned and amnestied in Azerbaijan. During the 15 years between 1995 and 2010, 48 orders on pardon were adopted, on whose grounds 5,121 were released from prison, among them: 2,623 convicted for intentional crime, 29 sentenced to life imprisonment. Between 1996 and 2009, on the basis of 9 acts of amnesty, 48,437 criminals were released from prison, 3,394 of whom served out their sentence in places of detention. Humanism is undoubtedly necessary, but a man cannot sacrifice social safety so often and so plainly, since it creates an even stronger idea of impunity.

In the science of criminal law, this question on the subject of the threat of punishment is still debated. In his day, Ferri divided the social classes of criminal sociology into three categories according to their attitude towards criminal punishment. The first group consists of highly moral classes of people. They never commit crimes and belong to the largest group of the population. This category comprises people for whom criminal penalty is completely useless. The second group comprises the lowest class of population, most of them being natural-born criminals. Punishment as a threat is useless for them because this threat is aimed at a mind deprived of social conscience, thus making punishment a mere matter of risk. And finally, the last class of individuals have no natural inclinations towards crime, yet their honesty fails the test of temptation. Punishment as a psychological impact may have a certain effect on them.[51] Garofalo, while agreeing with the ideas of Ferri, believed that it is necessary to separate the class of criminals that are able to feel the horrifying power of punishment from the criminals that are not affected by this power.[52]

According to the opinion of the modern theorist of general deterrence Andenaes, the population can be divided into three theories: law-abiding citizens who do not fall from grace notwithstanding any threats from the law, potential criminals who would have broken the law absent the threat of punishment, and criminals who might fear the law but only to an extent that does not prevent them from breaking it. The deterring effect of

50 Ibid, p155.
51 Ferri, E. Op. cit, pp 258–259.
52 Garofalo, R, *Criminologia*, issue 2, Turin, 1886, p217.

punishment is effective only to the second category, i.e. potential criminals.[53] Back in 1914, Timoshev came to the conclusion that the absolute majority of the population in tsarist Russia was deterred from crime only under the threat of punishment.[54] This kind of claim attests to the high significance of the general deterrence factor in criminal punishment, although there are no facts that can prove it. According to S. I. Kurganov, the target audience for the threat of punishment are not all of the subjects, but those of them who do not commit crimes only out of fear of punishment.[55]

V. M. Kogan believes that from the point of view of the threat of punishment, the population may be divided into three categories. The first category comprises people who do not deem the threat as a motivating factor, because they do not commit crimes due to their consciousness or other circumstances not related to criminal interdictions. The second category comprises people who do not deem the threat as a motivating factor, because they do commit crimes—the threat of unfavourable consequences notwithstanding. The third category comprises people who do deem the threat a motivating factor, because they do not commit crimes only out of fear of unfavourable criminal law consequences. They belong to the main subject of the threat of punishment.[56]

A survey conducted among people sentenced to imprisonment, i.e. among those people not deterred by the threat of punishment, showed the following. According to data collected by A. I Martsev, 58 per cent of the 200 people surveyed were indifferent to the punishment hanging over them,[57] and according to data collected by I. S. Noy, 64 per cent of the 245 people surveyed did not think of punishment while committing the crime.[58] The statement that the threat of punishment may deter some people from committing crimes might be deemed an axiom,[59] but you cannot quantitatively define this part. And it is not just criminal punishment, it is more a matter of the current impossibility of explaining the reasons for crime at all.

Criminal law science in its new form is first and foremost looking for the

53 Andenaes, J. *Punishment and Crime Prevention*, p125.
54 Timoshev, S. N. *Criminal Condemnation*, Saint Petersburg, 1914, pp 304–306.
55 Kurganov, S. I. *Punishment: Criminal Law and Penal Aspects*, Moscow, 2008, p172.
56 Kogan, V. M. *Social Apparatus of Criminal Law Impact*, Moscow, 1983, pp 160–161.
57 Martsev, I. 'General Crime Prevention', *Legal Science*, 1970, no. 1, p73.
58 Noy, I. S. *Essence and Functions of Criminal Punishment*, p153.
59 Korobeev, A. I., Uss, A. V. & Golik, Y. V. *Criminal Law Policy: Tendencies and Prospects*, p114.

natural causes of the abnormal social phenomenon called crime, thus it tries to find means if not to eliminate then at least to limit it. Hippocrates once wrote: "Those diseases which medicines do not cure, iron cures; those which iron cannot cure, fire cures; and those which fire cannot cure, are to be reckoned wholly incurable."

Crime in its modern sense is an incurable phenomenon, since humanity has been using all the means at hand, including the essential one—criminal punishment, which can be compared to 'fire'. Threat of punishment comprises everyone, not only one category, for the legislator is not able to determine the direction of the threat. But people perceive the existence of criminal punishment differently. For someone it is a warning, yet for someone else it is leverage for deterrence from criminal intentions. But the fear of this threat is universal. This conclusion is based on psychological data on the rational, emotional and conative spheres existing in the human mind. Human behaviour in terms of individual deeds is dictated by their internal psychological activity. At that, wilful acts of the mind are induced both by thoughts and emotions that interrelate with each other. By affecting a human mind externally, you can order his will, form it from inside, and force it to produce a wilful action.

The task of horrification is to provoke such a behavioural motive that would oppose other motives and incline the subject towards lawful behaviour. Usually, this motive is fear of the unfavourable consequences of misbehaviour. But one can only discuss this in regard to crimes preceded by some kind of estimation, an assessment of all pros and cons, i.e. a duel of motives. Therefore, K. A. Sych is completely right in stating that "for fear to have the meaning of a truly-efficient motive capable of changing human behaviour, deterring him from a socially-harmful deed, there must be a real category constantly affecting the mind of the individual".[60] Degree of horrification impact depends on the level of the social and moral neglect of the subject. Undoubtedly, the more neglected the individual is in this respect, the less socialised he is, the more difficult it is to affect him with the threat of punishment. Better educated and more moral citizens can be as efficiently impacted by lenient punishments as another country's citizens notable for their savageness, ignorance and barbarism would be impacted by severe punishments.

It should be especially noted that the threat of punishment affects human psychology. Therefore, if psychologists were interested in the influence of

60   Sych, K. A. Op. cit, pp 16–17.

the threat of punishment on humans, it would lead to important practical and theoretical results. Here, we speak of learning the psychological relationship of the 'human threat of punishment' system. For only in such a manner can psychological attitude towards this threat be understood. This issue requires a brief detour into the psychology that studies relationships and the work of human mental activity. Originally, psychology developed as an integral part of philosophy, and it was only in the mid-nineteenth century that it evolved into a separate science.

V. P. Tugarinov noted: "Philosophy is a result, a generalisation of all the previous advancement of science and practice. This fact makes philosophy the theoretical basis, the ideological framework for all the social sciences."[61] Philosophy helps to solve a number of important issues, including issues about the nature and levels of the mental, as well as the concepts of person and identity. We regret to report that the law nowadays does not fully use the results of these studies in relation to the field of investigating the causes of human criminal behaviour.

With regard to the study of the issues of the mental impact of punishment on a person and the mechanism of threat perception by an individual, as well as the deterrent role of punishment, they have almost never been subject to scientific review. It should be noted that studies in the field of legal psychology over the past thirty years have had a broad range. We know that nowadays such legal psychology areas as forensic psychology, the psychological basis of preliminary investigation, the psychology of judicial activity and correctional labour psychology are explored deeply enough. It seems that by means of general psychology, together with criminal law, it is necessary to research and develop scientific criteria and methods of the 'person–threat of punishment' system. This will help the legislator to formulate evidence-based guidelines in setting criminal and legal sanctions.

Certainly, punishment does not stop all criminals from committing crimes, just as medicine does not cure all patients. We have no doubt that solely and independently of the existence of punishment, the person is capable of finding the right solution to the current legal situation, because even with no reference to criminal law, people can distinguish the legitimate and lawful from the illegitimate and unlawful. But we also have no doubt that the individual often does not commit crimes because of the existence of criminal penalties. The *effectiveness* of the deterrent properties of punishment

61 Tugarinov, V. P. *The Laws of the Objective World, Their Knowledge and Application.* Leningrad, 1954, p98.

has always been a matter of dispute among progressive thinkers of all times, i.e. lawyers, philosophers, psychiatrists, writers and so on. In recent years, many works have been published on the effectiveness of criminal punishment. Despite the fact that the authors express a variety of views on this issue, eventually they all agree upon following the 'Goal–Result' formula in order to determine effectiveness.

We also believe that it is reasonable to determine the degree of implementation and efficiency of punishment by comparing the goal and the achieved result. Of course, it should be borne in mind that between the *goal* set by society (a systematic decrease in the state of criminality in general, its grievous and extremely grievous kinds in particular) and the actual *result* there is quite a considerable distance which should be overcome. Herewith, a set of interrelated circumstances affecting the efficiency of achievement may occur. The complexity of determining the utility of punishment is also associated with the indefinite and uncertain goal in contrast to the result, which is freely and accurately expressed in numerical terms.

In other words, if the result of achievement may be 'materialised' or 'objectified' by introducing appropriate indicators that give it a quantitative and qualitative certainty, then in relation to the *goal* this cannot be done. Therefore, in order to measure the goal's value, it is necessary to find the ratio of the measured value to a different uniform value taken as a unit of measurement. In other words, in order to carry out the measuring procedure, it is necessary first of all to carry out their comparative analysis, i.e. firstly, to find an immediate evaluation standard, and secondly, to express in single units of measurement both the goal and the results. Therefore, in order to measure, at least approximately, the effectiveness of punishment, it is necessary to express the preliminary goal set by society and the results in the corresponding units of measurement, for which a system of indicators must be developed. For example, in order to determine the effectiveness of the life imprisonment that replaced the death penalty, we can conduct a comparative analysis of the indicators of the level of crimes for which this punishment is imposed in accordance with applicable law. If the level of this category of crime grows systemically, it can be assumed that the death penalty was more effective than its substitute.

This same method can be used in determining the effectiveness of imprisonment in the event of a change of its boundaries, i.e. by increasing or decreasing its limits. Therefore, measurement of the effectiveness of punishment by numeric indicators is impossible. They can be based on the relative values of low, medium, maximum; worst, average, best; small, medium, large. We propose distinguishing four relative stages of the effectiveness of criminal penalties depending on the existing criminality result: high effectiveness, average effectiveness, poor effectiveness, inefficient (zero effectiveness).[62]

Unfortunately, the level, nature and dynamics of crime over the past twenty years show the poor effectiveness of criminal punishment in achieving social goals. It is understood that the effectiveness of punishment cannot be narrowed down to the actually occurring desired results, because it is hard to imagine a situation where the goal and the results would fully coincide. However, it would be better if the result moved towards the desired goal, i.e. to the level of high efficiency, not to zero effectiveness. It should also be noted that the results of punishment may not be achieved, not because of the fact that it is ineffective but because of the fact that it is poorly implemented—for example, because of the failure to ensure the principle of the inevitability of punishment.

The goal, for which the criminal penalty is applied, is aimed towards the future. This is why many issues of the effectiveness of punishment nowadays are directly related to its prognostic essence. Consequently, there is no doubt that the future of punishment is associated with the use of prediction in the doctrine of punishment and its practical application in legislative and judicial activities, as well as in the process of execution of the sentence.

To a large extent, the effectiveness of the deterrent effects of punishment and the overall achievement of the goal of crime prevention depend on the prediction of its future results. Therein lies the problem, because we face the prediction, i.e. the foresight of the future results of punishment at the decision point, starting with the adoption of criminal law sanctions and ending with the execution of the judgment. Therefore, without scientific prediction, it is almost impossible to remove the obstacles that prevent the increase in effectiveness of criminal penalties. And this means that lack of efficiency is the result of the non-usage of scientific achievements in forecasting in the process of criminal law-making, in judicial activity on fixing sentence and in executing the judgment.

Having considered the essence, substance and properties of punishment, one can give it the following philosophical definition. Punishment is a

---

62   For details see: Ragimov, I. M. *Criminality and Punishment*, Moscow, 2012.

specific executive medium for deterring people from committing crimes. The essence of punishment is retribution, its substance is penalty and its properties are prevention and horrification.

*

3

The Right of Punishment

The time came when the state took control over the right of punishment. But how and for what reason did it become the body carrying out the functions that once belonged to the community and to the individual? Who gave that right to the state? Although these philosophical questions have long existed, they still remain a matter of interest and controversy. As Golik points out: "The correct answer to the question of the right of the state to punish will facilitate understanding of the role of the state in a modern, rapidly-changing world, the role and importance of criminal justice and criminal prevention; it will construct a system of punishments to be accepted by everybody and, most importantly, it will work."[1]

The right of punishment also entails the right to define the goals which the subject of this law is going to achieve through punishment. Therefore, these issues are not purely philosophical but also practical, because the definition of criminal policy depends on their solution. The philosophical issue of the right of the state to punish was once the focus of philosophers, religious representatives as well as many thinkers. However, nowadays this topic is not the subject of serious discussion and research. Golik explains this situation as follows: "The right has grown into an obligation. That is why the search for the grounds of the right of punishment has terminated."[2]

So does the right to punish originate in religion, morality or simply in the public interest? The theory of the divine origin of the right of punishment seeks the grounds for the right of punishment not in the origin of morality, in the public interest, in retaliation nor in the attributes of a particular

1 Golik, Y. V. 'Philosophy of Criminal Law: Modern Formulation of the Problem', *Philosophy of Criminal Law*, Saint Petersburg, 2004, p21.
2 Ibid, p50.

individual, but in the conditions of the emergence of human communication, in the laws of the universe, that is, in religion. The essence of the argument lies in the following: God himself, with the creation of the world, took the trouble to manage all the affairs of physical life, spiritual life, in politics and in religion; He alone made people the way they are now; He is their legislator, teacher, their lord and judge.

Representatives of theories of the divine origin of the right of punishment argue that the right of vengeance, belonging to God, may at the same time be delegated to spiritual and social rulers. The latter are vested with the obligation to punish. Thus, it appears that the right to punish belongs only to God and that without His powers nobody, not even society, has the right to make an attempt on the life of a person and his freedom. It should be noted that the canonists in the Middle Ages, referring to the Holy Scriptures, as well as to the considered theory, could carry out indescribable cruelty, execution and torture with the help of punishment in order to achieve their goals.

Logically, the right to punish belongs to the subject that established the rules of behaviour and determined what behaviour should be deemed correct and what, on the contrary, should be deemed illegal, i.e. criminal. Therefore, in order to prove that the right of punishment belongs to God, first of all it is necessary to take a look at the divine messages which are also considered legislative acts. If they stipulate what constitutes a crime and what punishment shall follow it, then surely it is God as a subject of law who has the right of punishment on the basis of these Scriptures.

Let us start with the Christian doctrine of crime and punishment. The fact that this religion, like all others, provides a certain pattern of behaviour is indisputable, though it is not of a public nature, it cannot represent the state or address its dogmas to the whole society as mandatory. This is why Christianity cannot be considered as a means of regulating social relations. This is also why Christianity as a norm of behaviour is related to a specific person, who accepts this doctrine that reflects his attitude toward other people. Among the religious sources of historical importance should be distinguished the Law of Moses, which is the law passed on to the Jewish people by God through Moses.

The Law of Moses is a systemic formation, the key element of which lies in the Ten Commandments of God. It is written that Moses received the text of the Covenant from God on Mount Sinai (Ex. 20: 1–17) and declared it to his people together with the laws (Ex. 21: 1–36; 22: 1–31; 23: 1–33). Both the Covenant and the laws were in the form of a contract, hence in the form of a legally significant act. We can therefore assume two positions: the author of the legislation is not only God but also the Jewish people, or the subject of the first act is only God and Moses acts as an intermediary in relations between the Jewish people and God. We shall proceed from the fact that Old Testament law comes from God and is therefore regarded as divine right. Undoubtedly, the Law of Moses has a number of parameters characteristic of criminal law. The most important of these are the definitions of crime, the determinations regarding guilt, punishment and the circumstances precluding responsibility. For example, the law provides a detailed description of the signs of homicide with forensic and evidential significance. Punishment is an integral component of the Law of Moses; it is sanctified by God and taken by the Jewish people for granted. So, it was originally established by God as a means of influencing the human being created by him.

So there was the Law of Moses which was related to only one nation, the Jewish nation. The author of this legal act was God. Therefore, before that historical time, so long as this law had not lost its legal (but not spiritual) power, the right of punishment belonged to God. It is clear that God does not carry out punishment by himself, at least in this life. In a certain period of historical time, this task was performed by the Church on behalf of and at the behest of the Almighty, in strict accordance with the standards set forth by the Founder and his immediate disciples. As the visible head of the Catholic Church, the visible Vicar of Christ on Earth, the Pope duly castigates for crime in the form of retaliation in the sense in which God carried out this retaliation toward Himself saying, "Vengeance is mine, I will repay!" Unlike the Catholic Church, the Orthodox Church, not having any other head except the invisible Christ, cannot pass vengeance for the crime into the hands of any visible government in the form of satisfaction of divine justice, reserving this vengeance to the immediate judgment of God.

Unlike the Law of Moses, which ceased to act as a legal means but continues to act in a spiritual way, the Quran as the law sent by Allah for Muslims is valid for many people up to now. After the divine revelation, the Arabs began to obey the Quran. This meant that they have to do as Allah orders; otherwise they can expect severe punishment. However, in real life, people met circumstances that put them in difficult and hopeless situations, i.e. the Quran 'kept silent' and they did not know how to act in such situations. Yet, unlike the Law of Moses, the law sent to the Prophet Muhammad regulates criminal and legal relationships more specifically and actively. In such situations, the Sunnah served as the basis of human behaviour and their responsibility. The Arabic word, *al-sunnah*, has many meanings, such as customs, temper, traditions and lifestyle.

In this respect, one can argue with Oppenheimer, who claimed that "the grounds of Muslim criminal law laid down in the Quran are extremely scarce and scholars do not agree with each other on the interpretation of the few texts relating to this subject."[3] Firstly, the Quran is a message to humanity transferred by the Prophet Muhammad, not the product of human creativity. Secondly, as was unanimously confirmed by modern scholars, the Quran very clearly states what Allah considers a crime and what kind of punishment he demands for it. Unlike the Quran containing the message of Allah to Muhammad, the Sunnah is a collection of *adats*, traditions associated with the actions and words of the Prophet himself. The Sunnah was the addition to the Quran in the field of criminal law and was applied when in the Quran there was no specific reference to the resolution of certain incidents of legal life. The Sunnah included messages about the Prophet's companions and followers. Figuratively, one can say about the importance of the Sunnah: "To follow the Sunnah means to imitate Muhammad."

The Prophet Muhammad in the name of Allah addressed some basic rules of conduct, standards and punishments to Muslim believers. Another part of the legally relevant standards was developed as a result of the life and work of Muhammad. After Muhammad's death, his rulemaking work was continued by his closest supporters, the righteous caliphs Abu Bakr, Umar, Uthman and Ali. Based on the Quran and the Sunnah, they set new rules of conduct, appropriate, in their view, to the will of Allah and the Prophet Muhammad. In the case of non-responsiveness to emerging issues from the field of crime and punishment, criminal law standards were established by the joint discretion of caliphs or solely by each caliph, as the Prophet recommended.

So, in the seventh–eighth centuries, the Quran, the Sunnah and the statements of the Prophet's companions were the sources of Islamic criminal law. This means that the right of punishment by that time belonged to Allah as the author of the Quran, to the Prophet Muhammad as the author of additions to the Message of Allah in the field of criminal law, and to the Companions of the Prophet. Actually, one should agree with the statement that Muhammad did not try to create some kind of law in the strict sense; he taught people how to act in all life situations, how to react to this or the other event, fact, action and so on.

It should be emphasized that it was only in the eighth century that Muslim jurists managed to separate the criminal and legal provisions from the religious, in other words they developed Islamic law, including criminal, trying to justify the decisions arising from the Quran or the Sunnah. However, there are many examples where it is confirmed that the religious and criminal

---

3   Oppenheimer, H. *Historical Research on the Origin of Punishment*, Moscow, 2012, p47.

law regulating similar relationships formed on its basis could not fully match the content of their documented rules of conduct. So, for homicide and bodily injury, the Quran essentially allows blood vengeance and punishment in accordance with the principle of retaliation. Islamic criminal law, rejecting the application of the principles of the Quran regarding punishment, insists on the payment of bond and only in extreme cases allows for the death penalty. Beginning in the ninth–tenth centuries, the role of Islamic law gradually shifted to the doctrine that has developed the large majority of criminal law standards of Islamic law.

The first step towards the emergence of Muslim legal doctrine was 'heaven', a relatively free discretion, which was used in the interpretation of the Quran and the Sunnah, and the formation of new rules of conduct in case of the silence of these sources. However, by the end of the tenth century, Muslim judges lost their right to make decisions on their own in the absence of criminal law standards in the Quran, the Sunnah and other relevant sources. It was necessary to be guided by the doctrine adopted by the national population. By the thirteenth century, Islamic criminal law almost lost its integrity and became a half-doctrine law divided into different branches.

Thus, by the end of the fifteenth century, Islamic criminal law in the form of doctrine (conclusions of the major representatives of the major sects) was the leading source establishing a system of punishment for crimes and regulating the procedure for its application. With the formation of the Ottoman Empire, the expanding legislative practice of the rulers significantly influenced this branch of law. The rulers made laws on matters not covered by the Quran or the Sunnah. Publication of legal acts on criminal matters took place with almost all the Ottoman sultans, but only Mehmed the Conqueror systematised them and put them in place in the form of two consolidated laws, the *Kanun-name*, the second of which contained an extensive section on criminal penalties.

From the second half of the nineteenth century, major changes took place in the position of Islamic criminal law, primarily due to the fact that in the legal systems of the most developed Muslim countries, it was gradually ceding its leading place to legislation based on West European examples. In particular, in 1840, a Criminal Code was published which took French legislation as its basis. The code was applied to almost all Arab countries forming part of the Ottoman Empire. However, with the collapse of the empire after the defeat of Turkey in the First World War, some of these adopted new criminal legislation, also based on European models.

By the mid-twentieth century, the most developed Arab countries adopted criminal legislation which focused on bourgeois examples and replaced

Islamic tort law as the primary source in solving criminal cases. In Saudi Arabia, there is still no unified penal code. In Yemen, criminal law is not codified either. The Islamisation of criminal law is most pronounced in Pakistan, Iran and Sudan, while the legislation of Morocco, Jordan and Pakistan still stipulates criminal liability for Muslims for failing to fast during Ramadan. Special Muslim courts in Iran, established to deal with so-called moral degradation, may apply penalties for neglecting Muslim traditions in terms of attire or violating Sharia norms of social behaviour.

So, the right to punish belongs to the state, as it determines the rules of conduct for the members of society. But how did the state obtain this right? The right of punishment belongs to the state out of necessity. Manouvrier writes: "I think that the right of punishment is none other than the need for punishment. Society should strive if not to destroy, then to reduce this need. Until then, the word 'punishment' should express nothing but a concept of useful and necessary reaction to those acts that are harmful to overall well-being and social progress."[4]

According to N. D. Sergievskiy, "'the state has the right of punishment on the grounds that it cannot exist without criminal justice. Legal justification of the right of punishment for criminal jurisprudence is as follows: if there is law and order, then *eo ipso* criminal justice has to exist."[5] Y. V. Golik, just as Foinitskiy, believes that the right of punishment owned by the state is its duty, from whose exercise it cannot abstain.[6] A. Frank answers the question of who owned the right of punishment prior to the state and how this right was passed to the state as follows: "Should we not think that the right of punishment, taken in and of itself, in principle, abstracted from all historical reasons that forced its wresting from the individual and assignment to society, is nothing but the right of vengeance? . . . The right of punishment exists everywhere, where the obligation to obey is assumed and where the obligation to obey, in turn, implies the right of coercion and punishment."[7]

Currently, in all civilised countries, regardless of their political organisation, the supreme state power is the specific carrier of public criminal law. Therefore, the issue is not whether evil deserves punishment, as this is obvious, but how can society punish and to what extent, in what area and for what is society entrusted with this right?

4   Manouvrier. Op. cit, p116.
5   Sergievskiy, N. D. 'Russian Criminal Law', *Philosophy of Criminal Law*, Saint Petersburg, 2004, p231.
6   Foinitskiy, I. Y. *The Doctrine of Punishment in Connection with Prison Study*, Ibid, p305; Golik, Y. V. *Philosophy of Criminal Law: Modern Formulation of the Problem*, Ibid, p50.
7   Frank, A. Op. cit, p116.

In the period of the family and tribal life of nations, the right to punish children, sometimes wives, for crimes and misdemeanours committed within the family, belonged to the head of the family or tribe. In fact, there was no community that did not have its binding rules and did not support itself using coercive measures, nor is there any. The leaders of tribes, clans, and unions were initially not only legislators but also judges and executors of their own judgment. The right of punishment belonged only to them. In place of the clan and its members, the government gradually began acting in the progressively-developing state as a reactionary factor against illegal, or more precisely, malicious actions in the course of historical development. It took over the duty of the protector of the inner world commanded by it from all sorts of violations. Solely to it belonged the right to ban known acts and omissions under penalty, as well as the right of appointment and execution of punishment. Thus, the right of punishment passed from the leaders of tribes, clans and unions to the state, because all members of society waived it in favour of that authority.

However, this does not mean that the state has occurred or formed as a result of the arbitrariness of people. Moral necessity lies within its structure. People, by nature, are forced to live in the state as, in order to provide for human wellbeing, development and cultural growth, the jointly-organised life of people called community life is necessary; it is unthinkable without legal order. And legal order can only exist in a state that has been granted the right to stop those who violate its laws, i.e. society has entrusted the state to protect it with the appropriate tools against illegal acts. We are talking about such remedies as criminal penalties. Therefore, it can be stated that the natural beginning as the basic principle of the right of punishment stems from the need to protect both the social organism and its separate individual. The right of punishment owned by the state is its responsibility, duty to the individual members of society, as well as to the whole society. On the other hand, any violation of the established legal standards causes a reaction not only on the part of public opinion, but also by the state exerting its power to protect any law proceeding from the public authorities. Thus, the right of punishment belonging to the state on the basis of the social contract is as undeniable as the right of punishment belonging to the head of the family, with the only difference that the former may not have the same goal as the latter.[8]

In the hands of the state, punishment becomes a means of protecting public order and preventing crime through coercion and intimidation. It should be specifically emphasized that we are not talking about granting to the state the right to take revenge on the offender for his actions, but about

8   See: Ibid.

the fact that the punishment represents the same moral necessity. That sense of recompense (not revenge) requires the existence and application of criminal penalty without which the state cannot exist. This is why punishment is lawful and fair. For the sake of eliminating lynching, lawlessness and revenge, society, represented by the state, assumes the obligation to punish the criminal, since this is required by the person who suffered from the evil, became the object of violence or offence, lost his property and so on. Finally, in order to make sure whether the punishment is necessary or not, whether it is useful or useless in today's society, it is enough to imagine what would happen the next day after the announcement of the abolition of criminal penalties for criminal behaviour. Thus, according to Foinitskiy, "the right of punishment belongs solely and exclusively to the state as a subject".[9] As for the divine right of punishment, it can be used within the Holy Scriptures— the Laws.

We have not set the goal of considering in detail the theories regarding the right of the state to punish existing in literature. However, we consider it necessary to note that, according to N. D. Sergievskiy, starting with Hugo Grotius, there are up to twenty-four philosophies and around a hundred individual theories of different jurists who joined either direction.[10] Among them there are also schools of philosophers and legislators who absolutely reject the right to punish, as they deny the existence of the object of this law, that is, the moral evil. Representatives of another direction, in particular V. D. Spasovich, as a sign of denial of the right to punish, recognise the denial of free will and include in this group all determinists with theologians and materialists. There is also a school which, while not denying the right of punishment, does not recognise that this right could be used by society or any human power in general. Thus, it is concluded that the right of punishment is the area of medical art.

No one therfore has the right to punish criminals; they should be treated with a variety of tools, exercises, which gradually return to the sick body missing strength and health or correct its wrong shape distorted by the whim of nature. But are there medications for this? Prisons will be replaced by a special kind of hospitals, and justice and criminal law will be cast down from the throne in favour of a new therapeutic and hygienic system.

*

9   Foinitskiy, I. Y. *The Doctrine of Punishment in Connection with Prison Study*, p302.
10 See: Sergievskiy, N. D. *Russian Criminal Law*, Saint Petersburg, 1890, p77.

4

The Future of Punishment

Punishment and Non-Punitive Action

Recently the West has seen a spread in the idea of moving from punitive justice to restorative justice, i.e. to non-punitive punishment. In his day, Sorokin wrote: "We would not be so bold as to predict, but as history shows the gradual and accelerated extinction of punitive acts and improvement of the social psyche and human behaviour, so far there are no grounds to suggest that it would no longer take place. And if so, then, obviously, the limit of evolution, which the variable of penalties is seeking, can only be *zero*, i.e. the disappearance of penalties."[1]

In fact, the history of punishment indicates the tendency of its gradual softening. Blood vengeance is replaced by the law of retaliation, i.e. by the establishment of equality between crime and punishment. The system of bond is introduced. Nowadays, the process of abolishing the death penalty is being terminated, and so on. This is perfectly normal, since with the growth of culture, less violent ways of influencing people are required. But the nature of punishment does not change, it is a fair reward, what changes is the substance, i.e. the punitive action. What does non-punitive action mean? It is almost a destruction of the punitive substance of punishment, i.e. the rejection of suffering inflicted by punishment against the person who committed the crime.

In Oslo, Norway, two prominent criminologists lectured in front of the same group of students. In the morning, Nils Christie, member of the Norwegian Academy of Science and Letters and the Royal Swedish Academy

---

1   Sorokin. P. Op. cit, p374.

of Sciences, told the audience: "Personally, I would believe that now is the time when it is necessary to stop further advancement of the theory of general prevention, as well as to prevent further strengthening of the influence of neo-classical ideas, at least here in Scandinavia."[2]

In reply to a student's question on the reasons for such a way of thinking, Christie provided the following affirmative statement: "I do not see any serious reasons to consider the current level of inflicting pain as fairly legitimate and natural, since this issue is very important and I have to make a choice; I do not see another position that could be defended, but to fight for the reduction of pain."[3] The students realised that the academic was not a utopian, because he did not denounce criminal penalties. It is about minimising pain as much as possible, since one of his basic prerequisites is that the struggle for the reduction on Earth of the pain caused by people is a justified cause.[4]

What did Christie suggest? Firstly, to understand the essence of punishment, which he defines as inflicting 'pain', suffering, restrictions, deprivation, etc. Secondly, to solve the issue of the limits to this pain, for which self-regulatory communities should be created instead of punishment. While the lecturer did not openly express his sympathy for the theory of non-punitive action, the students grasped this nonetheless. What Christie says indeed attracts many with its humanism, since the imposed and executed sentence is a conscious deliberate infliction of pain, which, in his opinion, "stops or slows the spiritual growth of man, makes him angry".[5]

The lecture ended with these beautiful words: "One of the rules that should be followed is: one cannot inflict pain when in doubt. Another rule should be to inflict the least possible pain. *Look for an alternative to punishment rather than for an alternative punishment.*"[6]

It is clear that Christie actually rejects punishment since he doubts any fair reward due to the problem of accurately determining the correspondence between the severity of a crime and its punishment. Instead, he refers carefully to the unconditional recognition of the correct return to the concept of general prevention. At the same time, instead of punishment, he offers nothing specific—the main thing is to cause as little 'pain' as possible. He therefore sees the essence of punishment in the inflicting of pain against the criminal, i.e. in misery, deprivation and so on. This means that the

2   Christie, N. *Inflicting Pain. The Role of Punishment in Criminal Policy*, Saint Petersburg, 2011, p47.
3   Ibid, p20.
4   Ibid.
5   Ibid.
6   Christie, N. Op. cit, p21.

reduction of pain indicates the variability of the nature of punishment, while the essence of the phenomenon does not change. However, the substance of punishment, i.e. its punitive side, is changeable as evidenced by the history of the doctrine of punishment. Christie writes: "My position . . . can briefly be summarised by saying that social systems should be built in such a way as to minimise the need for causing pain for the purposes of social control. It is sorrow that is inevitable but not the hell created by people."[7] But can this be achieved? Where is the limit to this pain? Non-punitive action is compared with somatic medicine and is seen as a blessing. Treatment, and according-ly, non-punitive action in the criminal justice system, are meant to improve human health. There is a noble goal: to return social health to the person, to cure him of crime.[8] Non-punitive action as the 'treatment of crime' has lost its credibility, even though non-punitive action as assistance has proved its worth. This is recognised by Christie himself. At the same time, he is deeply convinced that "the welfare state in the future will be able to provide more effective assistance to those who make it difficult and troublesome to the community without resorting to the use of prisons".[9]

The theory of non-punitive action, in fact, is a denial of punishment as deterrence, i.e. it is directed only at the identity of the criminal and not at potential criminals. On the other hand, this theory leads to hidden punish-ment, to the secret infliction of pain under the guise of the proposed treat-ment. The infliction of pain could be permitted by the theory of non-puni-tive action, but only as a link in the chain of events which eventually had to improve the fate of the one suffering. How should this theory be approached in a practical way? It can be done by discarding prisons, places of detention and other suffering or by reducing to a minimum the pain of those suffering, limitations, and so on. How, then, should we achieve deterrence and warn-ing against committing crimes? Christie notes: "The debate on the general warning is a discussion not of how directly pain is impactful but mainly of how A is influenced by the fact that B was subjected to punishment."[10] It is clear that punishment is the deliberate infliction of suffering and hardship, not a treatment for their illnesses. And pain is inflicted as vengeance for com-mitted acts, as well as in the interests of others. Another case is regulation of the infliction of pain, which becomes a more important issue and should be the focus of the public and science.

Plato spoke about the importance and usefulness of punishment for the

7   Ibid.
8   Ibid, p41.
9   Ibid, p130.
10   Ibid, p36.

prevention of criminal manifestations in his *Laws*: "If the legislator notices that the person cannot be cured, he sentences him and sets another law. The legislator is aware that for those people themselves it is better to cease to exist by losing their lives; thus, they would bring a double benefit to all other people: they would serve as an example to others in the sense that one should not act unjustly, and besides, it would save the state of the presence of evil men."[11] The *Naradiya Dharmasastra* states that "no one stays on the right track if there is no punishment".[12] And in the Laws of Manu, punishment is given special attention and its exceptional role is emphasized: "Punishment rules over everybody, punishment protects, punishment is awake when everyone is asleep; the wise declared punishment the embodiment of Dharma . . . If the king did not tirelessly impose punishment against the ones deserving of it, the stronger would have roasted the weak like fish on a spit."[13]

Later that day in Oslo, in the same auditorium and in front of the same audience, Johannes Andenaes, prominent in the same field of law as Christie and president of the Norwegian Academy of Science and Letters, delivered a lecture on the merits and necessity of the theory of general prevention. He began with the fact that the idea of non-punitive action applied to the criminal instead of his punishment was a noble thought that has had a strong influence on legislators in many countries. "However, in the long history of crime and punishment, the dominance of the concept of non-punitive action is presented as an interlude of less than one hundred years. This does not mean that efforts to rehabilitate criminals should be abandoned, but they should be undertaken within the framework of a just punishment. The original purpose of punishment is not the change of the criminal's personality but the assertion of social norms. And it means a general warning."[14]

When a student posed Andenaes with the question, "What do you mean by the term 'general warning?' ", the reply came: "The ability of criminal law and its application to provide for the law-abiding behaviour of citizens."[15] Therefore, the simplest way to make people more law-abiding is to strengthen punishment. When legislators and courts try to restrain significant growth in the crime rate, they usually reinforce the severity of punishment.[16]

Around the same time, students of the law school at Saint Petersburg

11   See: Plato. *Laws*, p350.
12   See: *Naradiya Dharmasastra*, translated with commentary by A. A. Vigasin & A. M. Samozvantsev, Moscow, 1998, p62.
13   'Laws of Manu' (vii, 18, 20), *Anthology on the History of the State and Law of Foreign Countries*, 2 vols, ex. ed. N. A. Krasheninnikova, vol. 1, Moscow, 1999, p105.
14   Andenaes, J. *Punishment and Prevention of Crime*, p18.
15   Ibid, p29.
16   Ibid, p261.

University were attending a lecture by D. A. Shestakov on the same subject, where he stressed that by the end of the twentieth century, the institution of criminal punishment as a regulatory tool of mass human behaviour acquired critical evaluation. As a result, criminology in the twenty-first century should pay heed to the prospect of non-punitive sanctions by including them in the context of the individual prevention of crime,[17] and so future punishment is viewed by the science of criminal law and criminology in two directions: the transition from criminal penalties to non-punitive action, or the improvement of punishment as a means of preventing crime in modern conditions.

Looking at non-punitive action, the fact of the ineffectiveness of criminal punishment has brought into question its future in the fight against criminality starting with Lombroso, who, drawing on anthropology, criminal statistics, criminal law and the study of prisons, proposed abandoning punishment as a useless means and replacing it with other measures. But what is offered in return for deterrence or punishment?

The doctrine of the criminal anthropology school, in recognising the biological properties of crime, proposed replacing criminal penalties with 'security measures' and the criminal sociological direction with 'social protection measures'. This replacement was reduced to finding a universal means of overcoming criminality as a sociopsychological phenomenon by psychomedical and social impact on the mind of the criminal. Thus, A. Prince tried to theoretically justify the need for the replacement of criminal punishment with measures of social protection which in his opinion have a fundamental feature.

Due to the fact that, at the present time, the theory of criminal punishment more and more insistently recalls the idea of social protection, there is a necessity and a practical need for differentiation between the institution of punishment and social protection measures. As we know, the concept of social protection measures traces a long history, but up till today neither the nature of their relationship to punishment nor their volume have been established. Again, views on the nature of social protection measures existing in literature can be reduced to two directions: recognition of the fundamental difference between punishment and social protection measures, or the denial of it. Considering the external expression of this institution and recognising its substance, we understand that social protection measures are a completely independent institution that occupies a special place among other forms of criminality. In contrast to punishment, the application of measures of social protection is not caused by the need to assess a previously

17   See: *Criminology of the Twentieth Century*, Saint Petersburg, 2000, pp 5, 12.

committed crime but only by the need to prevent the committing of a new crime on the part of the person against whom they are applied. This is followed by the fact that a purely preventive nature is inherent in this institution. Therefore, it can be stated that the concept of punishment is a narrower concept in the sense that social protection measures represent a wide range of opportunities to achieve this goal.

Gogel identified punishment with repression, the source of which is undoubtedly revenge: "With the emergence and development of the state in the modern sense of the word, revenge in the form of repression passed into the hands of public authorities . . . Repression, the performance of which was the responsibility of the state, was totally powerless in the fight against criminality and little by little it was recognised, although not definitively, as unserviceable in the fight against criminality."[18] It appears to be erroneous both from the legal and sociopolitical perspective to equate repression with punishment. Repression is solely a political event caused by the state and it has no direct relation to justice. At the same time, even the most severe criminal penalties applied in the fight against criminality cannot be called repressive if there are no political goals. Thus rejecting punishment, Gogel offers a transition from repression to prevention: "In favour of the possibility of such a transition and, moreover, a complete one, from repression to prevention, are found the following considerations. Committing a crime in most cases is not an accident in the life of an individual, but the result, the completion of a slow and gradual process of economic, physical and moral weakening."[19] Dril in his day was arguing along the same lines: "The results of a careful study of the phenomena of live reality loudly object to the use of repressive measures meant to inflict pain and suffering in the fight against the bred criminal bequeathed to us from antiquity."[20]

As we see, there is no major difference between the concept of social protection and prevention, because in both cases we are talking about crime prevention not by means of punishment but by non-punitive impact on the causes and source of criminality. In 1945, in Genoa, the followers of the concept of social protection at the initiative of the Italian lawyer Filippo Gramatica founded the Centre for Social Protection while the Frenchman Marcel Ancel arranged a 'new social protection' trend. Gramatica's ideas are a new, modern version of the Italian positivist school that was developed

18   Gogel, S. K. *The Course of Criminal Policy in Connection with Criminal Sociology*, Moscow, 2010, p142.
19   Ibid, p139.
20   Dril, D. *Crime and Criminals: The Doctrine of Crime and Measures to Combat It*, p158.

through the works of Garofalo and Ferri. Gramatica denied the right of the state to punish criminals while Ancel proceeded from the fact that against criminals should be used only humane enforcement measures in order to correct and re-educate them. Thus, the proponents of the new movement of social protection acknowledge the concept of sociologists on social protection and agree with their rejection of the classical understanding of punishment as a liability for fault. Meanwhile, in contrast to the sociological school's supporters, the representatives of the new direction are trying to find a balance between society and the individual, accusing the classical and the neo-classical that they believe that punishment is the only possible and fair kind of reaction by the state. A. A. Piontkovskiy vigorously refuted the theory of the 'new social protection', seeing in it excessive subjectivisation and psychologisation of the institute of punishment.[21]

One idea today is that "criminology of the twenty-first century should pay attention to the prospect of non-punitive sanctions by including them in the context of individual crime prevention."[22] But what is this non-punitive action that has recently become such a fashionable subject in criminal law and criminology? For some, it means to engage psychiatrists, doctors and other professionals in order to restore the personality of the offender, rather than punitive methods. Others suggest including the methods used during the execution of punishment in prison. The most radical reformers proceed from the fact that the system of non-punitive action was founded upon the principles of personality restoration—where possible, of course. Otherwise, a person must be isolated until restored in order to deprive them of the opportunity to commit a new crime. This means that people found guilty of the same crimes should be sentenced to various corrective actions in the name of rehabilitation, and punished not for the act but in connection with the terms of its commission.

In other words, the idea to punish not for an act, but in connection with the terms of its commission, varying the penalties in accordance with the alleged hazardous features of the criminal's personality, eventually gave birth to the theory and practice of non-punitive action. This system is based solely on the principles of restoration of the criminal's personality and, if this is impossible, his isolation as long as it is necessary to prevent him from reoffending. In order to do this, some representatives of this theory propose engaging psychiatrists and psychologists in order to restore the mind of the perpetrator.

21 Piontkovskiy, A. A. 'On the Theory of the "New Social Protection" in Criminal Law', *The Soviet State and the Law*, 1968, no. 4, p14.
22 *Criminology of the Twentieth Century*, p12.

In fact, non-punitive action when applied to the criminal and measures to restore his personality, as compared to criminal penalties with a long and often 'dark' history, seems enlightened, humane and modern. This is why some see the future issue as replacing punishment with corrective measures without punishment elements.

Therefore, non-punitive action is seen as noble and humane, because it has a single goal: to return social health to individuals, to cure them of crime. Now in order to treat and cure a disease it is necessary first to know its cause, and yet still have we failed to determine with any exactitude the cause of criminal human behaviour. Additionally, even if that cause lies within man himself aside from any external factors, then it is important to identify that specific source hiding within such a complex biological organism. As to whether such identification is possible, science is still searching for the answer.

The idea of non-punitive action has another advantage. The fact is that not only theoretically but also practically crime prevention through criminal punishment is a more complicated process in terms of determining its effectiveness than non-punitive action because it is, in this case, about a specific object. The proponents of non-punitive action tend to argue that experience teaches us that punishment has precisely the opposite effect on the criminal, since it is characterised by a tendency to demoralise the convict. It often puts him in a class of social outcasts. Perhaps the process of punishment enforcement actually has a negative effect on a certain portion of convicts, which ultimately leads to relapse. However, the positive role of punishment is to prevent others from committing crimes, that is, prevention through a frightening and preventive impact.

It would seem that attempts made with the best intentions to replace punishment with non-punitive measures may cause uncertainty and arbitrariness. It should also be remembered that ethically the concept of non-punitive action breaks with traditional notions of justice, good and evil, proportionality of guilt and responsibility and so on that have existed for thousands of years.[23] Christie, as one of the best modern representatives of this theory, notes that "the theory of non-punitive action removed issues of a valuable nature extremely successfully. Based on an analogy with somatic medicine, non-punitive action was perceived as an obvious benefit. Treatment and, therefore, non-punitive action in the criminal justice system was meant to improve the health status of the customer. Therefore, it was inappropriate to ask whether non-punitive action causes suffering."[24]

---

23   Nikiforov, B. S. 'Introduction', in J. Andenaes, *Punishment and Prevention of Crime*, p9.
24   Christie, N. *Limits to Pain*, Moscow, 1985, p45.

K. A. Sych rightly adds: "The concept of non-punitive action is, in our opinion, an example of the continuation of the development of positivist ideas in the form of the doctrine of the 'innate criminal type' (Lombroso), the concept of 'dangerous condition' and the 'criminal as a sick person' to be treated (Ferri, Garofalo)."[25]

Thus, the essence of the theory of social protection, the concept of prevention and ideas of non-punitive action, except for some fundamental differences, lies, as we have seen, in denial or disbelief in punishment as a means of combating criminality. It seems that we can talk not about replacing punishment with some other measures, but about the improvement of its efficiency, as well as about the parallel existence of various measures to combat criminality. Without a doubt, it is theoretically possible that there may come a "time when punishment loses its intensity to such an extent that the need would arise to introduce new terminology".[26] However, by abandoning intimidation, the causing of evil and suffering, it would be logical to give up punishment, which is currently not a defamatory phenomenon; on the contrary, it is considered an inevitable and necessary consequence of a certain profession.

Speaking of punishment, absolutely normal and natural arguments are often set up: mankind has tried all means of repression, including the qualified types of the death penalty and refined torture, but for some reason, neither criminality nor other forms of deviant behaviour have disappeared. After all, when talking about punishment as a means of combating crime, we are not talking about some miracles, about the elimination of crime, but, mainly, about the suspension of its further growth. It should also be borne in mind that sometimes the achievement of this goal depends not only on whether it is set correctly, but also largely on the efficiency of the use of available means of achievement at our disposal. It may be, in fact, that punishment when considering its objective possibilities is a very useful tool, but we do not know how to use it to the maximum extent. We agree with Gogel, who points out that "penalties are excluded by the legislator from the ladder of penalties if they do not correspond to the views and morals of society as a result of the mitigation of these morals not admitting the further commission of cruelty and violence, whether in private or in public life."[27]

At this point I would like to ask the question whether the level of our morality and ethics and our development in general in the broadest sense corresponds to abandoning punishment and replacing it with non-punitive

25 Sych, K. A. Op. cit, p60.
26 *Criminology of the Twentieth Century*, p225.
27 Gogel, S. K. Op. cit, p129.

action. Once, in the science of criminal law of the Soviet period, there was a direction which believed that criminal policy is on the path of narrowing the scope of application of criminal penalties due to the measures of social influence and education. So, as Karpets out it: "In accordance with the improvement of public relations and with people's increasing awareness, the need for various forms of state coercion will fade away. Punishment will absorb more and more features not of punitive but of educational measures."[28]

Some authors have pointed out that the development of the process of replacing punishment with social influence measures includes as a prerequisite their gradual mitigation; that the growth of the cultural level of the workers not only leads to a decrease in crime, to the process of replacing punishment with educational measures, but also to the mitigation of measures, because more stringent measures appear to be unnecessary in an increasing number of cases.[29] According to N. A. Belyaev, "the main way of replacing punishment with measures of social influence and education is to reduce the range of criminal offences and criminality".[30] The concept of 'measures of social influence and education' in its essence is identical to the concepts of 'social protection measures' and 'non-punitive action'. The term 'social protection measures' appeared earlier than the term 'non-punitive measures'. With regard to measures of social influence and education, this term was in trend during the Soviet period and was usually used for ideological and political purposes.

Supporters of the gradual replacement of criminal punishment with measures of social influence and education, wrongly, in our opinion, believe possible the existence of punishment generally devoid of punitive elements, which is actually impossible because punishment means, above all, the presence in its substance of penalising elements. Therefore, believing that punishment should be deprived of all the elements that cause physical suffering or humiliation is absurd. Mokrinskiy wrote: "As a fact of sensitive life, criminal penalty is an act of coercion to suffering. From the moment when the state ceases to react to certain facts by causing suffering, this historical concept is bound to disappear from the legal lexicon."[31]

It seems that a change in the substance of punishment by gradually reducing to zero all its punitive elements is an almost untenable measure

28   Karpets, I. I. 'Social and Legal Aspects of the Doctrine of Punishment', *The Soviet State and the Law*, 1968, no. 5, p68.
29   See Noy, I. *Issues of the Theory of Punishment in Soviet Criminal Law*, Saratov, 1962.
30   Belyaev, N. A. *Selected Works*, Saint Petersburg, 2003, p76.
31   Mokrinskiy, S. P. *Punishment, Its Objectives and Suggestions*, p3.

which is even harmful in the present conditions; this is also evidenced by the state, structure and dynamics of criminality. We cannot speak of the gradual replacement of criminal punishment with measures of social influence and education, rather of the parallel existence of non-punitive measures with criminal penalties, which stems from a fundamental view on the historical fate of the state and law, on the role and place of coercion and persuasion in society. It should be emphasized that nowadays, the active use of measures of social influence instead of punishment without comprehensive and deep preliminary preparation may lead to undesirable consequences.

A significant role in the development of scientific thought in this area should be played by the revision of long sentences of imprisonment, as well as radical changes in the substance of the penalty. This way, we cannot accept the position which argues that "social systems should be built in such a way as to minimise the significant need for inflicting pain for the purposes of social control".[32] This approach is a denial of the common preventive impact of criminal penalty, which is known to play a significant role in preventing criminality. Without suffering, pain and hardship, which are the elements of the substance of punishment, it is hardly possible to influence people's behaviour in terms of social utility. We can only talk about the limitation of these punitive features of punishment for the perpetrators of minor crimes. However, in the short term, the possibility of limiting the role of penalties in the prevention of crime is excluded and the attention to the other measures of impact, especially to those able to influence personality not only directly, but also through changes in the socio-economic, cultural and so on conditions in which it lives and forms, is increased.

Thus, we would like to remind those who say now is the time when the further advancement of the theory of deterrence shall be stopped, that the theory of horrification is completely acceptable if it is a choice between two extremes: all or nothing. If no action is taken in response to offences, if they are not to be deterred, then, we repeat, it will undoubtedly lead to an increase in the overall criminality level. We must not forget that at the present time, the ability to effectively confront crime is not a private problem, but a problem of the survival of society in general. Nowadays, there is no need to prove that positive results in curbing crime can be achieved not only by means of rational social policy, but also by affecting the personality of the criminal.

The social control of criminality, therefore, involves fighting through

32 Christie, N. Op. cit, p12.

punishment and prevention. In this regard, I would like to make one very important clarification. When talking about deterrence, we are not talking about the use of measures of severity, but we have in mind an impact on the certain unstable part of the population by means of appropriate penalties to help them adapt to the conditions of life in society. Nevertheless, one would with great pleasure take a non-punitive action and refuse punishment, if there could be at least some kind of confidence that after this, criminality would gradually decrease. As there is no such certainty, then criminal penalties should be considered as the prevention of crimes in the nearest future as well. The truth is that actual crime figures indicate the low efficiency of the preventive effects of punishment, but at the same time, they do not answer the question of the number of people who have not committed crimes because of this particular threat.

Based on this, the legislator does not think whether to apply a punishment or not, although he knows that the threat of punishment does not work exceptionally for everybody. Therefore, it is almost impossible to isolate the fear of punishment and deterrence from the totality of the circumstances due to which the person refused to commit the crime, or to determine exactly what proportion the threat occupies in the general scope of causes.

The effect of criminal punishment cannot be numerically determined. It operates insignificantly. The reality is that for the modern legislator, the motive of prevention plays a major role when determining criminal penalties. Hence, there is no doubt that the deterrent and preventive effect of punishment increases in certain categories of crime. Out of the experience of the fight against crime in the Soviet period we can produce facts that indicate where in fact due to increasing the punishment for a particular type of crime (such as hooliganism, bribery, theft of state and public property) there was a sharp decline in its level. However, it is absolutely unacceptable to draw conclusions about the impact of punishment on crime, taking into account the cruelty of repression and conviction dynamics. In practice, there cannot be a situation in which the crime rate fluctuated only under the influence of the severity of punishment. A multivariate analysis of the circumstances having an impact on crime in the specific conditions is necessarily required.

So, talking about the future of criminal penalties and the possibility of replacing them with non-punitive measures, we support the position of Andenaes when he says: "I choose the criminal law of an open and direct punitive nature that does not try to hide behind the benevolent rhetoric of remediation and restoration of the individual, i.e. the criminal law that is based primarily on general retention and considerations of fairness, and I predict that the future belongs to it."[33] This is why we should not talk and argue about the 'crisis of punishment', but we should deeply examine and understand the mechanism of action of the threat of punishment on the person. Can we yet discover something previously unknown? Can a positive truth be restored and reinforced with new evidence? American criminologists claim that "in the end, it is not so important whether punishment works or not, because it is falling out of use".[34] Why? Because punishment is becoming less compatible with the prevailing morality, as they believe. "And one can imagine a time when punishment loses its intensity to such an extent that there would arise the need to introduce new terminology."[35]

In Russia, there was a time when penalty was regarded as social protection measures. However, the state reaction to crime did not change and remained the same retaliation. The Danish Penal Code of 1954 rejected the term 'punishment' for Greenland and replaced it with the term 'measure'. The proposal to abandon the term 'punishment' was seriously discussed after the Second World War in Sweden, although the new Penal Code of 1962 retained the term 'punishment.' It seems that such views on punishment in the West express significant changes of moral evaluations, which in post-Soviet countries are associated with democratic reforms. Surely now, national legislation on the response to crime needs real reform compared with the depths of reform of the late-eighteenth to early nineteenth centuries, when humanity was freed from maiming penalties and qualified types of the death penalty.[36]

However, the attempts to invent a new term instead of 'punishment' will not change anything, and cannot be recognised as the least bit serious. In connection with this, Andenaes remarks: "I do not think there will be major changes if a progressively-adjusted legislative department of the government decides to replace the term 'punishment' with a term that sounds more neutral, such as 'sanction' or 'social measure.'"[37] What would change if we were now to agree with Christie and instead of the concept of 'punishment' we used the term 'infliction of pain' in the Penal Code? Absolutely nothing, because the essence of society's response to crime will remain unchanged. It is quite another thing if we try to put to thorough investigation the usefulness of the role of punishment in the prevention of crime and build a

33 Andenaes, J. *Punishment and Prevention of Crime*, p261.
34 Bittner & Platt. 'The Meaning of Punishment', *Issues in Criminology*, 1966. vol. 2, p79.
35 *Criminology of the Twentieth Century*, p225.
36 Shestakov, D. A. 'Introduction', *Criminology of the Twentieth Century*, p12.
37 Andenaes, J. Op. cit, p260.

renewed concept of punishment, taking into account the socio-economic, ethical and religious, national characteristics of any nation. One thing is clear: the ineffectiveness of criminal punishment in the fight against crime is becoming more obvious.

Thus, the rejection of the term 'punishment' and its replacement with another, more humane, democratic, modern name does not change anything substantially. This is evidenced by the history of the doctrine of punishment. Therefore, the future of punishment is not associated with a change in its name, but with many factors, both objective and subjective. We must proceed from the fact that the future of punishment cannot be defined outside the context of the causes of crime. Until then, until we can answer the question of the causes of human criminal behaviour, we can hardly talk about fundamental changes in the punitive nature of punishment.

Non-punitive impact on criminals will take the place of criminal penalties only if it is proven that a man commits a crime against his will, for reasons beyond his control, and that these causes can be eliminated without punitive action. The future of punishment, in terms of the degree of its punitive effect, will depend directly on the nature, dynamics, and level of criminality in the given country in general. This will lead to the emergence of new alternative forms of punishment due to the appearance of currently unknown criminal acts. The percentage of persons sentenced to imprisonment remains almost at the current level, based on the level and nature of criminality.

The future of punishment is associated with the expansion of judicial discretion, because the boundaries of the lower and upper limits will be increased, as well as with the emergence of new, alternative punishments. Short-term punishments will eventually fall out of fashion and be replaced with major penal sanctions. Some countries will once again return to the death penalty because of an increase in grievous and extremely grievous crimes. The future of punishment is also directly associated with the determination of the level of its efficiency. If it is proved that the punishment hardly gives the result that society expects from it, then there are substantial grounds to abandon it and to find other measures of influence on criminal behaviour, including those of a non-punitive nature. However, if we see that punishment brings some benefit, then we should look for ways to improve it. In fact, the future of punishment does not exclude, along with punishment, the application of non-punitive methods for certain categories of crimes and criminals.

The Future of the Death Penalty

Nowadays, in almost every country, both among those keeping the death penalty and those abolishing it, acute controversy occasionally erupts. This applies to Europe, the United States and the post-Soviet states. For example, in the parliament of the United Kingdom, since the final abolition of the death penalty in 1969, proposals for its restoration have been made on a full eighteen occasions.

At the time, A. Berner wrote: "Over the past ten years, almost everywhere where the death penalty was retained, it was solemnly declared that the time for its complete elimination would come."[38] This penalty is known to exist and is actually carried out in many countries, although the number of opponents of the death penalty is much larger and their arguments are of sufficient strength. In particular, many experts who oppose the death penalty, including Beccaria, try to base their positions by bringing proof of the life and history of various nations: in order to prove the futility of the death penalty, they point to the fact that it does not make people better nor terrifies criminals, that criminality is not reduced due to the existence of the death penalty. So, for example, Berner notes: "The bloody performance of private executions completely demoralises the morals of a nation: it develops rudeness in it, drowns human compassion, provokes cruelty and blood-thirstiness."[39]

Even Nero, the true embodiment of human cruelty, when asked to sign the death sentence for a particular criminal as expected, found himself exclaiming: "I wish I did not know how to write!" So wrung his heart at the thought of condemning a man to death. At times, opponents of the death penalty cite More, saying that human life cannot be compared with all the riches of the world. However, More had in mind the uselessness of the death penalty in respect of economic crimes, and he wrote: "In my opinion, it is unfair to take human life for the withdrawal of money. I believe that human life in its value cannot be balanced against all the benefits of the world. And if they say that this punishment is not vengeance for money but for the violation of justice, for the violation of laws, then why cannot we rightly call the supreme law the supreme injustice. God has forbidden killing anyone, and we kill so easily for taking an insignificant amount of money."[40]

38 Berner, A. *On the Death Penalty*, pp 90–91.
39 Ibid, p30.
40 More, T. *Utopia*, Moscow; Leningrad, 1958, p68.

The argument in favour of abolishing the death penalty is often linked to the fact that the death penalty has occurred because of the custom of blood vengeance. Thus, S. V. Zhiltsov believes that "the objective basis of the death penalty as a criminal punishment is vengeance for killing, the principle of retaliation, equal for equal. As for any other crime, the death penalty cannot be objectively assigned."[41] This approach does appear to be erroneous, although in science there is a view that there is in fact a genetic connection between the death penalty and the custom of blood vengeance, which is characterised by features that are not inherent and cannot be characteristic of the death penalty. Blood vengeance was considered a moral duty, whose failure entailed disgrace and recognition as unworthy of one's ancestors. Therefore, in contrast to the death penalty as revenge, blood vengeance aims to maintain the authority of the clan, tribe and family. V. V. Esipov correctly believed that the death penalty cannot be derived from blood vengeance, since the latter "naturally evolved into a system of compositions, which existed long before the introduction of the death penalty".[42]

The difference between blood vengeance and the death penalty is not only that one is done at the behest of a private person and the other at the behest of the state, but lies in the fact that in the case of blood vengeance, the subject enjoys the committed offence and he commits it merely for the satisfaction of senses of pleasure and justice, both his own and those of his relatives, tribe, clan and so on. In the case of the death penalty, this component is missing. However, we can talk only about satisfying the sense of justice of society members, including relatives of the victim. In addition, blood vengeance did not require any mandatory proportionality between harm and revenge. The offences could even be paid off. If the subject of the death penalty was directly the criminal, the object of revenge could not only be the offender, but also any other member of the clan, tribe, family and so on. Thus, the sources of blood vengeance are national customs and traditions, and of the death penalty are the protection of public and private interests.

The main argument of supporters of the immediate abolition of the death penalty has always boiled down to the fact that this punishment has no warning value. Tarde believes that the strongest argument against this punishment lies not in arguments for it uselessness to society, but in the moral and aesthetic revulsion that it causes: "I have tried to overcome a sense of horror of the death penalty and could not."[43] To say that people are not

41   Zhiltsov, S. V. Op. cit, p7.
42   Esipov, V. V. *Crime and Punishment in Ancient Law*, Warsaw, 1903, p42.
43   Tarde, G. D. Op. cit.

afraid of death means to lie, to rebel against nature, to declare the sheerest nonsense. Kistyakovskiy rightly notes that "nothing is clearer, simpler and more obvious as the terrifying nature of the death penalty. The person feels terror at the mere mental representation of this punishment."[44]

Fear of death is a serious barrier to the criminal. Simply on the basis of common sense, people fear death more than other forms of punishment and therefore the death penalty inhibits criminals more than any other punishment. V. A. Zhukovskiy's opinion was as follows: "Execution is nothing but a representative of the strict truth, pursuing evil and saving from it the public order established by God himself. The death penalty, like Nemesis menacing with her sword, like the fear of possible death, like a ghost haunting the criminal, is awful in its invisible presence, and the thought of it abstains many from wickedness."[45] Arguments therefore to the effect that the death penalty is absolutely not dangerous—because it is the destiny of everyone, because different sages believed it to be a sedation, because of physiological considerations over the painlessness and even some pleasantness of taking away life via the guillotine or gallows—even if they were scientifically fair, are contrary to the common sense of the common aim.[46]

The next argument of supporters of the abolition of the death penalty is that the death penalty is a contrary punishment, one based on power not on truth or humanism. Of course, it is foolish to oppose humanism, and we would fully support this argument, were it not for two essential points. Firstly, if we consider the death penalty as an inhumane punishment and so demand humane treatment of the criminal, we should not however forget the victims of the crime. Is it humane to leave a woman whose husband was brutally murdered by criminals with two, three or more children to the mercy of fate? Somehow, in that moment, we think more about humanism in relation to the criminal. Humanity and justice will triumph completely when the state takes on its full provision the family of the victim of the crime. Secondly, if the death penalty is inhumane then the humanity of its substitute, i.e. life imprisonment, is unquestionable. Therefore abolition of the death penalty should take place if we see that this is the most inhumane punishment but ensuring at the same time that its alternative is no less dissuasive. Unfortunately up to this date we are not convinced of this, but certainly, in comparison to the death penalty,

---

44 Kistyakovskiy, A. F. Op. cit, p55.
45 Zhukovskiy, V. A. 'On the Death Penalty', *Works*, vol. xi, Saint Petersburg, 1857, p186.
46 Kistyakovskiy, A. F. Op. cit, p57.

life imprisonment is a more humane measure although it condemns the criminal to life in torment.

However, it should be recognised that fear of the death penalty is stronger than fear of life imprisonment. This is an undeniable fact, although some would disagree. A criminal who was sentenced to death would have preferred the most severe and prolonged imprisonment, the hardest work and conditions of serving than the death penalty. Therefore, even the fear of life imprisonment cannot keep people from committing crimes to the extent that the death penalty does. The reasonableness of the death penalty may be recognised only if it has proven its necessity and indispensability. And vice versa: the reasonableness of the death penalty is only questioned if it has proven to be inappropriate and substitutable. Denying the death penalty from the standpoint of humanism, we, nevertheless, state that this measure of criminal punishment has the highest quality of intimidation.

What then is the future of the death penalty? Societies that have renounced this punishment will return again to the question of its restoration, and the countries that have retained the death penalty up to this day will be even more convinced of the correctness of their position. To reach such a conclusion there are religious, philosophical and legal grounds.

Religious Grounds for the Death Penalty

Although issues of law, in particular criminal law, should not be resolved on the basis of religious trends and the sacred divine books, their importance when considering the issue of preservation or destruction of the death penalty, as well as the nature of punishment, criminal in particular, cannot be left unattended. Addressing these theological views, we frankly find it incomprehensible how an educated, enlightened, civilised man might build a defence of the death penalty on such an outdated principle as 'whoever sheds man's blood, by man his blood shall be shed'. Everyone knows that the people's voice—i.e. the opinion of the people, which cannot be ignored—demands blood for blood. But where does this people's voice come from? From religious feelings, because the divine message of 'an eye for an eye and a tooth for a tooth' lives in the human mind as a symbol of justice and fairness.

Life confirms through many historical facts that "people pathologically like to watch the punishment of their own kind".[47] If it were announced that in the afternoon someone would be executed in the square, people would start to gather there early that same morning. Why? The theory of revenge as people understand it, based on the Sacred Books, in deriving from it the

47   Golik, Y. V. *Philosophical Issues of Punishment*, p37.

absolute necessity of the death penalty, may be wrong in its basis and fitness for use, but it exists and has serious grounds that are not only religious but also philosophical and legal. At the same time, it should be fairly noted that the first respectable votes against the death penalty were constantly heard in the Christian world. Incidentally, when sentencing Adam to death, God prefers imprisonment as an indeterminate sentence and not the immediate death penalty, in other words He transfers Adam to a different life, from paradise to the ground, from eternal life to mortal life. Punishment thus "is portrayed as providing complete freedom of action to the forces of nature, seeking to lead to the collapse of a living organism".[48] At the same time, because of Adam's sin, for God he died—not physically but spiritually, because there was a breakdown in man's connection with God.

In exhorting not to kill, the Quran says: "And do not kill the soul which Allah has forbidden, except by right" (Surah 17: Al-Isra' [The Night Journey], ayah 33). Hence the severest form of punishment according to the Quran is the death penalty, its basis being the postulate of 'a soul for a soul': "And do not kill the soul which Allah has forbidden, except by right. And whoever is killed unjustly, we have given his heir authority, but let him not exceed the limits in [the matter of] taking life. Indeed, he has been supported [by the law]" (Surah 17, ayah 35).

In the Holy Book of Allah 'painful punishment' is a very common expression. It seems that we are talking about the death penalty. The mention in the Quran of the legend of death should be understood clearly as the actual loss of life, as the death penalty. At the same time, according to the Quran, the concepts of 'murder' as a crime and the 'death penalty' as a punishment are not identical. In murder, arbitrariness and the will of one man are always the case, and in punishment in the form of death, i.e. deprivation of life, it is the highest will of Allah ensuring higher justice.

Providing the death penalty in retaliation for a killing, the Quran at the same time provides a choice to the victim's party. "If someone's relative is killed, he may choose one of two things: either get a bond for the killed, or to avenge him elsewhere" (from the *Sahih* of al-Bukhari, a collection of hadiths of the Prophet Muhammad, 92, 'The Book of Belief'). Special punishment is stipulated in the Quran for the murder of believers. Allah speaks to the people with this appeal: "And never is it for a believer to kill a believer except by mistake. But whoever kills a believer intentionally, his recompense is Hell, wherein he will abide eternally, and Allah has become

48   Golbiti, E. & Piazza, A. 'Complicated Pages of the Bible (Old Testament)', *Christian Russia*, Milan; Moscow, 1992, p97.

angry with him and has cursed him and has prepared for him a great punishment" (Surah 4, ayahs 92–93). And it is not only Islam but other religions that consider the death penalty a fair punishment on the basis of the divine messages

Philosophical Grounds for the Death Penalty

The requirement for the death penalty is based not only on the religious requirement of 'blood for blood', but also on the principles and ideas of the philosophy of Kant and Hegel. Thus, the retention of the death penalty is not only a religious principle of *retribution*, but also a requirement of philosophy. Can we consider Kant and Hegel as advocates of the death penalty on the basis of their philosophical position: equal–for equal, life–for life?

As we know, this theory has existed for thousands of years, i.e. since the time of primitive humanity, and Kant lays down in the foundation for determining the measure of penalty the principle of balancing the crime with the punishment. From this it follows that the death penalty must necessarily be sentenced for murder. Hegel also seeks to establish a certain balance between crime and punishment. But this balance should not be a specific equation, only an equation according to a crime which is defined by estimates. B. N. Chicherin wrote: "Just punishment is taking away that which has the same price. If, despite the fact that the death penalty is sometimes cancelled and replaced by other penalties, it does not happen because of the demands of justice, but for other reasons."[49]

Another interesting fact is that both opponents and advocates of the death penalty refer to *justice*. Hence Kistyakovskiy notes: "What kind of total equity leads to two opposite conclusions, and some say, the death penalty is a sacred institution, it meets my requirements; and others say, the death penalty disgusts me, it is based on power, not on the truth."[50]

Legal Grounds for the Retention of the Death Penalty

With the growth of criminality and the nature of crime, new modern methods, means and instruments of murder becoming widespread, more and more jurists are forced to think about the appropriateness of the death penalty as a deterrent. Chicherin had the following opinion: "If the protection of society requires the deterrence of criminals, in this respect the death penalty is valid as the strongest factor. It can stop even the most

49 Chicherin, B. N. Op. cit, p156.
50 Kistyakovskiy, A. F. *Studies of the Death Penalty*, Tula, 2000, p13.

hardened villains who even look at a life sentence rather indifferently. It is useful for society to cut the infected member off. If there are incorrigible criminals, it is best to get rid of them at once."[51]

Even Lombroso in the last edition (1907) of his *Crime, Causes and Treatments* returns to the issue of the death penalty and finds it necessary "for though the prospect of the death penalty hangs like the sword of Damocles over the heads of the most horrific villains who have already been sentenced to life imprisonment, they repeatedly infringe upon the lives of others". In these cases, in his opinion, "there is nothing more but to resort to this grave means of selection". The death penalty in such cases is "relatively fair, like all other punishments". It was his belief that "the death penalty is inscribed with bright letters in the book of nature and history and even the organic process entirely rests on the struggle for existence".

How then do criminals themselves relate to the death penalty? Do they agree to a life sentence instead of the death penalty? No one has ever answered these questions and would hardly ever succeed, because we are talking about people with a different psychology, character, will power and so on. Here we have shown that in some cases criminals prefer the death penalty to life imprisonment, although the death penalty has the strongest effect on the human soul: it makes a man deepen into himself in the face of eternity and repent of his crimes. But it is also clear that many criminals are completely indifferent to death. When we say that we dread death, we think first of all about the pain that is its predecessor. Death either took place or will take place, it is not relevant to the present, and death itself is less sensitive than its expectation. As Montaigne said: "The trees also kind of groan when they are injured. As for death, then we cannot feel it; we grasp it only by reason, because it is separated from life by a moment."[52] The same thought is expressed by François de la Rochefoucauld: "The equanimity sometimes manifested by those sentenced to death, as well as their scorn for death, speaks only of their fear to look it straight in the eye; consequently, we can say that to their minds, both are like a bandage for their eyes."[53]

The impact of mitigated punishment on citizens with a higher level of development can be as strong as the impact of heavy punishment on uneducated or under-educated people. Logically, this implies the following statement: if we want the penal system to be softer, then care must be taken in order to raise the moral and educational level of citizens. And from this we

---

51 Chicherin, B. N. Op. cit, p156.
52 See: *On Human Nature: Montaigne, La Rochefoucauld, Pascal*, Moscow, 2009, p32.
53 See: Ibid, p201.

can conclude that abolition or retention of the death penalty depends on this foundation. Therefore it is necessary to be sensitive to those countries where this kind of punishment still exists. In fact, the demonstration of the death penalty makes a painful impression on people with a higher level of development in moral, legal and political terms. It affects uneducated or under-educated people quite differently. For them, it is a common phenomenon, a performance.

In our opinion, legislation should provide for homicide under aggravating circumstances, as well as for the rape of minors under extremely aggravating circumstances, two kinds of punishment: the death penalty and life imprisonment. The right to choose should be given to the defendant whose guilt is proved.

Imprisonment and Its Future

There is no criminal code in any state where imprisonment would not have been provided as a punishment. Moreover, it is more likely than other types of penalties applied in practice. Each country defines different imprisonment limits. For example, in Belgium the minimum term of imprisonment is five years and the maximum thirty, given the fact that there is a life sentence. In the Netherlands, a fixed term of imprisonment begins on the first day and cannot exceed fifteen years (in exceptional cases twenty years). Swiss criminal law provides punishment by imprisonment of the convicted prisoner for a term of one year to twenty years, considering life imprisonment in exceptional cases. Besides convict prisons, the system of penalties also includes imprisonment from three days to three years. In China, in addition to the punishment term (six months to fifteen years), criminal law also provides for life imprisonment, i.e. for life, although the system of punishment also includes the death penalty. Incidentally, instead of life imprisonment, Georgian law uses the term 'termless (indefinite) imprisonment'. In San Marino, the minimum term of imprisonment is three months, and the maximum is thirty-five years. Attention is drawn to the fact that some states, instead of the term 'deprivation of liberty', use the term 'imprisonment', which, in fact, are identical.

At the turn of the eighteenth and nineteenth centuries, the 'triumphal procession' of the modern prison system began. It is known that before that there were terrible corporal punishments and the death penalty (hanging, beheading, breaking on the wheel, mutilation); imprisonment in convict prisons where the perpetrators of various crimes were held (robbers, thieves, prostitutes, vagrants and so on). In other words, until the second half of the eighteenth century, terrible conditions reigned in prisons. The main purpose of society was to warn, to frighten people. Imprisonment for a long time and forced labour as a punishment did not exist.

John Howard was the first who studied in his homeland of Britain and in other countries conditions of serving the sentence, and drew up a public accusation of prison orders. In parallel, many scholars began to recognise the fact that the criminal was also a victim of society, so it was not necessary to destroy him but to try to save him. Subsequently, Philadelphia even built the famous example of a prison with solitary cells. As today, the number of prisoners at that time exceeded the number of available places. The emergence of prisons was also contributed to by a rapid increase in crime, which was impossible to fight by penalty executions and corporal punishment alone. At the same time, there was a need for cheap labour, and so imprisonment with strict forced labour for many years was a new punitive tool for the protection of society. This kind of punishment during the nineteenth century acquired a dominant position in the penal system and became so deeply rooted in the public mind that its utility was considered almost certain. Differences could only arise in determining the best system of imprisonment. Representatives of science as well as practitioners began to search for ways to improve and enhance the effectiveness of prison (which continues up to this day) towards the humanisation of serving the punishment, reducing the pain and suffering of prisoners.

But to what extent? After all, without inflicting pain and suffering on persons who committed crimes, execution of the penalty of imprisonment is not possible, and it should be recognised that modern institutions of this type are based on the recognition of the need for retribution and the infliction of suffering, and not on the correctness of convicts. Therefore, the actual modern prisons are only required for the isolation of criminals. Inflicting pain and suffering on convicts absolutely does not mean their suppression or humiliation. At the same time, when organising the system of imprisonment, we should consider the general standard of living. Convicts should feel the difference; otherwise, the punishment will have no deterrent impact either on the criminal or on society in general.

Punishment by imprisonment, without losing the essence of causing suffering and pain within reasonable limits, must at the same time through a variety of reforms become a system of correction, education and rehabilitation of the person. Unfortunately, modern correctional facilities are not able to solve this problem. They are not only unable to reduce recidivism, but rather generate a new number of criminals. Nowadays, these institutions cannot protect the public from further crimes, because they have lost the deterrent power they once had.

A subtle and practically acceptable system of corrective treatment accompanied by the humane execution of punishment is needed. Indeed, in modern institutions, convicts are not explicitly included in the labour process, although the places of deprivation are of sufficient liveability. Why could a certain category of convicts not be used for work at private companies if there are no opportunities in prison? One should not forget that only that work which the convict chooses himself and which brings him joy will benefit in correcting him. Are we able nowadays to go for it and solve this issue? The aforementioned is worth considering.

Compared to the places of the deprivation of liberty that existed in Soviet Azerbaijan, modern prisons look much better from the outside. Changes for the better have also occurred in the interior of these institutions. However, in their essence and social meaning, they have become much worse, i.e. the punitive and educational process virtually falls short of its goals. Noteworthy is the fact that the number of persons sentenced to imprisonment every year not only has not decreased but rather increased. If the average number of persons sentenced to imprisonment over the 1960s was 28–32%, starting from 1970, it started to grow rapidly and by 1983 was already 55%. Analysis of the punitive practices of courts shows that the percentage of persons sentenced to this penalty in 1971–1991, that is, before the collapse of the USSR, ranged from 35–55%. Thus, in 1971–1977, it was 41–45%. Between 1980 and 1997, there was an increase in this figure to 50–54%. The drive to widely use this punishment was associated with the desire to reduce the level of crime. However, the results were negative. Crime kept on growing. For example, the average crime rate for the period from 1961 to 1970 amounted to 13,600 crimes, in 1971–1980 it was 14,650, and in 1981–1990 15,850.

Since 1976, there has been a notable growth in grievous crime and other crimes of violence. So, in 1980, the figure of persons sentenced to imprisonment for grievous crimes was more than 25%. The ineffectiveness of criminal policy in the Soviet period was not only in the mistaken position of the effectiveness of imprisonment in the prevention of crimes, but also in the rather wide use of this punishment for committing minor offences that do not pose a major public threat leading to an artificial increase in the percentage of persons sentenced to imprisonment.

Before the collapse of the Communist regime, in Azerbaijan, every year between 6–10% of the total number of convicts were sentenced to imprisonment for profiteering from agricultural products and the same amount for cheating customers. In particular, in 1982, out of the number of all persons sentenced to imprisonment (54.2%), the percentage of persons who committed minor crimes and of non-persistent criminals was 58.4%. The criminal policy of sovereign Azerbaijan remained unchanged regarding the use of imprisonment for criminals. Over the past thirteen years (2000–2013), the rate of imprisonment for a fixed term has been within 42–49%, although there are currently no such crimes as profiteering and cheating customers.

The need to refer to these statistics is related to the validity of conclusions that the deprivation of liberty has always been the most popular and practised type of criminal punishment. This is why the future of punishment is directly related to imprisonment. And if we talk about replacing punishment with non-punitive action, then it is possible only with a gradual decrease in the role of imprisonment up to its complete disappearance as a means of influencing criminal behaviour. But is this possible?

Unfortunately, crime statistics, in particular in Azerbaijan, over the past ten years cannot give a positive answer because there is a tendency towards its growth. So, if in 2000 the state registered 13,958 crimes, in 2010 this figure reached 23,000, and in 2011 24,000. It should also be considered that during the indicated period, the number of grievous and extremely-grievous crimes, homicide, rape, i.e. all kinds of crimes against the person, not only have not decreased but rather have tended towards growth. Can we abandon the use of imprisonment if 50% of all committed crimes constitute crimes against the person?

Imprisonment in the future will remain the main form of punishment for serious violent crimes and persistent criminals. At the same time, the need will fall away to isolate away in prisons certain categories of offenders who have committed non-violent crimes: economic crimes, crimes of negligence, and crimes related to drug possession. And this would reduce the percentage of imprisonment and increase the share of such penalties as fines, corrective labour and the restriction of freedom. It seems that the future of punishment is also associated with the abandonment of short-term imprisonment, because it is absolutely unable to achieve any positive results. This is clearly evidenced by the practice of this form of imprisonment.

If, in current conditions, by imprisonment we understand certain restrictions on the freedom to dispose of oneself, of one's rights, but not their complete withdrawal, i.e. the infliction of suffering, then the future of punishment is related to the limitation of its punitive substance. However, if prisons start looking like motels, like recreation centres built at the expense of taxpayers, it will lead to the complete disappearance of this form of punishment per se, and hence to the loss of the main and almost sole deterrent impact.

So, nowadays, no state has refused using places of detention, imprison-ment, jails, penitentiary institutions, no matter what are they called, as conceived and created in 1780 in Philadelphia with the aim of the complete isolation of criminals, although everybody questions their effectiveness.

*

Conclusion

The history of the doctrine of crime and punishment is evidence of the success that mankind has attained in solving the issues that occupy this field of criminal law. It is surprising therefore to find statements such as those made by Khavronyuk at the Scientific and Practical Conference on Punishment Issues, held in Beijing in December 2012: "Thus, over the centuries, over the millennia, the best human minds and legal scholars have not progressed much on the issue of criminal penalty: in fact, they have only stated that punishment must be just and merciful . . . Not much has been done to ensure that the penalty in each case would indeed be so. We still do not know the way to punish a criminal in order to attain the purpose of punishment and to ensure that the person is corrected and will not commit crimes anymore."[1]

As noted in this volume, because of the predictive nature of punishment, we are unable to predict the future outcome of punishment at the stage of lawmaking or in the process of the appointment and carrying out of punishment. For this reason, it is impossible to determine the effectiveness of individual forms of punishment or of the entire system of punishment as a whole.

Consequently, it may be concluded that jurists do not fully make use of the achievements of other sciences in order to improve the efficiency of criminal penalty. This is incidentally referred to by Khavronyuk himself, who wonders: "Why are the advances of criminalistics so insignificant? What are the reasons for this lag of legal sciences and of criminal law in particular?" And then he answers: "Or is it that criminal and legal science, like any other legal science, forgets about the need to consider the natural laws of development

---

1   See: Khavronyuk, N., 'What Should Criminal Penalties Be, Or Why Does Jurisprudence Fall Behind Physics?', *Materials of the Scientific and Practical Conference on Punishment Issues in Beijing*, 2012, Dec 1–3, p13.

of society and the individual that is possible only at the intersection of the sciences; it also forgets about the need to find opportunities for the most precise reflection of the advances of other sciences in the norms of the law, primarily of sociology, criminology, criminal statistics, psychology, psychiatry, medicine."[2]

The results and value of the humanities, unlike the natural sciences, cannot be determined immediately but require a sufficiently long period of time to come to fruition, since they are directly related to public and political processes, historical conditions, and human consciousness, including justice. Undoubtedly, Copernicus' theory of the heliocentric system (1543), Mendel's laws of heredity (1865), the cellular structure of plants discovered by Hooke (1665), the basics of embryology developed by von Baer (1828), and space discoveries and so on are the greatest achievements of mankind, which are truly tangible and visible. Well, are the ideas of Beccaria as set out in *On Crimes and Punishments* not as great for the development of human society as the theory of relativity, or Darwin's theory of evolution? Is the modern system of criminal law not built on his ideas and principles?

The classical trend in criminal law was a natural product of the Enlightenment, which gave the world such thinkers as Rousseau, Voltaire and Montesquieu. In the field of criminal law, the specified direction proceeded from the fundamental requirements: to reduce to a possible minimum the impact on human behaviour, in other words the punishment should not exceed the requirements of fairness; crime and punishment should be clearly defined in advance; the punishment should fit the severity of the crime. From the point of view of the development of human civilisation and culture, these ideas are no less great than the discoveries of the scientists we have just mentioned.

Khavronyuk is right only in the fact that, while using the theory of relativity in practice, we are still unable to find the criteria for distinguishing crimes by their public danger and gravity or build on this basis a fair system of proportionality of punishment to the committed crime.

We should agree with the author's statement that we have still failed to develop an efficient and fair 'tool' that allows a judge to appoint and determine the punishment not off the mark but on a scientific basis. And yet significant changes in the direction of the humanisation of the system of definition, application and enforcement of criminal penalties should be

2   Ibid, p2.

related to the merits of the best thinkers and experts in law. We need but mention simply the rejection by the majority of the world's nations of the death penalty. Does the credit lie with physicists, biologists, physicians or astronomers?

We need now to consider the future of punishment, to formulate ways of finding new, more efficient but less harmful forms of punishment that reflect our current conditions and the level of development of society today.

*   *

*

Appendix

Aphorisms on Law

Laws are masters of the state.
—*Alcidamas*

Law is a web; little insects die in it, large ones break away unharmed.
—*Anacharsis*

There are a thousand ways to be a very bad person,
while still obeying all the laws.
—*Anne Louise Germaine de Staël-Holstein*

Dura lex, sed lex.
(It is a tough law, but it is the law)
—*Ancient words of wisdom*

Courage is a virtue that makes people in danger commit beautiful deeds,
motivated by the law and obeying it.
—*Aristotle*

Cruelty and fear shake each other's hands.
—*Honoré de Balzac*

Bad laws are the worst type of tyranny.
—*Edmund Burke*

Fear before people is the seal of love for laws.
—*Luc de Clapiers, marquis de Vauvenargues*

Freedom is in obeying only the law.

A multitude of laws in the state is like a multitude of treatments:
a symptom of illness and feebleness.

Laws are meant not only for the horrification of citizens,
but also for helping them.
—*Voltaire*

The world of laws is a still depiction of the existing world,
the world of phenomena.
—*Hegel*

To not to obey any laws means to be deprived of any protection,
for the laws are intended not only for our protection from others,
but for protection from ourselves as well.
—*H. Heine*

Law is strong, but need is stronger.
—*Johann Wolfgang von Goethe*

Men create laws, women create customs.
—*F. Guibert*

Law-making is a millstone that mills the poor and is driven by the rich.

To be complete, the law should not only punish, but reward as well.
—*O. Goldsmith*

What is the use of ineffective laws when there are no customs?
—*Horatio*

Laws are stupid fiction. Laws are created by people,
nature creates atoms and void.

Laws are useless both for the good and the bad.
The first do not need laws, the second are not improved by them.
—*Democritus*

The one who makes the laws should be the first to obey them.
—*Geoffrey Chaucer*

The laws are made for ordinary people, that is why they should be based
on ordinary rules of common sense.
—*Thomas Jefferson*

Law is a supreme manifestation of human wisdom that uses
people's experience for the good of society.
—*Samuel Johnson*

Endure the law that you created.
—*Charles L. Dumoulin*

The best of laws evolve from customs.
—*Joseph Joubert*

A people without laws is similar to a man without principles.
—*Zachary*

The law that exists within us is called consciousness. Consciousness is the application of our deeds to this law.
—*E. Kant*

Law and justice are two things united by God and separated by man.
—*Charles Caleb Colton*

People confuse laws with rights.
—*Heinrich Friedrich Emil Lenz*

Law should be expressed in words that strike with awe.
—*Titus Livius*

Create little laws, but take careful note of how they are obeyed.
—*J. Locke*

Laws are sovereigns above sovereigns.
—*Louis XII*

Law has to be short so that it could be easily memorized even by the ignorant.

The laws are useless for those who have no power and money to defend them.
—*Thomas Babington Macaulay*

Law (juridical) is a friend of the weak.

Law (juridical) is a compromise of state and jus.
—*Thomas Mann*

A law that commands a person who has nothing to respect a person who has everything, cannot be just.
—*Marquis de Sade*

Only the mind can create binding and lasting words.
—*Honoré Gabriel Riqueti, comte de Mirabeau*

Oppressive legislation contributes to loyalty.

Laws should have an equal meaning for everyone.

It is the law that can make wealth as burdensome as poverty.
—*Charles-Louis de Secondat, Baron de La Brède et de Montesquieu*

It is easier to make laws than to obey them.
—*Napoléon Bonaparte*

Cruelty is inherent to laws dictated by cowardice, for cowardice
can be vigorous only while being cruel.
—*Karl Marx*

Justice that is not backed up by power is weak. Power that is not
backed up by justice is tyranny.

Laws that are not based on justice have no power. Power that is not
backed up by justice is tyranny.
—*Blaise Pascal*

The wise legislator begins not with making laws, but with learning their
feasibility for the given society.
—*Jean-Jacques Rousseau*

Laws are like a web that catches little flies, but is no obstacle for
wasps and hornets.
—*Jonathan Swift*

Some imperscriptible laws are stronger than all the written ones.
—*Seneca the Younger*

Shame may restrain what the law does not prohibit.
—*Seneca*

The power of time is the law that cannot be ignored. Time dictates the
laws. Time is a juggernaut.
—*Publilius Syrus*

He that turneth away his ear from hearing the law, even his prayer shall be
abomination.
—*Solomon*

The closer the state is to collapse, the more numerous are its laws.

Good customs matter more than good laws.
—*Tacitus*

Law is a majestic statue, before which everyone takes his hat off, but then
just passes by it. Jurisprudence alters every ten years.
—*Hippolyte Adolphe Taine*

Fools rush in where angels fear to tread.
—Proverb

Along with the state laws, there are moral laws that make up
for legislative flaws.
—Henry Fielding

Laws that are too lenient are rarely obeyed, laws that are too tough
are rarely performed.
—Benjamin Franklin

Obey the laws.
—Chilon of Sparta

Extreme severity of the law makes an extreme injustice.

To become free we must become the slaves of the law.

To know laws is not to remember them by heart, but to know
their meaning.

When arms are rattling the laws remain silent.

Welfare of people is the ultimate law.

Law is nothing but a true command of the mind, conforming with divine
essence, ordering to act in good faith and forbidding to behave without
honour.
—Cicero

Laws based on fear are lawless.
—Nicolas Chamfort

Divine law is a changing law.
—George Bernard Shaw

When offences are hidden, it means that people have mastered law,
but when the crimes are gravely punished, it means that
law has mastered people.
—The Book of Lord Shang

People need even the worst of the laws, for if there were none, people
would have devoured each other.
—Epicurus

Aphorisms on Crime

Where there is no law there is no crime.
—*Paul the Apostle*

All crime needs is an excuse.
—*Aristotle*

People get into trouble like they get into a trap, all at once. But it takes a long way to descend to a crime.

Will is nothing but a thought evolving into action!
—*A. A. Bestuzhev-Marlinskiy*

Society prepares the crime, the criminal commits it.
—*Henry Thomas Buckle*

Opportunity makes a thief.
—*Francis Bacon*

The one who forgives a crime becomes an accomplice to it.

In the most superstitious times, there were always the most horrible crimes.

Only the weak commit crimes. The strong and the joyful
do not need crimes.

It is necessary to have crimes and disasters, and that they would
be the destiny of good men.
—*Voltaire*

Crimes are evil trespassing the borders of the soul.
—*V. Gavrilov*

Every religious dogma is a seed of crimes and discord among people.
—*Claude Adrien Helvétius*

Terrible crimes lead to terrible consequences.
—*A. I. Herzen*

History is nothing but an entry journal of human crimes, stupidity
and disaster.
—*Edward Gibbon*

Deeds are fruits of thoughts. When the thoughts are good,
so are the deeds.
—*Baltasar Gracián*

If everything that people say about good and evil is true,
then my whole life is a crime.
—*Khalil Gibran*

Look through the history of all the peoples of the Earth: everywhere
religion turns innocence into crime and declares crime innocent.
—*Denis Diderot*

The most serious problems of a modern man are based on the fact that he
lost the feeling of conscious cooperation with God in His intentions
regarding humanity.

There are moments when people love crime.
—*F. M. Dostoevsky*

If you do not want to experience fear, do no harm.
—*Qaboos*

Every crime has a dual meaning—towards the personality of the
condemned and towards society.
—*A. F. Kony*

Do not break the laws, for Allah does not care for those who do not
observe borders.
—*Quran, Surah 5: Al-Ma'ida [The Table Spread], ayah 87*

If poverty is the mother of crimes, then the simple mind is their father.
—*Jean de La Bruyère*

There is a great deal more likeness between geniuses and criminals on the
one side and madmen on the other side, then between geniuses, criminals
and healthy normal people.
—*Cesare Lombroso*

The general audience is only interested in three things: money, love and
crime.
—*Martti Larni*

A man incapable of a great crime can hardly believe that others are quite
capable of it.
—*François de la Rochefoucauld*

Evil begets evil.
—*M.Yu. Lermontov*

Where there is continence there is mistake, where there is indifference there is crime.
—*Georg Christoph Lichtenberg*

People are prone to evil.
—*Niccolò di Bernardo dei Machiavelli*

One day, when the science of anatomy advances, there will be a possibility to associate people's behaviour with their favors.
—*Marquis de Sade*

Whatever they say, there is something unusual in men—something that no scientists are able to explain.
—*Jean-Baptiste Poquelin (Molière)*

Crime is a surreptitious destruction through external deeds.

Crime is a sin of an unjust society.
—*Thomas More*

Not the crime of a criminal, but his cowardice and recklessness in committing it make us treat him with contempt.

Statistics claims that a woman commits ten times fewer crimes than a man, therefore a woman is ten times better morally than a man.
—*Friedrich Wilhelm Nietzsche*

Better crime than the nauseous emptiness of existence, vain and exhausting.
—*Romain Rolland*

Once bethought, even a crime that has not been committed is still a crime.

A severe mistake often becomes a crime.

One crime paves the way for others.

A person that has an opportunity to prevent a crime but does not do that, becomes an instigator for it.
—*Seneca*

We always strive to get what is forbidden and wish to do what is illicit.
—*Ovid*

A crime that has become a common phenomenon ceases to be a crime
and becomes a norm.
—*E. Sinegut*

The bad consequences of crimes live longer than the crimes themselves.
—*Walter Scott*

When asked 'How can crime be extirpated among people?,' Solon
answered: 'It would take to create conditions when victims and those
unharmed suffer equally from crimes.'
—*Solon of Athens*

Wishes manifest the essence of man.
—*Baruch Spinoza*

Those who have committed a crime twice deem it permissible.
—*Talmud*

Nine tenth of all the crimes that blemish humanity are committed under
the influence of wine.

One of the most common seducements that nevertheless leads
to the most terrifying consequences is the seducement expressed
in the words: 'Everyone does that.'
—*L. N. Tolstoy*

No benefits gained at the cost of crime can compensate for the loss of
internal peace.
—*Henry Fielding*

Even the greatest number of accomplices cannot justify crime.
—*Thomas Fuller*

Felonious intentions are the ultimate misery. It is less regrettable not to
receive what's desired than to achieve what's criminal to desire.
—*Cicero*

Aphorisms on Punishment

There is no punishment so tormenting as not to be punished.
—*Ryunosuke Akutagawa*

Justice is the constant and permanent will to pay everyone his due.
—*Ancient aphorism*

I am not afraid of punishment, I am afraid of committing something
culpable of punishment.
—*Karl Ludwig Börne*

Honest confession does not differ from any good deed, it also returns in
reward.
—*Pierre-Augustin Caron de Beaumarchais*

Ignorance of the law is no excuse for punishment. Knowledge of the law is
no excuse for abuse.
—*Nikolay Borskiy (nom de plume of the Russian poet N. Ludyakov)*

One unjust sentence leads to greater disasters than many crimes committed
by honest men. The latter spoil only separate streams, while the unjust
judge spoils the very source of the spring.
—*Francis Bacon*

Punishment of criminals has to do good. Yet when a man is hanged,
he is good for nothing.
—*Voltaire*

Pangs of consciousness begin when impunity ends.

Cruelty is always a result of fear, weakness and cowardice.
—*Claude Adrien Helvétius*

Penalty enters the human heart the very moment the crime is committed.
—*Hesiod*

Justice is the basis for all social virtues.

Retribution in the afterlife is nothing but a ghost invented to blur the
human mind, to deceive and lead people astray, to deprive them of peace
and turn them into obedient slaves of the clergy.

Fear before God deters from sin only those who are not able to desire
strongly enough or are already not fit to commit sin.
—*P. d'Holbach*

Do not punish those who deserve a mere whip with a dreadful scourge.
—*Horatio*

Those who are hastily condemned are often condemned wrongly.
—*Franz Seraphicus Grillparzer*

If your law punishes without guilt, be the judges for yourselves.
—*The Holy Gospel with comments of Saint Theophylact of Ohrid*
(Holy Dormition Pochayiv Lavra, 2008)

It is much better to prevent crimes than to punish for them.

It is better to justify ten guilty men than to condemn one innocent.
—*Catherine II*

It is not punishment that is shameful, but the crime.
—*H. Johann*

Dishonest scales are an abomination to the Lord.
—*Book of Proverbs*

Punish not for the fault itself, but for the intention as well.
—*Periander of Corinth*

Everything that was gained through training, pressure, violence is unsteady,
wrong and ineffectual.
—*Y. Korchak*

A punished criminal is an example for all wrongdoers. A wrongfully-convicted
man is a matter of conscience for all honest people.
—*Jean de La Bruyère*

Righteous people do not wish to commit sin because they love the good.
Bad people do not wish to commit sin because they are afraid of punishment.

A criminal that committed his crime in anger that was provoked by the
victim deserves a less grave punishment.

Those who commit crimes when drunk should be punished when sober.
—*Latin Juridical Quotations*

I punish you not because I hate you, but because I love you.
—*Latin proverb*

The purpose of punishment is crime prevention; it may never serve as a
motivation for good.
—*H. Mann*

The world was never improved nor horrified by punishment.
Punishment should not be more repelling than the crime itself.
—*K. Marx*

If there is a medium to prevent crimes then it is punishment, if there are
means to improve morals—then it's good examples.

Justice is paying everyone his due.

The means of fighting crime is punishment, the means of changing
customs is example.
—*Charles-Louis de Secondat, Baron de La Brède et de Montesquieu*

It is not crime that is punished, but stupidity.
—*Marguerite de Navarre*

The misery of all public executions lies in the fact that they teach us not to
commit deeds only because of their consequences.

The motives that justify the punishment can justify the crime itself.
—*Friedrich Wilhelm Nietzsche*

Make that the punishment for the crime be done inside the condemned—
and you will reach the ideal of moral education.
—*N. I. Pirogov*

The wise man punishes not because an evil deed was committed,
but for it not to happen again.
—*Plato*

A pardon by mistake is better and more useful than punishment by mistake.
—*I. Ragimov*

A criminal can sometimes escape punishment, but he can never escape
the fear of it.
—*Seneca*

A punishment imposed by a kind-hearted person seems much more severe.
—*Seneca the Younger*

As a person cannot begin eye treatment without thinking of the head, or begin treatment of the head without thinking of the whole body, so you cannot cure the body without curing the soul.
—*Socrates*

Sometimes it happens that punishment leads to crime.
—*S. Lem*

Every crime is redeemed by the sufferings it brings.
—*A. I. Urusov*

I'd better cancel *hadd* (punishment) when I am in doubt, than impose it when I am in doubt.
—*Umar ibn Al-Khattab*

Choose punishment over the death penalty, for the first one will grieve a man once, the second will grieve him once and for all.
—*Chilon*

Impunity is the greatest encouragement for crime.

It is a crime to take bribes for fixing sentences, and even a worse crime to take bribes from a person for justification.
—*Cicero*

Punishment is the flesh of power.
—*Zhuangzi*

In the same way as a drug does not help if the dose is exceeded, so reproof and criticism do not help when they go beyond justice.
—*Arthur Schopenhauer*

The first punishment for the guilty is his inability to justify himself before his inner judge.

A retribution for one crime was crucifixion, a retribution for the other was the imperial tiara.
—*Decimus Iunius Iuvenalis*

*

Index